PURE
BASEBALL

PURE BASEBALL

Pitch by Pitch
for the Advanced Fan

KEITH HERNANDEZ
and Mike Bryan

HarperPerennial
A Division of HarperCollinsPublishers

A hardcover edition of this book was published in 1994 by HarperCollins Publishers.

PURE BASEBALL: PITCH BY PITCH FOR THE ADVANCED FAN. Copyright © 1994 by Keith Hernandez and Mike Bryan. All rights reserved. Printed in the United States of America. No part of this book may be used or reproduced in any manner whatsoever without written permission except in the case of brief quotations embodied in critical articles and reviews. For information address HarperCollins Publishers, Inc., 10 East 53rd Street, New York, NY 10022.

HarperCollins books may be purchased for educational, business, or sales promotional use. For information, please write: Special Markets Department, HarperCollins Publishers, Inc., 10 East 53rd Street, New York, NY 10022.

First HarperPerennial edition published in 1995.

Designed by George J. McKeon

The Library of Congress has catalogued the hardcover edition as follows:
Hernandez, Keith.
    Pure baseball : pitch by pitch for the advanced fan / Keith Hernandez and Mike Bryan. — 1st ed.
        p.   cm.
    Includes index.
    ISBN 0-06-017090-5
    1. Baseball — United States.   I. Bryan, Mike.   II. Title.
GV863.A1H47   1994
796.357'0973 — dc20   93-33940

ISBN 0-06-092591-4 (pbk.)
95 96 97 98 99 ❖/RRD 10 9 8 7 6 5 4 3 2 1

To all the managers,
who are constantly being
second-guessed

PREAMBLE

First, I'd like to see you buy a real scorebook that has a place to chart the balls and strikes. The little scoresheet they print on page 37 of the official program just isn't good enough for the advanced fan. If you really want to get into baseball, you have to follow the game pitch by pitch. As a former batter, I'm biased, but it still seems to me that the cliché that holds that pitching is 80 percent of baseball is correct only as far as it goes. What percentage of pitching is hitting? I don't know exactly, but it's high. Good hitting can offset good pitching (an opposite-field double off a perfect pitch on the outside corner at the knees), and bad hitting can offset bad pitching (a comatose batter takes a hanging curve over the heart of the plate on a 3-1 count). For me, this battle of wits and balance of talent between the pitcher and the hitter is baseball. Everything else is secondary.

Of course, another baseball cliché holds that the little things, the fundamentals like hitting the cutoff man, win ball games and pennants. This is definitely true. I'm a stickler for these basics myself. My father drilled them into my brother, Gary, and me for hours on end. Dad was a former minor leaguer who believed that sloppy baseball was a serious sin. He gave us tests—written tests. The fundamentals Gary and I learned as kids are covered at length in this book because the strategic principles behind the hit-and-run, say, or guarding the lines late in the game aren't fully understood even by some

major leaguers (it's true), much less by many lifelong fans.
Boning up on these strategies will give you even more oppor-
tunities for that great American pastime—second-guessing.
Nevertheless, they are not the heart and soul of baseball.

Trust me here. The best way to delve deeper into a ball
game and to find more to think about and enjoy, even if the
score is 8-0 in favor of the despised visiting team, is to analyze the decision making and the execution of the pitcher
and the hitter on each individual pitch and then to watch and
analyze the resulting play with this understanding. The average at-bat in the major leagues requires three or four
pitches, my buddy Lenny Dykstra of the Phillies averages
about five, Wade Boggs with the Yankees maybe even more.
Many at-bats require six, seven, or eight pitches. Only one of
these usually results in a play by the fielders. Are all the others preliminary, without significance, a waste of time? Of
course not. What happens with the preceding pitches often
determines, in large measure, what happens on the final
pitch. They're vital. The fly ball to the left fielder for the easy
out on a full count may actually be the result of bad pitching
and good hitting. The players, managers, and coaches will
know; if you've watched the preceding pitches closely, you'll
know, too. In any event, the putout marked "F7" on the
scorecard doesn't begin to tell the story of that at-bat.

When we go to the park or turn on the local television or
radio broadcast, we don't watch generic "pitching," "hitting,"
and "fielding." We watch this pitcher throwing to this batter
with this glove work and this base running as a result. I can't
think about baseball other than in such specifics. That's why I
base this book on the action of two major league games
played one week apart in June 1993. All of my more general
observations and dissertations are set in this context. The
first game was a close one between the Phillies and Atlanta
at Veterans Stadium in Philadelphia. The second was a ten-
inning affair at Yankee Stadium between the Tigers and the
Yankees that ended with a dramatic and totally unexpected
home run. Each game was one of a series between the
respective teams, and I call on relevant events in the other

games as they reflect on the action of these two, and I also refer to innumerable other incidents from my years with the Cardinals, the Mets, and the Indians. But, mainly, I'm talking about how much you can learn from just two regular-season ball games featuring American League–style and National League–style play, grass and artificial turf, lefties and righties, power pitchers and junk ballers, sluggers and slap hitters, highlights and bloopers, fundamentals well executed and others thoroughly botched, shrewd managerial moves and a few dubious ones.

For better or for worse, most fans, even many serious fans, now follow baseball mainly on television, and it seemed advisable to take this fact into account in writing this book. Therefore, I wasn't even at the game at Yankee Stadium. I was in town, but in Manhattan, not the Bronx, and watching from the comfort of my living room with the volume off. (DeWayne Staats and Tony Kubek are one of the best announcing teams in the business, but I didn't want to be unduly influenced in my own analysis.) Watching baseball on television is not as much fun as going to the ballpark and it makes it tougher to follow some aspects of the game, such as the positioning of the defense, but TV is the perfect way to watch the pitch selection and analyze an at-bat. Hitters unfamiliar with a raw recruit on the mound often go to the clubhouse to watch a sequence on closed-circuit before stepping to the plate. If they can learn this way, so can we.

The closest possible scrutiny of these two games is intended to serve you as a guide to anticipating the plays, watching the action, and judging the strategy and the performance in any game you attend. If I have erred, it is probably on the side of providing more than you ever believed you wanted to know about the hit-and-run and the 2-2 count. My motto: Pay attention. Pay attention to the nuances of the game. I played this way because Dad drummed it into me and because it made the game more challenging and my job more fun. I think this approach will bring the same benefits to any fan. After reading this book, you should even be able to handle any of my father's tests.

CHAPTER 1

Wonderful night. Great seats. Sing the song. Have a dog. "Hey, let's play two!" as Ernie used to say. Danny Jackson's heater—that's the fastball—misses high and outside to Otis Nixon, the Braves' leadoff man, and we're underway at the Vet in Philadelphia. The Florida Marlins took Jackson from Pittsburgh in the expansion draft last winter and then immediately dealt him to the Phillies. That was a setup deal, I guess, and a good one for this team because Danny is one of the reasons for their success in '93. He's 6-3 with a 3.35 earned run average over fourteen starts—considerably better than his 8-13 record last year, 3.83 lifetime earned run average, and 81-92 record coming into the season. In spring training everybody said the Phillies might do okay if their pitching was decent. I guess so. The starters lead the league with seventeen complete games, and the team is eight and a half games in front of St. Louis in the National League East. But it's only June 22, you say, the pennant race doesn't start until August 15. Yeah, but that cuts both ways. There's a lot of time for other teams to make their run but just as much time for the Phillies to sew it up early. We did that on the Mets in '86, and it was a helluva lot of fun.

You have to like these Phillies. Manager Jim Fregosi and the gray suits in the front office have molded a team out of a bunch of in-your-face and down-in-the-dirt pros, quite a few of them castoffs from other cities, several with shaggy hair and a big chaw in the cheek. Nobody has thrown a complete

KEITH HERNANDEZ

game against them yet. They haven't been shut out. And their fans are getting greedy. Forty thousand of them— more than that—have come out to watch their favorites in the sharp red pinstripes and red caps get revenge for last night's rain-delayed 8-1 loss to the Braves. These fans are boisterous—in fact, they're the toughest in the league on opposing players, hands-down, ask anyone—and their team is boisterous, too. How could last night's blowout tarnish the best record in the majors, 48-21, and the second-best start in the club's history? The Phillies have a few games in the standings to play with, they could lose a few in a row and not panic, but they just don't want to. Right now, these ballplayers are having the time of their lives. Most of them haven't played on a big winner before. It feels good.

Meanwhile, Otis Nixon and the Braves must be wondering what they have to do in the West, which they won going away the past two years on the way to consecutive defeats to Minnesota and Toronto in the World Series. On June 22 last year they were 39-30 and trailing Cincinnati by one and a half games in the NL West. This season their record is about the same, 40-31, but they're seven and a half games behind the Giants. Ask manager Bobby Cox if the pennant race starts on August 15. The Braves' pitching, theoretically even stronger than last year's, has been good but not good enough because the batters haven't hit their stride and they're not driving in runs in the clutch. When and if they start to, will it be too late? They have to wonder. Winners now of three in a row, eight of ten, the Braves want to win tonight's game, too, to maintain some momentum. They're going to need it the rest of the way.

So what we have here besides perfect weather, now that the thunderstorms have cleared the muggy air from the City of Brotherly Love, is your basic midseason game between two good clubs that have good reasons to win. The Phillies have a chance to skip the pennant race in the East and the Braves are driving hard to get one going in the West. But you know where the real pressure out there comes from? The simple fact is that winning is better than losing, and

2

more fun. It's more difficult, too. Losing is easy. And then there are the fans in the stands and watching on television, waiting to see if you screw up. And the press—they're a lot easier to deal with when you're winning.

Danny Jackson had a tremendous season in 1988 with the Cincinnati Reds, when he was 23-8, but he's been less than a .500 pitcher since then. Much less. Jackson can be an effective, seasoned power pitcher—good fastball, hard slider, and a change-up that I'm sure has improved under the tutelage of Phillies pitching coach Johnny Podres, who had one of the best ever. Historically, though, Danny's problem has been that he can be a little wild around the plate, fall behind in the count, and therefore be forced to give the batter one or two good pitches to hit. He proves the point on his second offering to Otis Nixon on 1-0, another fastball, and this time right down the middle, but Nixon doesn't quite get around on the pitch and fouls it off to the right side. After two fastballs, Jackson introduces his slider but misses low. With the count 2-1, Nixon can now look for the fastball if he wants to, and I'm sure he does. Jackson will almost certainly throw the cheese, as we say, for these reasons: He features the fastball and it's his best pitch to throw for a strike, he doesn't want to walk the leadoff batter, and he isn't concerned about Otis's home run power. Nixon has zero homers and six doubles in almost two hundred at-bats, and he's batting .237. So make him earn his way on. Plus Otis has a bad right foot tonight, which won't help him.

Here comes the fastball, maybe high, but Nixon swings anyway and again fouls it back to the right side. With the count 2-2, the same philosophy applies for the pitcher: Go after the leadoff hitter, especially when the guy has yet to get around on the pitches.

Slider! There you go. Danny has as much confidence in this pitch as in his fastball. That selection is a message to the Atlanta hitters in the dugout: "I can throw something else for a strike." But there's one problem here. The message doesn't get through because the pitch is low. One thing every decent

hitter watches from the dugout is whether the pitcher is getting his breaking ball and off-speed stuff over the plate. If
not, the hitter has him by the short hairs and will sit on the
fastball when he's ahead in the count. However, one pitch
here in the first inning from Jackson proves nothing. Full
count. Again, I say you have to bet fastball here. Jackson
winds and the pitch is the fastball, probably high, but Nixon
can't take any chances with two strikes and fouls it off with
another late swing. Okay, throw the same pitch again. Nixon's
bat is just not quick enough for that pitch, not yet, at least,
and an inspection of the Phillies outfield reveals that they
don't expect the batter to get around on Jackson, period.
They're playing Nixon shallow and way around toward right
field. Plus he tends to hit the ball to the opposite field, anyway, especially off left-handers. But Otis does have more pop
from the right side. You wouldn't call him a slap hitter.

That positioning of the outfield is another reason for
Jackson to avoid anything off-speed. If Nixon is swinging
late on the fastball he might be right on the change-up and
pull it down the left-field line for a triple. The infielders
might shift to their right if the change-up is the pitch (more
on this subject later), but the outfield wouldn't be able to.
So don't throw it.

Phillies catcher Darren Daulton sets up on the outside
half of the plate and the fastball is right there, at the knees,
too, and Nixon lines the ball to Jim Eisenreich in right field
for the first out of the game. Otis got good wood on that ball
despite the fact that he was stepping in the bucket with his
butt out. He had every reason to expect the fastball outside,
so why wasn't he ready to take an aggressive swing, rather
than bailing out? I don't know. He's probably not in a good
groove right now. Batting right-handed, Otis has always
been a good high-ball hitter. You could conclude that the
late swings on these pitches almost prove that he's not in a
groove. How could he be? Because of that foot, his status is
day-to-day. Two weeks from now he might wear out those
pitches. In thirty-seven career at-bats against Jackson, Nixon
is hitting .351.

Batting second for the Braves is shortstop Jeff Blauser,

who gets better and better every year. He comes into tonight's game hitting a tidy .321. The Phillies' defense plays Jeff pretty much straightaway, average depth. You could know nothing about Blauser and still judge the kind of hitter he is from that alignment: His power is okay (14 homers in '92, but only 5 so far in '93) and he can pull the ball as well as drive it the other way, so play him straight up.

Jackson starts Blauser off with the fastball, just as he began with Nixon, but he locates this one over the outside half of the plate for strike one. Up in the count, he tries the slider and misses for the second time. Nothing doing so far with this pitch; the ball has very little break on it. If I'm Blauser, I'm satisfied right now because in my first at-bat of the game I've seen this pitcher's two main offerings—fastball and slider—and I'm even in the count. I'm ready to start hitting.

On the 1-1 count, Jackson chooses the fastball and there's another foul a little off to the right side. That pitch was also right down the pipe, but neither right-handed batter has caught up with it. Foul balls tell you a lot about what's going on at the plate. Right now, the batters are swinging late, but if and when they start fouling Jackson's fastball straight back onto the screen, we'll know they're "on the pitch"—perfect timing, but with the swing just a fraction low. Danny Jackson is a power pitcher, but he's not an overpowering strikeout pitcher these days—fifty-three Ks in ninety-six innings this season—so he'll have to get that pitch down at the knees as the game goes along. A pitcher like Sid Fernandez of the Mets can make a living off the high, riding fastball upstairs for fly-ball outs because his pitch has a lot of movement, but that's not Jackson's style anymore. He put up some big strikeout numbers in the mid-eighties, but now he's averaging about one every two innings. He still has what you would call power stuff, but you have to surmise that he's not throwing quite as hard as he once did. He's thirty-one years old. He might be able to blow his fastball past the hampered Otis Nixon tonight, but against Blauser and Terry Pendleton and Ron Gant, I have my doubts.

Ahead in the count 1-2, Jackson now goes outside with

PURE BASEBALL

5

another fastball but misses the corner low. Danny can come back with any pitch at all, but there's a little more pressure on 2-2 to make it a strike. As he did with Otis Nixon on this count, he tries to send a message to the Braves by throwing the slider when he needs the strike, but this time the message comes through because the pitch is a strike, and Blauser fouls it off. Anything is possible now and Blauser knows it, but Jackson makes a mistake with yet another fastball right down the middle—that makes three, at least—and this time he doesn't get away with it. Not a good pitch. Blauser turns on this one and drives it into the gap in left-center field for a double.

Just two batters into the game, the alert fan has an important clue about Danny Jackson that almost every batter in the National League already knows. He sometimes has trouble coming inside effectively to right-handed hitters, and the one mantra that any baseball fan has heard about effective pitching is that the pitcher has to "establish" inside. The battle between the pitcher and the batter for control of the inside part of the plate is bedrock. Nothing is more basic in baseball. The plate is seventeen inches across, and the umpires often call a strike zone wider than that, maybe twenty inches. But the sweet spot on the bat is about ten inches long. Figure it out: About half the strike zone can be covered by this piece of the bat. You can get hits when you're jammed on the hands or when you hit the ball near the end of the bat, but only these ten inches really drive the ball. So if the pitcher cannot effectively throw strikes with a hard pitch inside as well as outside, the batter doesn't worry about the inside half of the plate and focuses his attention and his swing outside. He can adjust to the breaking ball inside. But if the pitcher does establish hard stuff inside, the batter has a much more difficult time covering the whole plate, not just with the bat, but with the sweet spot of the bat.

When I first came up to the big leagues, pitchers had all too much success worrying me inside. Lou Brock, who worked with me a lot, sat me down one day and asked, "Where do you like the ball?"

"Inner half-away." That's the lingo for the outer three quarters of the plate.

"That's right," Lou agreed. "But worrying about your weakness—the inside corner—is taking away from your strength. Don't let it do that. Look into your strength."

Lou and I worked on this a lot. It's a mental thing. The pitcher tries to get the batter concerned inside in order to get him out outside. That's the vital point. A second point is that much depends on whether the hitter is sharp. You've heard many times that the pitch takes about a half second to reach the plate and less than that, usually. That seems like an impossibly short period of time in which to make any kind of decision at all. You'd think it would just come down to reflexes. And when you're slumping, that's about right. You don't feel like you have any time at all. But when you're sharp and seeing the ball well, you actually feel that you have all the time in the world. The half second seems like…I don't know, three or four seconds, plenty of time to identify the pitch and make the decision almost methodically about when and where to swing. That's when hitting is really fun. That's when you have a good chance against the fastball on the inside corner at the belt, the toughest pitch of them all.

After thirteen pitches tonight in Philadelphia, Danny Jackson hasn't come inside one time. One reason is that his fastball tends to run away from these right-handed Braves hitters. If that pitch does not start out three or four inches inside, if instead it starts out over the inside corner, it will run toward the middle of the plate and right onto the barrel of the bat. That's why it's dangerous for Jackson to throw his "tailing" fastball inside to right-handed batters, and he hasn't developed the fastball that stays straight. That's no disgrace, however, because Nolan Ryan never developed one, either, to use against left-handed batters in conjunction with his own tailing fastball.

In direct contrast to Jackson was the previous night's starting pitcher for Atlanta, Greg Maddux, one of the best and most aggressive control pitchers in either league. Greg is a right-hander. He throws a sinking fastball but also another variety straight over the top, a hard, straight bullet, and he knows that if he throws it inside to left-handed batters, the ball will stay inside. Last night he did so on two of the first three Phillies hitters and continued to do so all night. He got into their kitchen, as we say. Rattled the pots and pans. Made their hands sting when they hit the ball down toward the handle of the bat. Danny Jackson has a much tougher time doing this. His most effective inside pitch against right-handed batters is the slider, and it's a good one, but he can't throw it quite as hard as the fastball and it's not as easy to locate any breaking ball on the corners.

For almost every pitcher, the fastball is the most dependable pitch to throw for a strike or to throw on a corner. I'll draw this analogy: Is it easier to hit the target with a rifle shot or with a mortar lob? A rifle shot. That's why when the count is 3-0 and the pitcher feels he has a free shot at a strike with the batter taking the pitch, he throws the fastball, never the breaking ball. And that's why Danny Jackson has difficulty hitting the inside corner against right-handed batters. His fastball isn't suited for the job, and pinpoint control of the slider is never easy. He hasn't even attempted that pitch inside yet.

With Jeff Blauser on second base, Terry Pendleton comes to the plate for Atlanta. He's having an off year so far at .256, with only four homers and twenty-eight RBIs, but now he's heating up, with an eleven-game hitting streak. And from the right side of the plate—he switches—Terry has always been murder: .319 this year, .357 last year. By way of contradiction, however, Terry is hitting only .257 career against Jackson. Some managers place great stock in these *mano a mano* statistics, but I'm dubious, especially when the stat is a negative for the hitter. We're talking here about a total of thirty-five at-bats. Maybe Terry came up against Danny a couple of times when Terry wasn't swinging the bat well or Jackson was throwing great, or both. Or maybe Terry has just hit with bad luck against Jackson. I got quite a few key hits off Nolan Ryan, and a bunch of walks, so I was shocked to learn that I had something like a .170 batting average against him. I battled Nolan. I always felt I was a tough out for him, but you wouldn't know it from that batting average. Therefore, if I were looking down the bench for a pinch hitter to use against Danny Jackson in some future game, I wouldn't hesitate to go to Terry Pendleton, and I'm sure Bobby Cox wouldn't, either.

A high batting average against a pitcher means more, in my opinion. Jeff Blauser, for instance, was already hitting .391 against Jackson in twenty-three at-bats before his double tonight. It's safe to conclude that he feels confident against Jackson. The chances are good he's not bleeding and blooping Danny to death.

By the way, these and many of the other timely facts I use throughout this book come from the notes prepared for the game by the media relations departments of the Braves and the Phillies. Every organization writes them for every game, and they're invaluable, with up-to-date stats on each player, recent performance, streaks, and slumps. A few teams make these notes available to fans on a regular basis; I hope I don't make enemies around the league by suggesting that any serious fan could possibly arrange to get a copy "at the door." Give it a try by calling the media relations department of your team. These notes tell you a lot of stuff it's nice to know. I used them as a player. But also remember that cold statistics are not necessarily the whole story. They don't prove one way or another whether Terry Pendleton feels comfortable batting against Danny Jackson.

Jackson's first pitch to Pendleton makes you wonder whether his low average against Jackson means something after all. He pops up a fastball over the outer half of the plate. Lenny Dykstra comes in a long way from his post in center field, throws on the brakes, and swerves to his right before making the play. Some kind of rogue puff of wind up there, I guess; the flags on top of the stadium aren't exactly whipping on their poles. But that's secondary. The question on this play is why Pendleton swung at that pitch in the first place. With a runner in scoring position and one out, you want a good swing if you go after the first pitch in your first at-bat. That was always my theory, and it makes good sense.

The explanation tonight might be that Terry's RBI count, as well as the team's, is down a lot this year and he got overanxious. He's comfortable looking for the fastball on the first pitch of his first at-bat and has had success with this approach his entire career, and when he saw the fastball, he swung, despite the tough location. But I know Terry, and right now this former MVP is muttering to himself in the dugout. He wanted a better RBI at-bat than that. All things considered, would it have been better for him to get settled in, see a couple of pitches? In theory only. That's not the way Terry hits!

Regarding that fastball from Danny Jackson. It may have been "the cutter," which a lot of pitchers now throw. The cut fastball is held with the top two fingers slightly off-center to the outside. In effect, the cut fastball is just about the opposite of the tailing fastball. In the lefty Jackson's case, his natural tailing fastball moves away from right-handed batters, as I've described, while this cut fastball moves in on them a few inches. Watching on television, you could pick up the difference easily. Sitting here in the stands, it's tougher to see, no doubt about it. The cut fastball breaks the least of all the pitches that break at all, but that little bit is enough to be effective if located properly, especially in a lefty-righty situation, as in this at-bat, or righty-lefty. If Danny Jackson can throw this cut fastball inside to this right-handed-hitting Braves lineup, it will take some of the pressure off the slider. But it's imperative to keep this pitch on the corners; you can't miss with it over the middle. If it's not thrown correctly, the cut fastball doesn't run at all and is a bit slower than the regular fastball. In a word, trouble.

Two outs now, Jeff Blauser still standing on second base, Ron Gant up. Good, solid hitter. Pulls the ball with power. Ron had an off year in '92, but he's back on course this season, proved by his sixteen homers so far, only two less than in all of '92. You've got to mix it up on Gant. But before we go any further in this at-bat, let's consider the defensive alignment. The infield is shifted way around to the left, which makes sense, and the left fielder Pete Incaviglia and the center fielder Dykstra are pulled around, which also makes sense, but Jim Eisenreich in right field is playing just about straightaway, maybe even pushed toward that line a step or two. This leaves a gigantic gap in right-center field. The Phillies are playing Gant to pull the ball unless he hits it in the air to right field, in which case they think he'll go down the line. I'd like to see their charts on this. Hubie Brooks and Phil Garner come to mind as right-handed hitters who were (and still are, in Hubie's case) notorious for hitting line drives down the right-field line, but neither of them was a dead-pull hitter, like Ron Gant is. Even if Ron occasionally hits the ball down the line in right, you'll get hurt more often in the gaps than down the line. That's what I believe, and that's why I believe in bunching the outfielders. I did not like to look out from the infield and find the outfielders spread all over the place. If the guy's a pull hitter, like Gant, shift everyone around toward left. Take away the opposite-field gap. If the guy is an opposite-field hitter like Otis Nixon against lefties, push everyone that way. Unless some great charts on how Gant is hitting the ball this year convinced me otherwise, I'd move Eisenreich over toward right-center, at least in front of that "371" sign in the gap, maybe even farther. At any rate, mull this over the next time you see the outfield spread far apart. Then, when the ball rolls through the gap for a double, remember that Hernandez told you so.

After fastballs to start off the first three Braves batters, Danny Jackson is likely to throw his slider on the first pitch to Ron Gant. Not necessary, of course, just likely in the interests of diversity—and inside, too, because he hasn't been coming in, partially for the reasons I've just explained. Now's the time to give it a shot. And here it is, the slider, and inside, too—but low. Ball one. At the plate, Gant knows—or should know—that Jackson can have trouble coming inside with the fastball or the slider, so on this 1-0 count he's free to look for the fastball outside. Jackson needs a strike, and that's his safest location for getting it. Gant can sit on that pitch, go with it for a single to right field, and get the Braves on the board. One problem. I've just lectured about what a pull hitter he is. He's not very interested in going to right field. In that case, he can sit on the outside

11

pitch and pull it to left field. Contrary to popular wisdom, it is not hard for a good hitter to pull the outside pitch. Without getting too technical regarding hitting technique, it's simply a matter of rolling over the top hand earlier in the swing. You can test this with a handy broom or golf club. Roll over the top hand an instant before contact and the "bat" or club moves instantly from behind the plate to in front of the plate. You have just pulled the baseball or hooked the golf ball.

The 1-0 pitch to Ron Gant is indeed the fastball outside, and home-plate umpire Dana DeMuth gives Danny Jackson the benefit of the doubt on the call. Strike one! Gant glances back quickly, then down at the plate, a nice, simple way to send the ump a message without showing him up. This will no doubt be the first of many instances in which we'll observe that the umpire often has a wider strike zone on the outside than on the inside edge. Watching almost any game on television will verify this. I suppose the discrepancy results from the fact that the home-plate umpire sets up over the inside edge and therefore has a better view of the inside pitch. The National League umpires have always set up more inside, but the American League umps used to be behind the catcher, over the middle of the plate, when they wore that big balloon chest protector. In order to see over the catcher they had to stand fairly high, giving them a good view of the high pitch and the corners but a bad view of the low pitch. That's why the American League was a high-strike league. When they got rid of the big protector and moved inside they were able to squat a little lower, with a better view of whether the pitch is high or low, but I don't think the umpires in either league have a much better opinion regarding the outside corner from this location than the batter does. In fact, the batter may have a better angle. The catcher may sometimes block the umpire's view of the outside edge. The catcher has the prime spot.

On this same pitch from Danny Jackson, Darren Daulton rather noticeably pulled the ball in toward the strike zone a couple of inches. You see the catcher do this all the time, trying to help his pitcher get the call, but I don't think it will do much good. Does jerking the mitt in or out actually fool the umpire? On the contrary! If he sees the catcher jerking the ball around he's probably going to think, "Why's he doing that?…Ball two!" Much better on the pitch a couple of inches outside is to hold the ball right there, then drop the mitt and toss the ball back to the mound, "framing" the pitch for the umpire, who wants the catcher to catch the ball and hold it. Nothing fancy. Shifting the mitt in or out won't fool anyone. I came to the plate one day for the Mets with Terry Tata umpiring behind the plate, and Terry advised me to pass on a few words to our catcher—I forget who that was, some rookie sitting in for Gary Carter, I guess. "Tell him to hold the ball," Terry said. "Who's he trying to fool? Tell him he's in the big leagues now."

Shifting the mitt slightly up with the low pitch can be more effective because that movement is harder for the umpire to detect. That's almost a "timing" play, like the first baseman coming off the bag just as he catches the throw from the infielder, or maybe a fraction before he catches the throw. That smooth motion can get you the call on the close ones. You hear about pitchers like Dennis Eckersley who are famous for great control and therefore get the strike calls on the close pitches. Gary Carter was terrific at framing the pitch for his pitchers and getting more than his share of strike calls on the close ones. If a pitch was called a ball and Gary agreed, he tossed it right back to the pitcher. But if he thought it was a strike, he'd hold the ball perfectly still for a couple of seconds, a polite way to say to the ump, "Look again. I think you missed that one." Gary didn't abuse the privilege, so when he did this, the umpires paid attention.

In any event, Daulton and Jackson do get this call from Dana DeMuth, Ron Gant doesn't, but the count is still 1-1 and the batter is in the favorable position I mentioned earlier: He has seen Danny Jackson's two main pitches and is even in the count. The next pitch is a slider way outside. Nice try, Danny, but the strike zone doesn't extend *that* far out. The count is 2-1. Advantage hitter, and the thought surely enters both Daulton's and Jackson's minds that first base is open, there are two outs, and the struggling Brian

Hunter is on deck. He's hitting all of .125 after a month on the disabled list with a bad left hand, and he's had only forty at-bats all year. With one out the pitcher is less likely to pitch around the batter because he doesn't want to put two guys on with one out, regardless of who's coming up next, but with two outs, it's a possibility. Then again, do you want to put runners on base so early in the game? Jackson will be careful now with Gant, but he doesn't want to walk him, either.

But when you start pitching around someone, you do usually walk him because you're aiming for either corner, and if you miss, you want to miss off the plate, not over the plate. That's the whole idea of pitching around the guy. Specifically, when Darren Daulton sets up on the inside corner for the next pitch, the natural tendency is for Danny Jackson to miss either inside or low or both because he knows if he misses the target on the other side, the ball is right over the middle of the plate. And when Daulton sets up inside, you also suspect the pitch is going to be the slider, although Jackson could try to cut the fastball in there. But the slider it is, low. Three-and-one count now, and I'd be surprised if Jackson goes after Gant.

Oh! Slider on the hands, strike two. Gant glances back at DeMuth, but that was a good pitch and a gutsy one, too. It had *better* be a good pitch with Brian Hunter coming up. Now the tables are turned on Gant, in a way. I'll bet he was thinking that he might be standing on first base right now. I'll bet he was surprised at getting the good, hard slider inside on 3-1. Ron has yet to swing the wood, but this at-bat has been a good cat-and-mouse game, with pitcher, catcher, and batter all having to consider the empty base, the hitter coming up, the pattern of the pitches, and the successful inside slider that will now be in the back of every batter's mind for the rest of the game. The at-bat will be resolved with the next pitch unless it's fouled off, but as I said in the preamble, the previous five have been anything but irrelevant.

Jackson comes to his stretch and checks Jeff Blauser on second base. Let's see where Daulton wants the pitch ... same place, inside. I'm betting slider. The pitch is the slider ...

just inside. Gant's knees almost buckle as the ball zips past, then he trots to first. Danny Jackson doesn't look upset. If he missed, he was going to miss inside. Ball four but good "bait pitch." That was a perfect example of pitching carefully but aggressively. That sounds like a contradiction but it isn't, and Jackson just proved why. That slider was not an easy pitch for Ron Gant to lay off of.

So now Brian Hunter gets his chance. Jackson has to go after this guy, no fooling around. Again, the outfield aligns itself as it did for Ron Gant. Everyone is pulled around to the left except Eisenreich in right. Well, if that's the way they do things here in Philly …

The first offering, a slider, is low, but Hunter hacks away for strike one. You might suspect that Brian is known as a first-ball, fastball hitter and that Daulton and Jackson take advantage of this, knowing that he's hitless in his last fifteen at-bats, knowing he'll probably be a little anxious and pressing. This is almost spring training for Hunter, and the unhittable slider is the perfect bait pitch for the situation. Jackson comes back with a high and outside fastball, and Hunter swings again. Thank you very much! This is a batter in trouble, and indeed Brian concludes the inning by cuing a squibber out to Mickey Morandini at second base. That pitch was the low slider. This sequence is called "going up and down the ladder." It can work well for pitchers who have pop on their fastball and a good down-breaking ball low in the zone. Sid Fernandez is the classic up-and-down-the-ladder pitcher. Tom Seaver, Nolan Ryan, a lot of great pitchers get you to chase the high fastball, then the low breaking ball, then the high fastball, or vice versa—low, high, low. The batter can make an out against these guys and never swing at a pitch in the strike zone. Frustrating.

Brian Hunter doesn't run hard to first base, then flips his batting helmet off the back of his head onto the ground. Pick it up, coach. Poor form and a sure sign of disgust.

The matchup between the Braves' Pete Smith and the Phillies batters is a mirror image of the matchup in the top half of the inning. Smith throws right-handed and Jim Fregosi has loaded his lineup with left-handed hitters. Smith is Atlanta's fifth starter. Injury-plagued for years, still trying to post a full season of games following rotator-cuff surgery two years ago, he's off to a slow start in 1993, with a 2-6 record and a 4.23 ERA. Five losses in a row. It's nice to know these statistics, but the key stat I wanted to know as a batter about any pitcher was the ratio of walks to innings pitched. Half as many walks issued as innings pitched—fifty walks, one hundred innings—is about average. A higher ratio tells the batter that this pitcher doesn't have great command; the batter can work the count. In sixty-six innings pitched in 1993, Pete Smith has walked twenty-seven batters, not a bad number. Danny Jackson's numbers—thirty-two walks in ninety-six innings—are even better news for him, worse news for the batter. This is sharp control for Danny.

On the other hand, a pitcher's strikeout ratio means a lot to the fans but it doesn't tell the batter all that much. His approach may be very different against a strikeout pitcher with high walks, like Randy Johnson, versus one with low walks, like Tom Seaver, to cite one of the ultimate power pitchers with great control. The walks, not the strikeouts, are the key statistic for the batter.

Leadoff batter Lenny Dykstra knows this, for sure. He loves to take the count deep, and Pete Smith is a pitcher who will probably let him do it. Lenny and I played together with the Mets, who proceeded to trade him—a deal I assume they now regret—because he's a little on the wild and crazy side. The Phillies acquired him for just this reason. Lenny is pumped up with iron and energy, and he epitomizes this Phillies team. There's nothing corporate about the man. He's the only Phillie to start every game of the season, and that might be the biggest plus for the team this year because injuries limited Lenny to just eighty-five games last year, sixty-three the year before, and the dude knows how to play. (In New York, Dykstra was both "Dude" and "Nails." Here, he's just the dude.)

The fans are already stomping for a base hit when he

steps into the batter's box, but Dykstra will gladly take the walk. It wasn't always that way. Lenny got his head turned when he hit those three home runs for the Mets in the '86 postseason. One of them was a shot right down the line in the bottom of the ninth at Shea that won game three of the playoffs against the Astros. And this power display in post-season was after hitting just eight homers in the regular season. Lenny decided that he had home run power. Now, six years later, he understands exactly the kind of player he is and exactly what kind of production the Phillies need from him. They do not need for him to look for the low, inside pitch he can golf over the right-field fence. They need a solid batting average and a high on-base percentage, and this season he's coming through with a .284 average that's climbing as we speak and a .400 on-base percentage that includes fifty-three walks. He does have seven homers already, but they're coming naturally, and Veterans Stadium is a bandbox. The bottom line for any leadoff man is runs scored, and Lenny already has a phenomenal sixty-two, in just sixty-nine games. Before last night's loss, he had a streak of fifteen consecutive games scoring a run, two shy of the National League record.

Smith starts Dykstra off with a fastball high, then follows with either a cut fastball or a slider without a lot on it. Properly thrown by the right-hander Smith, the cutter will break a few inches in toward the left-handed-hitting Dykstra and the slider a few inches down and in. If the slider isn't thrown with authority, there's not much difference between these two pitches. Sitting in the stands, I'm not sure about this particular pitch. I'll call it a cut fastball, and Dana DeMuth will call it inside, ball two. Even the players on the field don't always know the pitch unless they've picked up the catcher's sign. From the vantage point on the field you know whether the pitch was high or low, but you may not know much else regarding location and pitch selection. After all, you aren't concentrating on the pitch itself. You're focused on the hitting zone because that's where the ball will come rocketing from.

Regardless what that pitch from Pete Smith was, Lenny Dykstra is happy. If, as a hitter, you like to work the count, the key is to get to two balls. It takes one more ball to walk a batter than strikes to strike him out, four against three, so the second ball tips the scales in the batter's favor, or at least evens them out. That was always my thinking, anyway. In my opinion, the hitter's absolutely ideal sequence to start off the first at-bat in the game is either the fastball for ball one, followed by the curve, or vice versa, the curve, ball one, followed by the fastball.

If the first ball is the fastball and the pitcher then follows with another fastball, you're ready to swing if the pitch is in your zone. You may not reach ball two in the count, but that's irrelevant if this second pitch is a good one to hit. But if the second pitch is the breaking ball, take it, especially in the first inning. If that breaking pitch is a ball, you've reached 2-0 and are sitting pretty; if it's a strike, you're okay at 1-1. Either way, you've had a chance to gauge the speed of the two basic pitches, and this is crucial for any batter in his first at-bat. He's extremely happy. I'm not exaggerating.

If that first ball was a breaking pitch, you'd be tempted to take the second pitch if it was also a breaking pitch and definitely take it if it was the fastball.

Maybe this sounds complicated, but the idea is simple: It's nice to see the different pitches as early as possible in the first at-bat. You get an idea what you're up against. You feel prepared. Granted, the change-up is still missing, but the change is usually the pitcher's third pitch. That's the case with both Danny Jackson and Pete Smith. The Braves and Phillies batters will see the change-up eventually, but it's not essential to see it early in the game because they can be mentally prepared for the fastball and still have a chance of adjusting to the change-up, while they can't be guessing change-up (or the breaking ball) and then hit the fastball. Highly improbable. You just can't catch up to it.

Since a lot of major league batters agree with me that seeing the fastball and breaking ball early in the first at-bat is ideal, why does the pitcher ever oblige them? Well, what are Danny Jackson and Pete Smith's alternatives? All breaking balls in the first at-bat? All fastballs? That doesn't sound like a good idea. They have to mix 'em up. In the top half of this inning, Otis Nixon saw two fastballs from Danny Jackson to start the game, Jeff Blauser saw the fastball and the breaking ball, Ron Gant saw the slider first pitch. Pete Smith will also alter his sequence from batter to batter, so some will get that preferred sequence of fastball, breaking ball or breaking ball, fastball.

I referred to Ron Gant's at-bat in the top of the first as a good cat-and-mouse game between him and Danny Jackson, even though Ron never swung the bat. To me, that game describes every at-bat. Some hitters—including some great ones—say they just go up there hackin'. Kirby Puckett comes to mind. But even with a hacker like Kirby, the count dictates his approach to some degree. The pitcher and the batter each has his preferred approach to the at-bat, but the count goes a long way toward dictating which of them is more likely to get his way. I look at it this way: After the first pitch for a ball or a strike, neither pitcher nor hitter is sweating too much. But if the second pitch makes the count either 2-0 or 0-2, somebody is in check, so to me the *second* pitch is more critical than the first one. If the second pitch evens the count, then the third pitch tilts the balance one way or the other, although 2-1 is not as bad for the pitcher as 1-2 is for the batter. If the fourth pitch continues the trend, either the pitcher is in trouble at 3-1 or the batter is struck out. If the fourth pitch evens the count at 2-2, this is better for the pitcher, but then if he fails to convert, the 3-2 count is a big lift for the batter (and for the base runner; I'll have more to say about this later).

Back and forth, back and forth, an extended at-bat is like a long rally in tennis, when first one player, then the other seems to have the tactical advantage; the idea is the same in each sport. Whoever has the initial upper hand wants to finish off the opponent, who in turn wants to even things out, then get the advantage himself. And to continue the analogy, this is why many hitters like to hit "first ball-fastball"—get all over that pitch like a cheap suit—and great returners of serve climb all over the second serve or weak first serve, going for the winner if at all possible: Strike early and try to wipe out the inherent advantage of the pitcher/server.

On the 2-0 pitch to Lenny Dykstra, Pete Smith throws a fastball at the letters for the first strike but another fastball runs away from the plate outside, ball three, and another misses high, ball four. Dykstra scurries to first base. Walking the leadoff batter: a cardinal sin. Something like 70 percent of all leadoff walks score, and the figure is probably higher than that for Lenny. With the Phillies' powerful lineup behind him, the dude loves to go deep in the count and get the walk.

Leadoff hitter on first base, nobody out, left-handed-hitting Mickey Morandini at the plate. This is the classic situation in baseball for putting on some kind of play, and the classic scenario for you to think along with the manager and then second-guess his decisions. The leadoff guy is fast, by definition—there are no slow leadoff batters in the major leagues. Wait a minute, Wade Boggs leads off every now and then. The number two hitter must be a good bat-handler because he may be required to make contact with the pitch on the hit-and-run, or he may be asked to take a pitch or two to allow the runner to steal. And this is tough. Say he takes two pitches and the runner doesn't go on either one, and both are strikes. Now he's in a big hole. It's very tough for the second hitter. Takes real patience and confidence. The number two batter is one of the unsung heroes of baseball, in my opinion, and no one has done the job better in the past than Willie Randolph with the Yankees and Ted Sizemore with the Cards. Among active players, Robby Thompson of the Giants is one of the best. So is Jeff Blauser, playing here tonight for Atlanta. The Phillies' Morandini already has forty-three strikeouts, more than you'd like from the number two hitter (Dykstra only has 22, in 50 more at-bats), but with all the runs Dykstra is scoring ahead of him, Morandini must be doing something right.

Jim Fregosi has five choices in this situation, ranked in what I consider to be the order of increasing riskiness (and most managers agree with me):

1. Bunt the runner to second base. This is the ultimate safety-first play, and I'd use it late in the
   game only. Early in the game, it's too conservative
   for me, and for Fregosi here, I'm sure.
2. Have the runner steal; if he's successful, bunt him
   to third base. The steal is risky, but the bunt is
   another safety-first play.
3. Have the runner steal. If he's successful, hope
   that the second hitter drives him in. Short of that,
   rely on the second hitter to hit a grounder to the
   right side of the infield, advancing the base runner to third, where he can score on a sacrifice fly.
4. No play at all. The runner stays put, and the hitter tries to hit.
5. Hit-and-run.

I consider no play a risky play because, as always, the
hitter is at a disadvantage and a ground ball risks the double
play that ruins the inning. The second hitter has to be a
good bat-handler, yes, but that doesn't necessarily translate
into a .300 average. It means you don't strike out much, you
direct the ball to right or to left, you put the ball in play.
Morandini is hitting .230. Putting on no play at all runs a
high risk of getting no results at all.

The riskiest option, the hit-and-run, is one of the more
strategically complex plays in the game. I don't know any
way to get into the subject other than at length because, as I
mentioned, experience has taught me that some big leaguers don't fully understand what the play is all about, when
it's a good idea, when it's a terrible idea. So here goes. Be
patient—the in's and out's of the hit-and-run go to the heart
of baseball strategy, and you have to understand them to
understand the game. We'll be back at Veterans Stadium in
Philadelphia in a few pages.

The phrase "hit-and-run" is actually a misnomer, as most
fans know. The runner runs, then the hitter hits, so it's really
the run-and-hit, but no matter. I'll stick with the standard
phrase. The basic idea is to force the shortstop or the second

baseman to cover second base, opening a large, inviting hole, usually to the opposite field, for the batter to shoot a hit through on the ground. The runner advances to third base easily on any single through the infield. Big inning brewing. And even when the play doesn't produce optimum results it usually produces acceptable results because the slowest man in baseball will be safe at second if he's breaking with the pitch and the batter hits a grounder to an infielder (with one exception, noted in a moment). So the second-best result of the hit-and-run yields the same result as a successful bunt: runner at second, one out. If the batter hits a pop-up to the infield or a routine fly to the outfield, the runner can get back to first in time. If the batter hits a line drive to the outfield, the runner has to hold on the base path between first and second, prepared to retreat to first if the liner is caught.

However, the hit-and-run is far from foolproof. The batter must swing in order to protect the runner. If he misses the pitch, the runner is thrown out at second base more times than not. In fact, if the pitch is two feet high and the batter does miss it, the likelihood that the runner will be thrown out is *greater* than with the straight steal because the runner does *not* try to get the best possible jump when this play is on. Why not? If the batter does his job and makes contact, the runner doesn't need a great jump in order to make it to second on a ground ball or to third on any base hit, so his first rule is don't get picked off. This caution costs him a millisecond. If the batter swings and misses, the runner is in jeopardy.

Another risk is a line drive at an infielder. The runner will be doubled off first base. The buzzard's luck. A third risk is the hard grounder hit right back through the box, directly over second base. If the runner weren't in motion and one of the fielders was not moving to the bag to cover, that's more than likely a single. But on the hit-and-run, it's a double play. When you do everything right but don't get the hoped-for results, we say, "Hang with 'em." The double play on the hit-and run is a *big* hang with 'em.

Since the batter must swing at anything on the hit-and-run, the play becomes a semisacrifice on a pitch a foot high or outside or in the dirt. This brings us to the key issue regarding the play and one that's misunderstood. The hit-and-run makes sense only when the pitcher needs to throw a strike or something close to it, for his own purposes. Thus the count in the at-bat is everything with the hit-and-run.

The counts on which the batter has the best chance of getting a decent pitch to hit are the first pitch, 1-0, 2-0, and 2-1. The pitcher wants to throw a strike with these counts because there's already one runner on and he doesn't want to dig a bigger hole for himself with the batter, risking the walk. On the other hand, the manager will seldom call for the hit-and-run when the count is 0-1 or 1-1 because the pitcher is even or ahead in these counts and has the opportunity to tease the hitter with a tough pitch just off the corner. Finally, it should be obvious that the manager will never put on the hit-and-run when the count is 0-2, 1-2, or 2-2. You can't force the batter to swing at anything with two strikes just to protect the base runner. Not done.

What about the three remaining counts, 3-0, 3-1, and 3-2? Again, not done, but for a different reason. With these counts, one more ball and the batter walks and the runner gets to second base the safest possible way. Why would you force the batter to swing at ball four? You wouldn't. It's true that the pitcher wants to throw a strike in these counts, but if your batter swings on 3-0 or 3-1, you want confident, aggressive, power swings. These counts are the batter's pitch. You don't want him going the other way for a single. Drive the ball! Now, the fast runner is often sent in motion on 3-1, and the batter often swings if the pitch is a strike, but this is not the hit-and-run. The batter just liked the pitch. On the full count, the runner will almost certainly be going on the pitch, but that's not the hit-and-run, either, because the batter can take ball four.

By the same token, the fact that the runner breaks and the batter swings on the 1-0 count does not necessarily mean that a hit-and-run is on. It could have been a steal with the batter swinging at his discretion. One way to judge which play it was is to watch the runner to see if he looks back at the plate on the pitch. If he does not, he's stealing. If he does, the hit-and-run is on and he's watching to see where the ball goes. This is a nice rule of thumb, but it's not surefire because some base stealers also look back at the plate on the straight steal, and some base runners on the hit-and-run do not look back, which is wrong.

The hit-and-run is usually put on with nobody out. With one out, you will try it only with an excellent hit-and-run man at the plate; the best. You have to like his chances for a hit because the second-best result, the grounder that moves the runner to second, makes the second out and leaves only one chance for the RBI. I hope it's clear that you would never hit-and-run with two outs. A defensive swing yielding a ground ball is the third out.

The hit-and-run is usually called for with the single runner on first base, but it's not unheard of with runners on first and second, and it's even tried with runners on first and third. With runners on first and second, there are two drawbacks to the play. First, a big inning may be brewing, by definition. Do you want to risk it by trying anything tricky at all? Second, a main point of the play with a runner on first is to force either the shortstop or the second baseman to cover second base, opening that big hole in the infield, but with a runner on second base, too, neither middle infielder has to cover. The third baseman breaks to cover third, but the resulting hole is not nearly as significant for the hitter. So the hit-and-run with runners on first and second is not popular.

With runners on first and third, you would only try it in a tie game, maybe a run down, and if the infield is playing back for the double play with one out. If the infield is playing in, you can't hit-and-run because the infielder could nail the runner at home, but if the infield is back, the runner on first breaks with the pitch and the runner on third breaks not with the pitch, but on contact. The defense won't be able to turn the double play, and the runner on third should score. You wouldn't try this particular hit-and-run with no outs. Let the batter swing away because if he makes an out, the next guy still has the chance for the sacrifice fly. But the first-and-third hit-and-run makes a little more sense with one out because if the batter makes an out otherwise, the chance for the sac fly is gone. Whitey Herzog put this play on quite a few times, with good success, as I recall. Buck Rodgers, now managing the California Angels, loves it, too, but I wonder if it's not too clever. After all, a sacrifice fly does score the run.

Whom do you want at the plate for the hit-and-run? Either the number two, three, or seven hitter in the lineup. The sixth hitter is a possibility, depending on what kind of power role he plays in the lineup. If he's a power hitter, he's not likely to be asked to hit-and-run. The fourth and fifth hitters don't hit-and-run, for the same reason you don't ask them to bunt. You want them swinging the bat with power. That's their whole purpose for being in the lineup. And there are individual hitters who simply aren't comfortable with having to swing no matter where the pitch is and so aren't good candidates for the hit-and-run.

At the bottom of the lineup, hit-and-run strategy differs between the two leagues. In the American League, the hit-and-run with any of the bottom three hitters is perfectly plausible. In the National League, with the pitcher batting ninth, the logic of putting on this play with the eighth hitter might be dubious. Even if the play is successful with the eighth hitter, will the pitcher be able to follow up? The play makes the most sense if the pitcher is a good bunter. If the hit-and-run is successful and produces runners on first and third, the pitcher can bunt the runner to second. Or you could pinch-hit for the pitcher late in the game and go for a big inning. Shortstop Rafael Santana got a lot of hit-and-run hits batting eighth for the Mets in the mid-eighties.

Many factors influence the decision to put on the hit-and-run, but the main one is the basic kind of team the manager has. The classic St. Louis lineup, loaded with good averages and speed but not featuring a great deal of power, is ideal for the aggressive hit-and-run. The classic Detroit lineup, or what has become that lineup in recent years under Sparky Anderson, will stand pat much more often.

The later innings in a tie game are the ideal time for the hit-and-run, when the team needs one or two runs. In the early innings, the manager might well decide to try to forgo the hit-and-run or the sacrifice bunt in the hopes of building a bigger inning. When you're six runs down, forget all these plays because you need all the opportunities for pure hitting you can get.

Conventional wisdom holds that the National League favors the hit-and-run more than the American League, the big-inning league. I haven't seen any figures to verify this, but over the course of a season you can easily come to a conclusion about the preferred strategies of your local manager in either league. Think carefully about the situation—the score, the inning, the personnel—and watch the count on the batter. If the manager seldom calls the hit-and-run in the late innings of close games with the leadoff hitter or any other fast man on first base, nobody out, and the count 2-1 on the next hitter, a good bat-handler, you know this manager is conservative, for whatever set of reasons. Maybe he prefers having the runner steal. If the runner seldom steals, either, this manager feels that his team is geared toward station-to-station offense. The classic example: Sparky Anderson and the Detroit Tigers, whom we will see in action in the second game of our doubleheader.

On the other hand, the manager can't become too predictable with the hit-and-run because the defense has one tremendous weapon to use against it: the pitchout. As noted earlier, the runner's first job on the hit-and-run is to make sure he's not picked off. A slow break from first base and an accurate pitchout to the catcher will produce an out at second 95 percent of the time. Therefore, the manager has to pick and choose. If he gets in the habit of calling for the hit-and-run at almost every reasonable opportunity, the defense will pitch out and nail the guy.

Recall the four conceivable counts for the hit-and-run: first pitch, 1-0, 2-0, and 2-1. One of these is the ideal hit-and-run count because the manager on defense will probably not want to risk a pitchout. Which is it? The 2-1 count, because if the hit-and-run is not on, the pitchout would be ball three, 3-1 is the best hitter's count of all, and the fast runner will be breaking on that pitch almost automatically. Nevertheless, managers do play their hunches and call for the pitchout on 2-1. Sometimes the catcher nails the runner at second, sometimes the pitchout looks silly when the runner stands at first while the batter gets an easy ball three. That's the problem with the pitchout. It can put the pitcher in a hole.

The opposing manager is equally leery of the pitchout on the 2-0 count, but the manager on offense wants his batter to drive the ball if he goes after the 2-0 pitch. On 2-1, the batter is up in the count but not as much as on 2-0, so 2-1 is the classic hit-and-run count. However, you may never get the 2-1 count, and that's why the manager intent on the hit-and-run often calls it on the only good count he can be assured of getting—the first pitch of the at-bat. But if he gets the reputation of calling the hit-and-run on the first pitch, the opposing managers will start pitching out. And the reverse also holds true. If a manager gets a reputation for pitching out often (as Roger Craig did with the Giants), the word will spread via the scouts, and the opposition will sit tight in obvious hit-and-run situations. By the way, the same holds for catchers. Ted Simmons, for one, became well known for calling pitchouts in certain situations. For this reason some managers don't authorize their catchers to call the pitchout. That play has to come from the dugout. This is why in any conceivable hit-and-run situation you can see the catcher look into his dugout for the instruction to pitch out.

That's about it for the hit-and-run from the offense's point of view. What about defending against the play? The issue is which fielder covers second base when the runner breaks on the pitch. Logic dictates that with a dead-pull left-handed hitter at the plate, the shortstop covers second because the odds are great that the guy will pull the ball toward right field. Vice versa with the dead-pull right-handed batter. But the dead-pull hitter is not likely to be participating in a hit-and-run in the first place because he's almost by definition a power guy and hitting fourth, fifth, or sixth in the lineup. More likely to be the batter in a hit-and-run is the scrappy line-drive hitter who can direct the ball just about anywhere. The defensive choice here requires some guesswork, but nine out of ten times the "opposite"

fielder will be covering second base: with a left-handed batter, the shortstop; with a right-handed batter, the second
baseman. With a good bat-handler notorious for taking the
ball to the opposite field—Wade Boggs is the classic example—you might very well have the second baseman cover. Or
say the pitch selection against a right-handed batter is the
fastball on the outside edge. That's not a tough pitch to pull,
as I've explained, but many batters still have a tendency to
hit that pitch up the middle or to the right side, especially on
the hit-and-run. In this case, the shortstop might cover so the
second baseman can stay put. Each manager has his own
thinking on this subject. In any event, when a runner is on
first and might be either stealing or involved in a hit-and-run,
note that either the second baseman or the shortstop will
watch the catcher's sign to the pitcher, then hold his glove in
front of his face and signal to his companion which of them
will cover second. A standard code is open mouth, you cover,
shut mouth, I cover. Television broadcasts routinely feature
this little bit of inside baseball.

Occasionally I called the coverage for the Mets, playing a
hunch, and one time it backfired and I heard about it from
Davey Johnson. With a left-handed batter at the plate, but a
guy who often took the ball to left field, I signaled for second
baseman Wally Backman to cover. The batter—I forget who
he was—made me look bad by pulling the ball through the
vacated hole on the right side. Back in the dugout between
innings Davey chewed me out. He believes that the only
time to cross up the coverage is against a right-handed batter. When you try to cross up a left-handed batter by having
the second baseman cover, as I had just done, the resulting
hole is enormous because the first baseman is holding the
runner. Also, the hardest line drive gets the runner to third
because the throw from right field is so long. But if the
shortstop covers against a right-handed batter and this guy
does pull the ball through the hole into left field, there is at
least a chance that the runner will have to hold at second
because the throw from left field to third is short. Also, the
hole on the left side of the infield isn't as large as the hole on
the right side because the third baseman isn't holding a run-

ner on. The bottom line is that the attempted cross-up against the right-handed batter isn't quite as risky as the cross-up against left-handed batters, should either backfire.

Very subtle, Davey. I hadn't thought about this point, and no one—not even Dad—had ever brought it up.

The question always comes up of whether the hitter can see in his peripheral vision which fielder has covered, and then try to direct the ball in that direction. This does sound possible, but all I can say is, easier said than done. Remember, the fielder breaks only when the runner breaks—when the pitcher is into his delivery. As an experiment, several times I tried to pick up the fielder and then get my attention back to the pitch in time. I couldn't do it. Hats off to anyone who can.

You can also watch the infielders on the hit-and-run try to trick the runner if the ball is hit behind him on the right side. If it goes into right field, the shortstop covering second may pretend there's a play at second base and the runner may slide (but not if he's paying attention). If the shortstop pretends the ball is being caught by the right fielder, maybe the runner will hesitate and lose the chance to go to third. The fielders can and do try this stuff, but the base runner who watches them makes a big mistake because he is taught from birth: find the ball on the hit-and-run; if you can't find the ball, watch the third-base coach.

All in all, the hit-and-run situation is one of the better mind games on the field. When the leadoff hitter gets on first base with nobody out, especially in the eighth inning of a 2-2 game, the proverbial wheels are turning in the two dugouts and they should be in the stands, too. The pitcher may throw over to first a couple of times. The batter and runner will check the third base coach for their sign. The catcher looks into the dugout for his instructions from the manager. The third baseman may move in to protect against the bunt. The odds for some kind of play rise and fall and rise again as the count shifts, and if you're awake, you're in just as good a position as the manager to call the shots. The players in the field are placing their bets, too. It's a kick to guess right.

29

CHAPTER 2

In Philadelphia, Lenny Dykstra has led off the game for the Phillies with a walk off Pete Smith. Left-hand-hitting Mickey Morandini is at the plate. The Braves play him like the Phillies played Otis Nixon: shallow and pushed around toward the opposite field, left field, in this case. They don't believe Morandini will pull Pete Smith. I concur. Morandini is not a pull hitter, and he doesn't have much power (for one thing, he chokes up about four inches). He's your basic number two hitter and therefore a good candidate for the hit-and-run except that it's early in the game and Dykstra has been successful on nineteen of twenty-three steal attempts. I assume that Lenny, like most if not all of the good base stealers, has a permanent green light. These runners are not told to steal on a particular pitch or at-bat; they may steal if they get the good jump. For these guys, the manager has a sign that says, "Don't steal." But that's not the case here. Dykstra can go. With him, the steal might actually be less risky than the hit-and-run because Lenny's odds of stealing successfully are excellent. If he does steal, Fregosi will then hope Morandini drives him in, or at the least moves him to third with a ground ball to the right side.

The sacrifice bunt? I'm sure Fregosi hopes Morandini can do the job by swinging the bat. In the first inning with a high-scoring team like Philadelphia, the bunt would be an extremely cautious play. Too cautious. It's early, these guys score runs, and Pete Smith is not Sandy Koufax. That's not a knock on Pete, either. The bunt is awfully conservative in the early innings even if the pitcher were Koufax. If it's 1968 and you're facing Bob Gibson when he had a 1.12 earned run average, maybe, just maybe. Or Gooden versus Valenzuela back in the mid-eighties, maybe (although these hyped pitchers' duels often have a way of disintegrating early). Early-inning sacrifice bunts by anyone except the pitcher are so conservative they're almost defeatist. I know that Kevin Kennedy, the first-year manager who did a great job with the Texas Rangers in '93, called for quite a few sacrifice bunts early in the game, and with excellent hitters like Rafael Palmeiro and Julio Franco, too. It's conservative to use that quality of hitter to bunt anytime; to use them early in the game, even if they're in a slump ultraconservative. The opposite approach to bunting was held by Davey Johnson when he was managing the Mets. He hated the sacrifice bunt in the eighth inning, much less in the first. I'm closer to that opinion. With rare exceptions, I wouldn't sacrifice with anyone other than the pitcher earlier than the seventh inning. I think a majority of major league managers would accept that as a rule of thumb.

But let's see what happens here with Jim Fregosi and the Phillies. Morandini and Dykstra study the signs from third-base coach Larry Bowa. It's also likely that one or more veteran coaches on the Braves bench are watching Bowa's signs, trying to figure out the code over the course of the series. It's great if you can pull it off. Manny Mota, a first-base coach himself, was famous for stealing the opposing third-base coach's signs. I wouldn't suggest that you invest a lot of effort in this enterprise because the odds for success aren't very good, but if you do feel like giving it a shot, here are the basics. Each of the four main situations—steal, hit-and-run, bunt, squeeze bunt—is assigned one gesture as its sign, and there is also the "indicator" sign. Standing in his coaching box, Bowa will make all kinds of meaningless gestures, and then he'll hit the team's indicator—maybe going to the bill of his cap with his left hand. After the indicator, the first sign is

31

usually the play, but it could be the second sign or the third sign. Usually, but not necessarily, both the indicator and the sign will be given by the same hand.

There is also the wipe-off sign, which nullifies the original sign. This is just another form of deception. You mix in a wipe-off along with an indicator and the actual sign, giving the potential sign-stealer a new headache. On the other hand, the wipe-off sign on every team I played on was the same: a hand swiped across the chest. Is this the universal wipe-off sign? I sometimes wondered.

The ultimate defense against stealing signs was devised by Preston Gomez, former third-base coach for Houston, St. Louis, and California. Preston was amazing. He had one set of signs for all the pitchers but a *different* set for *each* of the other players. Think about it. Fifteen guys, four signs and an indicator apiece, that's a lot of signs Preston had to keep track of. Touching the bill of the cap with the right hand might be the bunt for one player but the steal for another. With runners on first and second base and a bunt in the works, Preston had to flash three sets of signs, and quickly, too, with no mistakes. And he did it without a hitch. Awesome.

I suppose that if you have good seats in the first-base boxes you could train your video camera on the third-base coach every time he flashes the signs over the course of a homestand. Then go home and chart the gestures and compare them with the plays called or not called. With anyone other than Preston Gomez, maybe you could figure out the code, I don't know. Mota did, and I think he just watched carefully and relied on his memory. But don't forget, teams change their indicator and their signs every so often—and definitely if the first two hit-and-runs are greeted with pitchouts. On second thought, forget it. Don't waste your time.

The Phillies study their signs, Braves catcher Damon Berryhill looks for his sign, if any, from Bobby Cox. I'd be surprised if Bobby wants the pitchout. The managers will play this straight up, in all likelihood. Pete Smith throws to first. Dykstra steps back. Smith takes his stretch again, delivers to the plate, Dykstra holds at first base, Morandini squares to bunt but takes the pitch. Fastball, strike one. You cannot know for certain, sitting in the stands, but that was probably not an actual bunt attempt. I'd be shocked. Morandini didn't look serious, and the pitch was perfect to bunt. Instead, squaring around was designed to bother the catcher and keep him from popping up quickly to throw, should Dykstra be stealing. It might also keep Terry Pendleton, the Braves third baseman, pulled in tight at third base, but he would do this anyway in most situations against this left-handed batter, respecting his bunting and his speed.

After the bluffed bunt, Morandini is down a strike in the count, but that's not a disaster. The hit-and-run is definitely out the window, but the straight steal is still an option. Bobby Cox could order the pitchout. If Dykstra holds, the count would still be 1-1, okay for the pitcher. Therefore, the 0-1 count is not a great count to steal on. The same logic holds for the 0-2 count: Pitching out is relatively safe, therefore stealing is relatively unsafe. But let's see what happens. Berryhill checks the dugout. Pete Smith takes his stretch...Dykstra holds, fastball outside. The count is 1-1.

Those two fastballs bring up another bit of conventional wisdom: Throw a fastball instead of the slower breaking ball on likely steal situations, thus giving the catcher that extra split second to throw out the runner and also lessening the chance the catcher will have to dig a curve out of the dirt before he throws at all. Maybe Berryhill called for the fastballs for that reason. It would make sense. Certain catchers become known for calling for fastballs in steal situations, hoping to bolster their "caught stealing" statistics. Johnny Bench deservedly had this reputation, late in his career. I have a different theory about handling base stealers. Hold the runner close by throwing over on occasion. Vary your timing before you deliver to the plate, hold the stretch for a second one time, three seconds the next, and so on. Then just pitch your game. Simple as that. Throwing fastballs in steal situations may help the catcher or it may help the batter if he's thinking along with you and looking for that fastball. It can cut both ways. Davey Johnson occasionally warned the pitchers on the Mets against throwing too many fastballs when the speedy St. Louis Cardinals got on base. You can't throw a steady diet of fastballs to Jack Clark or any other strong hitter just to thwart stolen bases.

Pete Smith throws over to first base. It's increasingly popular in the major leagues for the manager to call these throws. The catcher flashes the signal, and the pitcher obeys. I don't know. That verges on overmanaging. But it's impossible for you to know whether a throw to first is the pitcher's, the catcher's, or the manager's brilliant idea. Or the first baseman's. I had a sign I used with some pitchers asking them to throw over because otherwise they never would, and you need to, occasionally. Tonight, Dykstra steps back to the bag.

On the third pitch to the plate, Dykstra holds again and Pete Smith wisely tries something besides a fastball: a curve on the outside corner, what we call the backdoor curve, strike two. I should explain the term "backdoor," which the announcers employ all the time without necessarily explaining what it means. The basic breaking ball thrown by a right-hander to a left-handed batter—Smith versus Morandini—or by a lefty to a right-handed batter cuts across the plate toward the inside corner. The backdoor breaking ball, on the other hand, starts off three to six inches outside, depending on the pitcher, and breaks onto the *outside* corner at the last split second for a strike. The tendency for the batter is to "give up" on this pitch, figuring it's a ball outside. Surprise! The backdoor curve or slider thrown consistently for a strike in a great location is a very effective pitch because it never actually crosses the strike zone. It just nicks the zone in passing—or maybe it doesn't even do that, if the umpire is calling a wide zone out there.

Morandini has now taken three pitches in order to help his teammate on first base, two of them were strikes, he finds himself in a hole, but Dykstra hasn't moved. What happened? Well, you can't steal every time. Lou Brock didn't. Rickey Henderson doesn't. Neither does Dykstra.

The dude doesn't have blazing speed. He relies on reading the pitcher and getting a good jump. He doesn't try to force the issue. If he doesn't get the good break, he doesn't run. And give some credit here to Pete Smith. He doesn't have a great reputation for holding runners on, but maybe this time he helped his own cause. Or maybe Dykstra is too tired tonight. We'll never know.

With two strikes on Morandini, Dykstra might not want to steal because most hitters don't like to hit with two strikes and the runner on the move. I didn't. With two strikes, you have to bear down at the plate. You don't want any distractions. Therefore, most hitters want you to do your stealing early in the count, and this goes double for stealing third base, when the batter picks up the runner breaking off second directly behind the pitcher. When I played in St. Louis with Lou Brock and Garry Templeton, I asked them please to go for third base early in the count. If they did, I'd take the pitch, even if it was a strike. (Imagine me telling Lou Brock when to steal!)

Pete Smith switches to the fastball for his fourth pitch to Morandini, and it's high for ball two. A 2-2 count, and now Dykstra will almost certainly hold at first base and hope for ball three on the next pitch, giving a full count and a situation guaranteed to put him in motion. But if Morandini doesn't object, Dykstra could steal because Pete Smith wants to throw a strike and avoid the full count, and Morandini will swing at that strike. The catcher has to wait for Morandini to finish his swing. But remember, if the runner does take off and the batter swings on 2-2, it is not a hit-and-run. The batter swung because the pitch was a strike.

As it turns out here, Dykstra holds at first base and the pitch is a fastball high and outside. Pete Smith grabs the return throw from Berryhill in disgust. He's in danger of walking a .230 hitter and on a 3-2 count, to boot. In effect, the 3-2 count is like a free hit-and-run. The runner will be off with the pitch, setting up runners on first and third on a single, and if the pitch is not a good one to hit—ball four. And if the infield should get a bullet on the ground and a chance for

35

the double play, the pivot man runs a much greater risk of getting creamed because the runner arrives at the base much quicker than if he weren't breaking with the pitch.

I'd like to emphasize this point because it's important and sometimes overlooked: Quite a few ball games every season turn on an at-bat in which the pitcher allows the count to move from 2-2 to 3-2 or from 2-1 to 3-1, also putting the runner in motion. Check it out. Pete Smith has every reason to be annoyed with himself.

Change-up! Pete's first one in the game, I think. The pitch is at the ankles, but Morandini swings anyway for strike three. Berryhill can't find the handle to make the throw, so Dykstra's headfirst slide into second base is beside the point. The net result here is the same as a bunt or hit-and-run grounder to the infield: Dykstra on second, one out. It just took him a little longer to get there.

And note the risky pitch. Pete Smith got the out, but Morandini swung at ball four. A change-up when you need a strike is a risky pitch, especially early in the game when you don't want to make trouble for yourself with walks and you haven't thrown the pitch before. Throwing the change-up for a strike is no guarantee. I don't think everyone realizes that the change-up from many pitchers, including Pete Smith, not only throws the batter off stride with its slower velocity, but it also breaks downward. Often the break is so gentle that "break" is the wrong word, sometimes the pitch just rolls downward. In any event, this kind of change-up often, if not usually, ends up out of the strike zone if the batter can only lay off. That's why it's a dangerous pitch to throw on a full count. On the other hand, it just fooled Mickey Morandini and earned Pete Smith his first out of the inning. A good eye is so important. I swung at my share of 3-2 change-ups in the dirt, but if Mickey had been able to lay off that pitch, Pete Smith would have been in a lot of trouble in the first inning with no one out, fast runners on first and second, and the three, four, and five hitters due up.

Did Morandini's at-bat last thirty minutes, or did it just seem that way? I didn't time it, but with all the checking of signs and throws to first Mickey was probably at the plate for three or four minutes. A long at-bat, and I've made it even longer. But it deserved the time. Now John Kruk walks to the plate, the dude Dykstra is on second base, one out. Kruk has one of the oddest stances in the major leagues. Swinging from the left side, he's deep in the box with an open stance almost directly facing the pitcher. If this isn't weird enough, he holds the bat straight up with his arms just about fully extended over his head. Waiting for the pitch, he waves the bat around like an excited tail. Carl Yastrzemski did something similar with the bat, but Yaz had a very closed stance. Kruk is more extreme.

You don't teach this kind of stance, you don't learn it, and, in Kruk's case, you don't change it. He can really hit— .297 lifetime average over seven years and a whopping .364 thus far in '93. When the pitch is delivered, John lowers his arms and strides into the pitch like every other good hitter. He's predominately a gap hitter who goes the other way with power, and he'll pull the ball occasionally.

Recall that in the top half of this inning, Danny Jackson pitched carefully to Ron Gant with first base open and two outs because slump-ridden Brian Hunter was coming up next. Pete Smith doesn't have that luxury with Kruk even if there were two outs, not just one, because another left-handed batter, Darren Daulton, is coming up next for the Phillies, and Daulton already has fifteen homers and fifty-seven RBIs. Smith has to pitch to Kruk. There's not even a question of pitching around him, and he starts him off with a curve, ball one. Now Kruk is probably thinking fastball, and here it is over the outside half, and John fouls it into the stands on the left side. He's up there to swing. He's a disciple of the "Thou shalt not pass" school of hitting.

I like that pitching. Even though Smith knew that Kruk was probably looking for the fastball on 1-0, he threw it anyway. Too many pitchers do not have enough faith in their fastball. This probably will not be the last time I make this point because it's a big deal with me. Pitchers just don't realize that if they throw hard enough—and most of them can in the major leagues—they may get away with the fastball if it's not in the greatest location. The batter may foul it off. I said earlier that the foul straight back over the screen is usually a high fastball that the batter just missed. That's true, but it was a miss. Now, hang the curveball right over the plate and see what happens. It may be fouled off but the odds are better it's going to be crushed.

As I understand it, "the hanger" doesn't have enough spin because the pither's hand snaps the ball too early in the release. If the release is too late, the ball may have a lot of break but it's in the dirt, but without the spin, the pitch doesn't break as much as normal, or at all, and "hangs" right over the plate a little below belt-high. It might as well be sitting on a T. The curve, the slider, the split-finger, the change-up—the pitcher can "hang" any of these and get hurt. The fastball is the only pitch that does not have this downside. One particular fastball may not have as much velocity or movement as normal, but it will not hang. It's true that batters want to hit the fastball if at all possible (unless they see a hanging curve), and many try to work the count so they'll get the pitch, but this does not mean the pitcher shouldn't throw it. Challenge the batter with cheese. That's power baseball and the kind I prefer. Unfortunately, in my opinion, the trend these days is in the opposite direction, with pitchers throwing fastballs when they're ahead in the count, breaking balls and off-speed when behind in the count. That approach began in the American League, but it's becoming all the rage in this league, too. Pete Smith just did it against Morandini. Full-count change-up! Morandini's not a really strong hitter. Why not challenge him with a good fastball rather than rely on tricking him into swinging at what would have been ball four? But that's the way many pitchers are going about their job these days. If you can pull it off, more power to you. But can you pull it off when the game's on the line? That's the question. I say the pitcher is better off in most of these situations throwing sharp cheddar cheese.

On 1-1, Pete Smith throws a good change-up on the outside corner that Kruk hits right back to him on one bounce. Clinic time. Smith fields the ball, turns to check Dykstra, finds him frozen between second and third base, and runs directly toward him, forcing him to break for one base or another. Dykstra correctly breaks toward third base. Smith correctly throws to Terry Pendleton, Dykstra reverses direction and races back toward second. Pendleton gives chase, then throws to Jeff Blauser at second base for the out. That rundown was played perfectly. The Braves' infielders forced Dykstra back toward the base he came from. They didn't let him run wild, thereby giving Kruk a chance to sneak into second. They used only two throws to do it. Mark this putout 1-5-6, with Kruk safe at first on the fielder's choice. The rundowns that go 1-5-6-5-4-1-5 are lots of fun for the fans but a coach's nightmare. They are not a credit to the base runner but a mark against the infield. Two throws on any rundown are ideal; three are acceptable, but not ideal.

Technically, Dykstra erred by getting hung up on the ball hit directly back to the pitcher. You're taught to hold at second base on any ground ball right up the middle until you're certain it has cleared the pitcher. But in practice, it's difficult to avoid that first instinctive step or two toward third base. You want to be aggressive. No one on the Phillies will fault the dude on this play. He really shouldn't have been trapped off second, but at least this was an aggressive, not a passive error.

Four paragraphs earlier I said that the hitter might foul off the poorly located fastball. I didn't say he *would* do so, and Darren Daulton, the Phillies' clean-up batter, doesn't. He jumps all over Pete Smith's first pitch, a belt-high fastball over the outer half (yes, you can pull that pitch), and lines it off the fence in the right-field corner. Kruk is running all the way, of course, with two outs, but the ball was hit so hard third-base coach Larry Bowa holds him at third. That's a judgment call. With two outs, Bowa could not be faulted for sending Kruk, even if he were then thrown out at the plate on a close play. With nobody out or one out, you're definitely going to be cautious, for the obvious reason that a fly ball scores the man. Bowa chooses to be cautious even with two outs, and correctly, because Kruk isn't fast and a good relay throw would have had him. Brian Hunter has a strong arm. Bowa isn't Carnac. He couldn't know that

Hunter's throw from the right-field corner would be too strong—a horrible throw way over cutoff man Mark Lemke and wide of the mark into foul territory, where first baseman Francisco Cabrera has to scramble to catch it, then fumbles it. If Kruk had been heading home, the Braves would not have had a play, but, again, how was Bowa to know?

Hitting the cutoff man is the most commonly cited "fundamental" that ball clubs work on, along with run downs; missing the cutoff man infuriates the manager like almost nothing else. The fielders work for hours, days, in spring training on their responsibilities when a cutoff might be in order. There are two basic situations:

- The drive to the wall, when a well-executed cutoff play holds the batter to a double and, perhaps, gives the catcher a play at the plate, or perhaps nails the hitter trying to stretch a double into a triple.
- The single hit directly or almost directly at the outfielder with runners in scoring position, when the cutoff throw holds the batter at first base while there's a play at the plate.

First, the long hit for a double. On the ball down the right-field line, the cutoff man is the second baseman, positioned between the outfielder and home plate, thirty to forty feet beyond the infield dirt (or, as in Philadelphia, beyond the white line on the artificial turf that marks where the infield dirt would be if this were grass). The first baseman backs up the second baseman, about twenty feet closer to the infield, within shouting distance. He's the "trailer" on the play. If the throw to the second baseman is accurate, the first baseman yells whether he should throw home for a play there or to one of the other bases—third, presumably—or whether he should hold the ball.

On the drive over the right fielder's head or in the right-center field gap, the second baseman is out in short right-center to take the cutoff throw from the outfielder. The first baseman is the second cutoff man, positioned on the infield grass directly between the second baseman and the plate. The shortstop is the "floater" out beyond second base, ready to cover second if there's a play there for some reason, protecting against a bad throw from the outfield, and, most important, ready to shout instructions to the second baseman. There are three of these:

"Cut three!" Throw to third for a play there.

"Cut home!" Throw to the plate.

"Cut. Run it in!" No play anywhere. Run the ball to the infield.

If the throw from the outfielder misses the second baseman and the shortstop, the first baseman fields the ball and makes the play—but there won't be one. It's too late. All the first baseman can do is pick up the loose garbage. We blew that one, boys. If the outfielder's cutoff throw to the second baseman is accurate but then the second baseman's relay throw to the plate is wide, the first baseman cuts it off and the catcher becomes the signal-caller.

On the ball to the gap in left-center field, the shortstop is the cutoff man in shallow left-center, the second baseman is the floater shouting instructions, the first baseman is the second cutoff man on the infield grass. In all of these situations, the third baseman covers third. The pitcher backs up the catcher behind home plate and reads the play as it develops. If necessary, he'll try to back up third, but he probably won't make it.

On the ball into the left-field corner, the shortstop down the line is the cutoff man, the third baseman is the floater or trailer, the first baseman backs up on the third-base line, about thirty feet in from third base, and the second baseman covers second.

On the shorter hit, the single to an outfielder, either the first baseman or the third baseman is the cutoff man stationed in the infield, directly in line with the throw from the outfielder. If the hit is anywhere between left-center and the right-field line, the first baseman has the honors; if the hit is to left, the third baseman takes over because the first baseman can't get in position in time, particularly if he was playing deep with runners on first and second. The idea is that when the batter rounding first base sees that the throw is on line to the cutoff man, he has to hold at first because the throw might be cut off. If the catcher shouts that he will have a play at the plate—"Let it go!"—the cutoff man lets the ball through but fakes the catch and freezes the runner at first. Doesn't the runner also hear the catcher's shout? No. He's a lot farther away. After the play at the plate the catcher springs up to throw to second base, but there won't be a play at second if the runner was properly frozen at first.

An accurate throw from the outfield is mandatory because the hitter, now the base runner, can tell from the ball's trajectory if it will overshoot the cutoff man, and he should take second base easily if it's going to. This is by far the most common mistake on the cutoff play: The outfielder overthrows the cutoff man on a single, allowing the batter to get into scoring position at second base, taking away the possible double play. A free base compliments of the defense. It happens all the time as an outfielder fires the ball all the way to the plate on the fly. Flashy, but anyone who knows the game isn't fooled. You can show off your arm just as well by throwing a one-hop strike that gives the cutoff man a play. Infielders can screw the play up, too, with poor judgment or a bad throw, but this doesn't happen nearly as often as the bad throw from the outfield.

And from the offense's point of view, the runner can also blunder by not taking advantage of the overthrow. Watch enough games and you'll see this happen: The throw from right field, say, is ten feet over the cutoff man's head but the runner does not take second base. Asleep at the wheel. Bad, bad, bad. The manager is hopping mad.

To sum up, the base hit with runners in scoring position is an invitation for you to change your viewing habits. Most of us watch the ball all the way. It's hard not to. But I suggest glancing from the ball to the infielders as they line up for the relay, then back to the ball. And by all means pay attention to the cutoff man as he makes his play. Does he cut the ball off properly, not with his back to the plate but instead "sideways," almost parallel with the first throw, so he can catch the ball and make the relay in one smooth motion? This is correct, but you'll see infielders with their backs to the plate have to catch—turn—throw. That's a poor fundamental that costs precious seconds, and seldom do you have much time to spare with a play at the plate. And try to glimpse the runner, too. Does he make as wide a turn as possible at first base? (When the first baseman is the cutoff man, there's no one there to hold him close, and he should take advantage of this.) More is happening on the field in these situations than at any other time in the game. Try to catch the broad perspective, like a quarterback reading the defense. You might feel you need a second set of eyes until you get the hang of it, but it can be done.

On Darren Daulton's double into the right-field corner, Brian Hunter's cutoff throw missed everybody, but the Braves got away with the mistake because Larry Bowa correctly held John Kruk at third base. As it turns out, Kruk scores on the next pitch anyway, as Damon Berryhill can't handle Pete Smith's slider in the dirt and the ball bounces away. There's the classic instance of a pitcher "overthrowing," trying to make too good a pitch. A theme throughout this book will be: How do the pitchers perform in a jam? A wild pitch is no big deal with the bases empty. Who even notices? But with runners on base? They'll kill you. Kruk runs home. Safe without a play. Daulton advances to third. The fans cheer like crazy. They lead, 1-0.

With Daulton now on third base and the score 1-0 Phillies, Pete Incaviglia is at the plate. Inky's career has been resurrected by the Phillies. He's always had great power from the right side of the plate, but he also has a tendency to chase bad pitches, strike out, and struggle against right-handers. In Philadelphia he seems to be curing these habits—only 37 strikeouts in 167 at-bats. Four Phillies have more than that. Incaviglia is one of these gritty, blue-collar guys the Phillies specialize in, and everything is working for Pete this year, by far his best in the majors, with a .293 average, eleven homers and forty-four RBIs on just forty-eight base hits in forty-seven ball games. That's tremendous production.

The idea for Pete Smith against Incaviglia is to throw him breaking balls and fastballs on the corners, predominately away, coming inside—way inside—occasionally to keep the batter honest. But throw nothing to hit in the middle third of the plate. Nothing. The pitcher wants to work just about everyone on the corners, but it's mandatory with a guy like Incaviglia, who can be an all-or-nothing batter.

The problem with this simple-sounding program was just proved by Pete's first pitch to Pete. Trying to put a lot on the slider, Smith threw it in the dirt. In tight situations (a runner on third qualifies) there's a natural tendency to overthrow, and the tendency with the slider outside is for it to end up way outside and in the dirt.

Nevertheless, with Darren Daulton now on third base, Smith's second pitch to Inky is another breaking ball, not in the dirt but still outside, ball two. Big trouble for the pitcher now. Smith can't be quite so careful about hitting the outside edge because he needs a strike. He hasn't been able to get that strike with a breaking ball, but he can't afford to groove the fastball, either, not against Incaviglia. Smith checks Daulton at third base and delivers...the fastball, low, ball three. On the 3-0 count, does Jim Fregosi give his slugger the green light? It's early in the game, and Incaviglia is not the most disciplined of hitters. Besides, the hot Jim Eisenreich, a left-handed batter, is due up next against Pete Smith. You want Eisenreich at the plate with a couple of base runners on. As great a year as Incaviglia is having, you've got to figure that Eisenreich hitting from the left side is more likely to hurt Pete Smith. Besides, Incaviglia will probably get just as good a pitch to hit on 3-1 as on 3-0. He's probably taking.

Strike one, right down the middle, and Incaviglia didn't look as if he were going to swing, but we can't be absolutely sure from the stands. Maybe he did have permission and just took the pitch. But I doubt it. Now on 3-1 he's swinging for sure. What's he looking for? Since Smith got behind with breaking balls, with Eisenreich protecting him, Incaviglia has got to be thinking fastball. If Pete Smith does throw a good curve or slider for a strike, taking his cue from the new style of pitching that throws breakers and off-speed behind in the count, take the pitch and tip your cap. It's still only a full count. But if it's a fastball or a hanger, jump all over it.

The pitch is a fastball down the middle at the knees, not a good pitch, and Incaviglia gets good wood on it, but the bullet is tracked down by Brian Hunter in right field for the third out. Nice hitting. What can you do? Trot out to your position in left field and catch the ball if it comes your way. Turn the page.

Batters are often declared to be either high-ball or low-ball batters, thus designating the hitting zone they prefer, given a choice, which they never are. Generally speaking, all reasonably good hitters can handle the low ball—and some, like Willie McCovey and Willie Stargell, are devastating on anything near the knees. You simply drop your bat on that pitch; if it's low and inside, you can golf it over the closest wall. A smaller number of hitters feast on the high pitch, even though, as Ted Williams pointed out, it should be the easiest to hit because the hands are held at that level to begin with. Simply extend them with a level swing. But right-handed batters find it easier to do this than their counterparts on the other side. Left-handed batters are almost always low-ball hitters. Maybe it has something to do with the left brain/right brain business, I don't know, but it's a fact that many more right-handed batters than left-handed batters can handle the high pitch. A level swing does the job, but a lot of hitters tend to swing up at the high pitch, obviously allowing less angle for good contact. A slight uppercut can lift the ball out of the park, but a lot of players overdo it and pop the ball straight up. I did it myself once or twice. More often than that. This is why the high, high fastball is often a good first pitch to a pinch hitter, who does not intend to let the pitcher get ahead in the count. He'll come out swinging, and the high heater out of the strike zone is therefore a good bait pitch to him. We saw it here in Veterans Stadium last night, in fact. The Phillies' Ricky Jordan batted for Joe Millette in the seventh inning with his team down 7-1, bases loaded, one out. A big hit brings the Phillies right back in the game. But Greg Maddux's first pitch was the fastball high and tight, and Jordan grounded into the inning-ending double play. That pitch selection was no accident.

Why isn't there a contradiction here? If most batters are low-ball hitters, why are the announcers always declaring— why have I just said about Danny Jackson—that the pitcher has to get the ball *down*? Why not throw more pitches *up* in the strike zone, where more batters don't like the ball? One answer is that good right-handed power hitters dream about the high pitch, almost to a man. Against them the mistake down in the zone may become a single or a double; the mistake up in the zone runs the risk of a dinger. That's why Danny Jackson needs to get his pitches down against Atlanta's right-handed power hitters.

Francisco Cabrera proves the point leading off the second inning for the Braves. He's definitely a high-ball hitter. I don't know what kind of pitch he drove into left field for the famous pinch hit that scored David Justice and the sliding Sid Bream to beat the Pirates in the deciding game of the playoffs in '92, but tonight in Philadelphia he drives a high fastball against the wall in left field for a double off Danny Jackson.

With Cabrera on second and nobody out, the textbook on offensive strategy says that Damon Berryhill has one main job. At the very least, he should move Cabrera to third base by hitting the ball on the ground to the right side of the infield. The runner will move up easily and then be in a position to score on a sacrifice fly to the outfield. If the ball is hit to the left side—third base or shortstop—the runner has to hold at second because the third baseman would just tag him out if he tried to advance, or the shortstop would have the short throw to third. Obviously, there is no point in advancing the runner to third if there were already one out because the batter is the second out and then there is no sacrifice fly. Also note that in this situation, the shortstop is designated to jockey behind the runner, trying to hold him

46

close, while the second baseman plays straight-up defense, under the assumption that the batter is trying to drive the ball to the right side.

If Ron Gant were the batter, forget moving the runner up because Gant is a strong pull hitter and an RBI man. You don't want him to semiwaste an at-bat moving the runner along. You want him to drive the runner in. But Berryhill is a platooning catcher hitting seventh in the order. He has fifteen RBIs for the year. He's not an RBI man. So everyone on the field knows—and everyone in the stands should know—that Berryhill will try to hit the ball to the right side. But I remind you of what I said regarding the hit-and-run. The ground ball that merely advances the runner is second-best. Best is to drive the ball hard to right field for the RBI single or double.

However, Danny Jackson also knows that Damon wants to take the ball to the opposite field, the right side of the diamond, so the textbook on pitching strategy says he'll try to pitch the batter inside. It's difficult for the right-handed hitter to drive this pitch with any power to right field; the tendency is to push it out there weakly. The opposite holds for the left-handed hitter trying to pull the ball to the right side to advance the runner. This is theoretically easier for him with the inside pitch, harder with the ball on the outside corner. But as I explained earlier, it's not really hard to pull the outside pitch. We just saw it with Darren Daulton's double in the first inning. If I needed to pull the ball to the right side, I wanted the ball either down and in or outside. Other hitters may not think like this, but this is the reason I had good success in this situation. The pitcher was thinking, "Well, Hernandez needs to pull the ball, so I'll throw it on the outside half of the plate." Fine with me. I'd just roll my hands. Up-and-in is a lot harder pitch for a left-handed batter to pull.

Berryhill versus Jackson. This fairly ordinary-looking situation on the field is actually a case study for honing your second- and third-guessing skills. Berryhill wants to do one thing, Jackson knows what it is, but his best pitch, his fastball, doesn't serve his purpose because it runs away from the right-handed-hitting Berryhill, out over the plate. So the stage is set for an interesting at-bat. Jackson starts off with the slider low and inside and Berryhill swings and misses and then steps out of the box shaking his head. He didn't use his bat well, or his head, either, and he knows it. He should have taken that pitch for a ball or a strike, either one. If it's a ball, Jackson will have to give him something better next time. If it's a strike, well, what's the harm because it was the toughest possible pitch to do his job with anyway. Hope for something better to hit next time. But this approach is easier said than done. Berryhill's reaction—swinging at the pitch—is common and understandable in this situation. Hitters know their job, they get defensive, they're not confident in their ability to use the inside-out swing to hit the inside pitch to the right side. (Briefly, the bat normally makes contact with the inside pitch in front of the plate. The inside-out swing is a means to delay the head of the bat through the strike zone so the bat hits the ball above, not in front of, the plate, directing it to the right side.)

Hitters don't realize that part of the answer for them when they're trying to move the runner to third is to be selective at the plate. Instead, they end up swinging at pitches like Danny Jackson's hard slider on the inside edge, one that Henry Aaron would have had trouble driving to the right side (not that Hank would have been trying to!). Early in the count, why not sit on something outside? Take that tough inside pitch!

Jackson now follows the slider with a fastball that starts out well inside and tails over the inside corner and up in the zone, too—his perfect pitch for the situation and not an easy one for Jackson to locate, as explained. Berryhill feels compelled to swing because he doesn't want to go to 0-2, and he comes close to doing the job, hitting the ball right back to Jackson. Cabrera has to hold at second base (unlike Dykstra, he does not take the initial, fatal step toward third base), Jackson checks him there, then throws to Kruk at first for the out.

In that at-bat, Jackson was in complete control, and this

became obvious from Berryhill's first weak swing. A similar

episode played out in the first game of this series, after Terry Pendleton doubled to lead off the second inning. Ron Gant came to the plate, Curt Schilling on the mound for Philadelphia. Ron took one good, aggressive swing on a fastball but two fairly weak ones in his attempt to move the runner to third. Gant struck out. Not a good at-bat. If I were the manager early in the game and I knew my man at the plate wasn't comfortable having to hit the ball to right field, I might tell him to forget it, especially in the case of my RBI man—Ron Gant—and especially if he's going to have an at-bat like that one. Swing the bat! Pull the ball! Later in the game, you have to try to go to the right side, but not in the second inning. I cringe when I see a right-handed batter just giving up an at-bat like this early in the game. Failing to hit to the right side would look like a blown fundamental, of course, and it would be one, but if the hitter has trouble doing it anyway, what's the loss? Why take the bat out of his hands?

In any event, Mark Lemke comes to the plate with one out, needing a hit, not a fly ball, to score Cabrera. With the pitcher batting next, the heat is on the number eight hitter, but on the first pitch he hits a hopper directly at Kim Batiste at shortstop. Cabrera takes off for third, and Batiste takes the easy out at first. This is a mistake by Cabrera. He made it to third, but there's still no percentage in the play at all. This high hopper will be the second out in the inning. With two outs, being on third is not that great an advantage over being on second, especially when you have Cabrera's speed. A single scores him from either base. Third base is better than second, but only if you're certain. On that play, Cabrera could not have been certain.

The rule is etched in concrete: The runner on second moves over to third on anything hit to the shortstop's left, except the ball hit right back up the middle, when he should read the play and hold if the pitcher makes the stop. Recall the play on Lenny Dykstra in the first inning. On any ball hit on the ground to the shortstop's right, the runner should hold at second. This grounder was hit directly at Batiste. He did check Cabrera going to third and had a shot at nailing him, but he used his head. Why risk the close play? Get the

49

sure out. Let the runner have third with two outs and the pitcher coming up, or even if Ron Gant is coming up. Besides, while Cabrera was breaking the rule by running to third, he also did a smart thing, intentionally or otherwise, something hard for us in the stands to pick up at the time, probably easier to see on a televised replay: He swerved slightly outside the base path, getting in the line of the shortstop's throw to third, making that throw even riskier.

You could assess this play in one of three ways. It reflects either the influence of speed on the game or youthful mistakes or weakness in the fundamentals—or all three.

With two outs and a runner on third, Danny Jackson has one and only one job with pitcher Pete Smith: Get him out, and don't fool around doing it. Slider, strike one. After all my discussion of Danny Jackson's fastball as the pitch he can most reliably throw for a strike, and considering the risk of overthrowing the breaking ball in the dirt, maybe scoring Cabrera, you might well ask whether Jackson's choice of a slider to the pitcher was smart, even though it yielded the strike. Yes, it was smart, because pitchers at the plate often assume they'll get the fastball and are ready to swing at it. When the pitch turns out to be the slider, they're probably going to get jammed or miss it for strike one. With the bases empty, Jackson might have come after Smith with three straight fastballs. But with Cabrera on third base, any bleeder scores him, and pitchers do get bleeders. A little more finesse in this situation is justified. As it happened, Pete Smith did not swing at this slider, but it caught the outside edge at the knees. Jackson switches to the fastball for ball one, then back to the slider, which Smith rolls to third base for the third out. Cabrera's leadoff double goes for naught.

Jim Eisenreich, another of the new acquisitions paying off splendidly this year for the Phillies, leads off the bottom of the second inning. A smooth swinger from the left side with a career .277 average, Jim has improved on that so far in 1993. His average is .333, with only 12 strikeouts in 131 appearances at the plate. That's a great strikeout ratio. You don't need special training in judging hitters to see that Eisenreich has a smooth, compact, level swing that should produce numerous line drives in the gaps. He's the ideal number six hitter. He could hit in other spots in the lineup, too; if he had more home run power (just two this year) you would definitely want him higher in the order. When Eisenreich starts against right-hand pitching, the Phillies usually win.

He has no holes at the plate that I'm aware of. No pitch is practically guaranteed to get him out, so all Pete Smith can do is throw good pitches to various spots, mix them up, and rely on his fielders. After all, there are nine of them out there, including the pitcher, and they're all poised for swift response. They all have big gloves, too, and that helps. Pitchers forget this. It's a pet peeve of mine (one of several that will come up as these two games progress). Go after the hitter, please! Nothing annoys batters, fielders, coaches, and managers more than pitchers who nibble, nibble, nibble. Rick Rhoden, formerly with the Pirates, the Dodgers, and some other teams, was nicknamed "Full Count." Ron Darling tends to be this way. Get two strikes on the batter, and you can wager a reasonable bet that the count would get to 2-2 or even full with Ron on the mound. I know. I played with him in New York. Aggravating, really, especially on get-away day when the airplane is waiting. Players do think about this kind of thing. They also get irritated when the pitcher can't find the plate, whether because he's nibbling or just wild, and they have to stand in the sun, or just under the bright lights of a night game, for twenty minutes when they're behind 6-0. That kills the offense, I can tell you.

With a disciplined hitter like Eisenreich, throw strikes. Pete Smith does just that with his first delivery, and a good strike, too, another backdoor curve precisely on the outside corner. That gives Jim something to think about. But Pete follows with a fastball down the middle, and Eisenreich strokes it smoothly for a single back up the middle.

With Eisenreich, an average runner, on first base, does manager Jim Fregosi want to put on the hit-and-run with Kim Batiste at the plate? Since Eisenreich only has three stolen bases, he won't be stealing, so the hit-and-run is more likely than it was in the first inning with the base-stealing Dykstra on first. Also, Batiste is not a strong hitter—until this year, when maybe he's overachieving with a .318 average in only eighty-five at-bats. And can he handle the hit-and-run? Frankly, I don't know. Fregosi may not know. All of us may be about to find out, or Jim may be content just to let this second inning unfold. He's not a great advocate of the hit-and-run with this team anyway.

If Fregosi does like the hit-and-run in this situation, I do not look for it on the first pitch in Batiste's at-bat, which otherwise might be the ideal count. Why not? Most managers will not force their hitters to swing at the first pitch of their first at-bat. Sure enough, Batiste takes a fastball for strike one, Eisenreich holds at first. Smith follows with yet another well-placed backdoor curve over the outside corner at the knees, and now he has Batiste where he wants him. Checking the stat sheet, we find that Kim has struck out ninteen times in those eighty-five at-bats, with only one walk. You would have to believe that the odds are pretty good we're about to witness number twenty. Smith wastes another curve just off the plate, then comes back with a high, hard one, and Batiste, almost predictably, chases it and goes down swinging. Smith just blew that pitch right by Batiste, ate him up. That's good pitching, up and down the ladder. After the low pitch, the pitch coming in around the level of the batter's eyes looks awfully inviting. It's hard to lay off that pitch, but it's also hard to hit it.

Now what? The next batter, Jeff Manto, is making his first start for the Phillies in the continued absence of the regular third baseman, Dave Hollins, who's on the DL with a broken hand. So this is Manto's first at-bat for the Phillies. He played a little in previous seasons with Cleveland. There will be no hit-and-run here, surely. The kid will be nervous. You want to give him every opportunity to hit a good pitch. The first pitch is a slider outside for a ball. Pete Smith throws over to first base. He throws over again. Once I can understand, but twice? Eisenreich has a short lead. He's not going anywhere because the odds are good he'd be thrown out. If he were and Manto made the third out, the pitcher would lead off the next inning, and you always like to avoid that. I wouldn't call this yet another pet peeve, but more or less unnecessary throws to first base are something I tend to note, perhaps because I played first base and had to catch them all the time.

Smith returns his attention to the plate. Oh, wow! That drive is way back in left field, way back...but Ron Gant catches the ball with a leap at the wall. Smith got away with one there, and what was the pitch? Fastball right down the middle. The fans behind the Phillies first-base dugout give Jeff Manto a standing O for the at-bat. Turns out he's a hometown boy.

Note where Eisenreich was on the base path. Standing on second base. That's good base running, but some guys would have been in the standard location for a regular fly, halfway to three-quarters between first and second. Eisenreich was correct to go farther, he could have even rounded the bag a couple of steps, because on that long drive he still had plenty of time to leg it back ninety feet to first base, but he also would have scored if Gant hadn't made the play. If he had stayed halfway between first and second, and with Otis Nixon backing up Gant properly, Eisenreich would not have scored if the Braves played the ball off the wall cleanly. That's a little example of base-running intelligence that didn't pan out in this instance for Eisenreich and the Phillies, but over the course of a season it will produce results.

Two outs followed immediately by a third as Pete Smith strikes out his counterpart Danny Jackson on three work-manlike pitches and the game moves to the third inning, Phillies up 1-0. Small point: Jackson, a left-hander, bats right-handed, thus exposing his breadwinner to a wild pitch. Baseball organizations don't like this, but what can they do?

CHAPTER ◆3◆

One of the many maxims you hear about pitching is that the pitcher doesn't want to throw the same pitch to the same batter in the same location in the same game. What a crock. Take Otis Nixon, leading off the third inning for Atlanta. Otis steps in for the Braves knowing that he'll be challenged with Danny Jackson's high fastball over the outer half of the plate. In the first at-bat, Otis fouled off two high fastballs and another one at the knees. He was swinging late. Three times in one at-bat might be a pretty good sign that Nixon cannot catch up to Jackson's fastball, not tonight. In any event, Danny should demand in this second at-bat that Otis prove otherwise. Pound a batter's weakness.

Another maxim is that the pitcher works the batter in similar fashion his first two at-bats, then changes for the third at-bat, then returns to the original formula in the fourth at-bat. This sounds reasonable until you really think about it. You're not going to throw the exact same sequence of pitches in the first two at-bats, are you? But substituting just about any pitch for any other pitch can totally change the complexion of an at-bat, so I'm not sure that maxim means anything.

Closer to the truth is this common sense: The pitcher knows his own and the batter's strengths and weaknesses, and he tries to match them up, and he tries to do this every at-bat, but not according to a formula. He'll usually mix up the pitches and the locations within each at-bat and among the at-bats in a game, always keeping the strengths and weaknesses in mind. Pitching a guy inside doesn't mean ten out of ten pitches inside. It means five or six out of ten, maybe, and no pattern, please. The great pitchers pitched you differently every at-bat. Then again, these are guys like Don Sutton and Tom Seaver, with great command of three or four pitches. Avoiding a pattern and mixing up four pitches is a lot easier than mixing up two. The key is that you have to be able to throw these pitches for strikes. If you have only one or two pitches that you can reliably throw for strikes, you're limited. How many different combinations can you come up with? Only the greatest, like Doc Gooden with the Mets in the mid- and late eighties, can thrive on two pitches. But after Doc lost a little off the fastball and the hitters began to catch up with him, he developed the change-up and the cut fastball and is now enjoying the closest thing possible to a resurgence on the embarrassing Mets. When Nolan Ryan couldn't get his curve over, the batters ignored it, geared fastball with confidence, and reduced Nolan to a one-pitch pitcher. Even he couldn't get away with that very often. But, like Gooden, Nolan eventually developed a change-up.

I happen to remember the day I first encountered that pitch. This was spring training 1987, maybe '88, I'm not sure, and the Mets were playing the Astros at their spring training camp in Kissimmee. (Ryan went over to the Texas Rangers in '89.) I was batting, and Nolan wound and delivered and the pitch broke down. Slightly off-speed, too. Good Lord, I thought, Nolan Ryan now has a traditional change-up, too. I looked straight out at him with a knowing but quizzical look on my face. He laughed, standing right out there on the mound, the sly dog! He knew it was a good pitch, and he knew he now had an alternative to his curve he could use to keep the batters from sitting on the heater. You know that if a pitcher like Big Tex needed these pitches, every pitcher does.

The guy who always amazed me because he did get by

with just two pitches—thrived, in fact—was Andy Messer-smith of the Dodgers and the Braves. He featured a regular fastball—I don't imagine it ever reached ninety mph—and the greatest change-up I've seen or heard about. That pitch just stunned me and a lot of other hitters. It was not a sinking change-up, either. It stayed pretty much on course, but the change of speeds was unbelievably effective. Andy was the rare pitcher who used his change-up to set up his fastball. Most pitchers use the harder stuff to set up the off-speed delivery, as Pete Smith did against Mickey Morandini.

And then there's Larry Anderson, who used to pitch for Houston and several other teams, and now is with these Phillies. Larry comes close to thriving on just one pitch. He lives and dies with his hard slider and throws it at least 85 percent of the time. He can do this because he has tremendous command of it, throwing it where he wants it time after time, biting hard and late on the outside corner at the knees to right-handed batters, on the hands to left-handed batters. And it helps Larry that he's a reliever. Batters usually see Larry's pitch for just one at-bat in the game, and that's it.

Facing Otis Nixon leading off the Braves' third inning, Danny Jackson might be able to get by with just one pitch, that tailing fastball up and out, but he still wants to vary things. Shrewdly, he starts Nixon off with a slider outside, ball one, before coming back with the fastball outside—but too far outside, ball two. Otis knows what's coming next, but he swings late on that fastball again and fouls it off. What can you say? Otis is not a .300 hitter. His career average is .257. He has that sore foot. He's not in a groove.

Me, I'm throwing a high hard one here, but Jackson tries...the change-up! Ball three. That's his first change of the game, by my count, and a strange time to try it. Now on the 3-1 count, he won't—he can't—fool around. The fastball is required. Nixon hasn't hit it fair yet. Jackson winds, he delivers...slider, low, ball four. Explain this, please. I cannot. A big mistake for Danny Jackson. It's easy to sit in the stands and second-guess, sometimes too easy, but in this case there's no other way around it. That choice of pitches was a mistake.

But, you ask, doesn't the catcher put down the signs? Doesn't the catcher "call the game"? Why not question Darren Daulton? Well, you could question Daulton, but the pitcher has the last word. The exception is when a rookie is throwing to a Johnny Bench. Then the recruit is going to throw what the future Hall of Famer tells him to throw. Otherwise, the only reason the catcher puts down the signs in the first place is that it's tough for the pitcher to do so without the whole world seeing it. If the pitcher doesn't like the catcher's sign, he should shake him off. Every pitcher is told a hundred times by his pitching coach, "If you're not happy with the pitch selection, don't throw it." On the other hand, the manager and the pitching coach want the battery mates to be in sync as much as possible. I know the Texas Rangers have worked hard with their catching phenom Ivan Rodriguez on calling a more strategic game.

When you see the pitcher swipe at his leg with his glove as he stares in to the plate, he's asking for another sign. Demanding one, really, but the veteran catcher may hold out. Maybe they'll meet halfway to discuss it. It's too bad Don Sutton is not still pitching or you could go out and watch him call the entire game this way. He's one of the very few pitchers I ever saw do this, and I don't know of any active pitchers who consistently call the game from the mound. Some will do it off and on. With Sutton, the catcher—Steve Yeager or Joe Ferguson—would drop the sign—"1" for fastball," "2" for curve, "3" for slider, "4" for the change-up, traditionally. Sutton had complete command of all four pitches, and he didn't care what Yeager or Ferguson called for. If he wanted something else, he signaled back with his glove swiped across his chest or down his thigh. Swipes on the chest meant add that number to the sign called: If the catcher flashed "1" and Don swiped twice on his chest, he was throwing "3," the slider. Swipes down his thigh meant subtract that number of swipes from the sign the catcher just flashed: If the catcher flashed "3" and Don swiped twice on his leg, that meant he was throwing "1," the fastball. Or he could change the formula so that swipes on the chest meant subtract, down the thigh meant add. Given Don's success, I might suggest more veteran pitchers try his scheme, even though it runs the risk of an error in arithmetic. If you do notice a pitcher swiping in this manner with any regularity, that's what he's up to. He's giving the signs.

Sometimes a shake-off is not really a shake-off. This ploy is hard to pick up at the park, easier on television. The catcher pretends to be giving a sign while shaking his head. This is a signal for the pitcher to shake his head as if he disagrees with the catcher. Then the catcher flashes the actual sign. Maybe they can get the batter to overthink.

Usually the pitchers acquiesce with the catcher's pitch selection because they consider the veteran catcher's judgment as good as their own, or even better. After all, the catcher sees the batters almost every game, not every fifth game, and he has worked with the pitcher long enough that the two are thinking along the same lines. But the bottom line tonight in Philadelphia is that Otis Nixon is standing on first base in the top of the third inning with an easy walk because Danny Jackson tried to get too cute behind the count.

Braves manager Bobby Cox's only likely play now, if any at all, is the hit-and-run. He will not have Jeff Blauser bunting because Blauser is too good a hitter to waste like that in the third inning, or in any inning, and the left-hander on the mound will make it harder for Nixon to steal, and maybe that sore foot will slow him down, too. Jackson snaps a couple of throws to first base, although "snap" is an exaggeration. Danny doesn't have a great move over there because it's obvious. Some shrewd lefties have their obvious move and their good move. They try to lull the runner with the obvious move for the first few throws over, maybe even for the first couple of times the runner is on first, then spring the good move in a late inning in a tight situation.

We'll watch as this game progresses, but Danny Jackson doesn't have the reputation of having such a move. That's too bad because this is one of the natural advantages lefties should enjoy over right-handers. They should be able to hold the runner closer. The second advantage they enjoy is that managers stack their lineups with right-handed batters, who have that extra few feet to run. And a third advantage many left-handers—but not Danny Jackson—enjoy is the ability to get away with quirky pitches and quirky deliveries and a lot of off-speed junk that drives right-handed batters to distraction. Charlie Leibrandt of the Rangers is a perfect example. Charlie doesn't throw hard enough to break cellophane, but he gets batters out. Maybe this talent of some lefties is more of that left brain/right brain business, like the preference of left-handed batters for low pitches, I have no idea, but the fact is that some lefties can pitch in the big leagues with stuff that would get a right-hander shipped out tomorrow. Whitey Herzog always said that he would have started five lefties if he could have found them. Maybe the White Rat was exaggerating, but maybe not. Left-handers are always in demand.

Returning his attention to Jeff Blauser at the plate, Danny Jackson fires the high and outside fastball. Nixon stands at first, Blauser takes. No hit-and-run. Jackson's control is failing him, and Bobby Cox has certainly taken this into account. You might not want to put on the hit-and-run with a pitcher who's having trouble finding the plate, for two reasons. One, he may walk the batter (Jackson just walked Nixon). Two, the batter may have to swing at a pitch in the dirt or over his head. So I doubt that Cox will put the play on with the count 1-0....He doesn't, and Blauser takes a slider inside at the knees. Nasty pitch, and gutsy when your control is shaky. But it's also Jackson's best way to come inside to right-handed hitters. Great pitch, but if I'm the batter I'm saying, let's see you do it again.

A high slider for a check-swing strike. That was an unusual pitch and a lucky strike for Jackson. The pitcher never wants the breaking ball up in the strike zone. That's

PURE BASEBALL

59

the infamous "hanger." In this case, the pitch was too high, out of the strike zone, but Jeff couldn't hold up. Vapor lock. It happens, and now Jeff is in a hole at 1-2, and the possibility of the hit-and-run is eliminated. Jackson comes in with a good slider on the outside edge that Blauser pops down the line in right. Eisenreich, Morandini, and Kruk converge on the scene from every direction, surround the ball, and Kruk just misses a nice over-the-shoulder catch at full speed. You can't fault him. That's a tough play. Sometimes you catch it, sometimes you don't. Still, you can't give good teams four outs.

Reprieve, batter, and Blauser makes the most of it by smoking the next pitch, a fastball, into the gap in right-center field. That pitch didn't seem to have a lot of steam behind it, and it was also in that "Ted Williams zone"—up and out over the plate. Maybe it was a totally misfired change-up. The ball bounces up against the fence, where Eisenreich fields it cleanly but makes a weak throw to Morandini, the cutoff man in shallow right-center. In fact, he misses him entirely— the ball skips under Morandini's glove—and the next fielder in line for the throw, shortstop Kim Batiste, has no shot at either Otis Nixon arriving at the plate or at Blauser pulling into the bag at third. There were two mistakes on this play. First, Jackson threw a nothing pitch when he was ahead in the count to Blauser; second, Eisenreich missed the cutoff man. You can't be sure that the Phillies would have gotten Nixon at the plate—probably not, with his speed, even with the bad foot—but they definitely would have held Blauser at second base. Only the guys with great speed like Deion Sanders should get a triple on a hard shot into the gap on artificial turf. That ball skips to the fence in a hurry. But Blauser is on third with nobody out, and the heart of the order is coming up. You have to figure his odds of scoring are excellent, thanks to a botched fundamental, hitting the cutoff man.

Score tied, 1-1, and "botched cutoff throws" also tied 1-1. Brian Hunter missed everybody with his throw from the right-field corner in the bottom of the first.

Terry Pendleton steps in, man on third, no one out. This is another situation—man on third base, fewer than two outs—that deserves close attention. Where are the infielders? Is the manager almost conceding a run on a ground ball by playing them back, or does he feel he has to take the risk of bringing them in in order to prevent the score? The closer in they play, the easier it is to hit the ball past them, obviously. The run scores, and the batter is on base, too. The rule of thumb holds that a drawn-in infield makes a .300 hitter a .400 hitter, and that seems about right to me. Generally speaking, the earlier the inning, the less likely the manager is to bring the infield in. The more confidence he has that his offense will score some runs off the opposing pitcher, the more confidence he has that his pitcher can hold the line, the less likely he is to weaken the overall defense by bringing the infield in. In a tie game in the middle innings, the infield might play in or halfway; in the late innings, definitely. All in all, this is one of the tougher decisions for the manager. He might want to fudge things, too. For example, in the rain-delayed game last night in Philadelphia, the home team fell behind 4-0 and Terry Pendleton was on third base, Ron Gant on second, one out, third inning, Sid Bream batting. Jim Fregosi brought his infield in at the corners. Perfectly feasible play, but it would also have made sense to bring Kim Batiste in at third while leaving John Kruk deep at first, protecting against the shot down the line.

With the infield drawn in, the opposing manager has a corresponding decision to make. Via the third base coach, what does he instruct the runner on third base to do on ground balls? There are three choices, in order of increasing riskiness:

- Go for the plate only if the ball gets through the infield. This is a cautious play that takes away an easy score on a high chopper, which is common on artificial turf.
- Go on any slow dribbler or high chopper, runner's judgment. This is the most common

PURE BASEBALL

61

instruction, and in practice the runner always uses his judgment on the high chops. Another judgment involves coming down the line on a grounder deep in the hole at short or up the middle behind second. When the fielder throws to first, break for the plate. You'll be safe unless the first baseman makes an instantaneous catch and accurate throw home. You might be safe anyway. It's a good gamble in most situations.

- Go on contact.

A host of factors affects how the manager decides to play this situation: the speed of the runner, the number of outs, the score, the inning, whether you're the home or the visiting team, and seat-of-the-pants hunches. Obviously, the faster the runner, the better the odds if you ask him to take off on anything hit on the ground. But with nobody out, you would never instruct even the fastest runner to run on contact, not when a fly ball from the next batter would still score him. At least I don't think I would, but I've seen Whitey Herzog do it, with success. With one out, you could have the runner run on contact. If he sees he's going to be out at the plate, he tries to get into an extended rundown that allows the batter to reach second base. That's a reasonable play. If his team is behind on the scoreboard, the manager is less likely to try to force the play. If his team is way down, he would never force it because the one run wouldn't be nearly enough to justify the risk. Then again, if he's way down in the score, the defensive team would concede the run by playing the infield back.

Of course, artificial turf changes everything in this situation. The fake grass in Veterans Stadium would allow Jim Fregosi to play his infield halfway in this situation—three or four steps behind the direct line between the bases. The ball gets to the fielders so quickly on turf they can play farther back and still have a shot at the runner at home. The shortstop and second baseman, in particular, can play halfway on artificial turf. This position on artificial turf is almost equivalent to an infield drawn all the way in—right between the bases or even closer—on real grass. Artificial turf takes a lot of the fun out of those situations that call for the drawn-in infield. It takes even more fun out of it for the fielders if the turf is wet, as it was for last night's game at the Vet. The baseball hydroplanes on wet artificial turf like you wouldn't believe. It can be scary playing in close, or even just halfway, with a runner on third. "Watch your lips" is the lingo. And check the outfielders on wet turf. They'll probably be playing a little deeper than usual, and cautiously.

As it turns out, early in the game here, Fregosi plays his men back, conceding the run on anything to second or short, but with a play at the plate still in order on shots to first or third.

At the plate, Terry Pendleton is in an interesting situation. A decent fly ball scores Blauser, a high chopper scores him, a slow roller scores him, just about anything scores him except the pop-up or a liner or hard smash on the ground to an infielder. This is as good as it gets in terms of notching an RBI, but for just that reason it's also dangerous. You go to the plate thinking you *should* get this guy in. To me, that's negative. Best is to know that you *will* get this guy in. What if I don't get him in? You can't let that thought cross your mind. In Terry's case, his RBIs are down this year, he missed an opportunity in the first inning when he popped the first pitch to Dykstra in center field, and he has to forget that and concentrate on the here and now.

What about asking Terry to squeeze Blauser home? With a runner on third, the possibility of the squeeze always comes up. It's an exciting play; fans love to see it. All true, but not here, not now, not with the heart of the Braves lineup coming up, even if they are struggling with runners in scoring position. With rare exceptions, the squeeze is restricted to late-inning situations with the pitcher or a weak hitter or a .240 hitter who's in a slump at the plate, but it could be called earlier if this questionable hitter is a dependable bunter. The squeeze can be a good play with a bad hitter, but it's hard to trust some of them to do even this correctly.

You try the squeeze with one out, never with two outs (forget the runner trying to score, throw out the batter for the third out), almost never with no one out. I say "almost" because I believe the old gunslinger Don Zimmer tried it with nobody out. But think about it. With no one out and the runner on third, the hitter can make an out and the next guy can still drive in the runner with a simple sacrifice fly. Recall that the same logic applies with trying the hit-and-run with runners at first and third and no outs. Either one is a rash play.

Even with one out the squeeze is rash because the sacrifice fly also scores the runner. That's why the batter trying the squeeze bunt has to be the pitcher or a struggling hitter and an adept bunter. As the manager, you like his chances of pulling off a successful squeeze better than his chances of hitting an ordinary fly ball.

To sum up, possible squeeze situations are fun—lots of guessing, lots of suspense—but you have to think about when it really makes any sense. The answer is, rarely. That's why you can watch for months and not see it tried, and that's in the National League. In the junior circuit it's an endangered species. And if you think the suicide squeeze is a dicey proposition, what about putting the runners in motion with the bases loaded, the count full, and one out? If the batter strikes out—hello! The catcher waits at the plate to greet the guy charging in from third. That amounts to a suicide hit-and-run and makes the squeeze look conservative by comparison. But Don Zimmer tried that play, too, at least once or twice. I think it's a horrible maneuver.

Terry Pendleton is not going to try to squeeze Blauser home. Forget that option. If I were in Terry's situation facing Danny Jackson, my strategy might be to sit on a fastball outside first pitch, and the entire at-bat for that matter. Terry knows Jackson has a hard time coming inside; on the other hand, the pitch he popped up in the first inning was a fastball on the outer half of the plate. For their part, Jackson and Darren Daulton might also be figuring that Terry Pendleton will be looking in the zone over the outer half on the first pitch, so they might start him off inside, hoping for a quick called strike. And that's what they do, and the pitch is that hard slider right on the corner. Pendelton bounces to short-stop and now we semiknow Bobby Cox's decision regarding the runner at third base. Blauser held on the sharp ground ball, so we know that he wasn't running on contact, but we can't be certain whether he held on his own judgment or because his instructions were to run only if the ball cleared the infield. Judgment, I'm pretty sure. Kim Batiste checks Blauser before firing to John Kruk for the first out of the inning.

Regarding Pendleton's swing, I see two possibilities. Maybe Terry crossed up everyone (or at least me), looked inside, got his pitch, and just didn't hit it well. If that's the case he'll take his seat saying, "Lucky you, pitcher." Or maybe Terry was overanxious, pressing, and swung at a pitch he now wishes he had taken. As fans, we'll never know. Only he knows. It's easy to sit up in the stands or watch on television or listen on the radio and pass judgment—knowledge-ably or otherwise—but this doesn't change the fact that per-forming on the field is difficult. Players have constant inter-nal battles between positive and negative thoughts, and eliminating the negative is not easy, especially when your batting average with runners in scoring position is .207, like Pendleton's, and when he can also look up and down the Braves lineup and see other guys in the same boat. Jeff Blauser has the highest such average among the Braves starters, at .298. The entire team is having trouble getting the runners home. (Four of the Phillies RBI men are hitting over .300 with runners in scoring position. The surprising statistic in this category is Lenny Dykstra's, at .137.)

Runner still on third base, one out, Ron Gant returning to the plate. When he came up in the first inning with two outs and Jeff Blauser on second base, Jackson pitched him care-fully before walking him to face Brian Hunter. You might jump to the conclusion that the same plan is in order this at-bat, but it's not. The differences this time are crucial. The runner is on third base, not second, and there's only oné out. Pitch around Gant, walk him, and he could steal second and you end up with runners on second and third with one out, and that's bad no matter who's up next. That sets up a big inning. So you have to pitch to Gant this time.

Ron knows this, too, and he, like Pendleton, is under pressure because he should get this guy in from third. His average with men in scoring position is .267. That's not bad, but Ron might be pressing a little anyway, trying to carry the load while most of the other guys are struggling. After fouling off a slider that was trying for the inside corner but didn't make it, Ron doesn't catch up with a fastball down the middle at the knees and lifts a short fly to Eisenreich in right. Too short to score Blauser, and take note that Blauser does not tag up on the play. Smart base running. Jeff knows he can't score on the catch. The play is too shallow. Instead, he comes halfway down the line and waits, ready to return to third when Eisenreich catches the ball, but prepared to trot home should he drop it. A lot of guys—or maybe just some—will stand on third base on that fly, accomplishing nothing if the ball is caught, and should the fielder drop it, they wouldn't necessarily be safe on a play at the plate. This base running yielded nothing, as it turned out, but it was still smart, like Jim Eisenreich's base running in the bottom of the second. These two examples show that the fine points of good base running reveal themselves only if you pay attention on all the plays, not just on base hits.

Two outs now, and the Braves are on the verge of stranding another runner at third. Brian Hunter steps in and takes a fastball high. Danny Jackson follows with another fastball, but this time it's in the strike zone, right where the one was to Gant, in fact, but Brian Hunter laces a rope to center field for the single that finally scores Blauser from third base. If it helps their pride, the Phillies can now believe that the botched relay throw that turned Blauser's double into a triple didn't cost them after all because Blauser would have scored from second on this two-out single.

I look around to see if any visiting Atlanta fans have the nerve to do their tomahawk chop in the middle of 40,000-plus Philadelphia partisans. I don't see any. But the Phillie Phanatic, the best mascot in the business, hands down, has no qualms about stomping on a dummy Brave right in front of Atlanta's dugout the first chance he gets. This guy can get away with anything on that scooter of his.

Danny Jackson's next pitch is a nasty slider on the inside corner that breaks Francisco Cabrera's bat and rolls to Jeff Manto at third for the final out. The Braves lead, 2-1.

Pete Smith and his catcher Damon Berryhill decide to give Lenny Dykstra something to think about on his second at-bat by showing him the change-up for a swing-and-a-miss strike. Well, why not? Pitchers like John Denny employ the change in almost every at-bat, while others want to save the offspeed pitch for a crucial moment when they really need the strike, the third or fourth or fifth pitch in the third or fourth at-bat, late in the game. From personal experience, I know those later at-bats were when the change was more effective against me, but no rule says the pitcher has to wait. You might wonder whether starting off with the change-up doesn't help set up the fastball. The answer is not really. The pitcher doesn't set up the fastball in this way because any hitter who knows what he's doing—Dykstra certainly qualifies—is always geared toward the fastball, as I've explained previously.

This pitch selection can work two ways. Pete Smith can say to himself, "Let Dykstra chew on that one from now on!" and Lenny can say to himself, "Okay, now I've seen that pitch. It's only one strike!" Mind games.

Smith follows the change-up with a fastball directly at Lenny's feet for a ball. Dude skips out of the way, lands on his face, leaps up, glares out at Smith, mumbles to himself, looks the catcher in the eye. But Smith wasn't throwing at him, and Lenny knows it. If you throw at a batter, you don't aim at his feet. Lenny is just horsing around, psyching himself up. But it's true that batters are a lot touchier about these pitches than they used to be. In the old days the brushback or the flagrant knockdown pitch was just part of the game—unless you were playing Frank Robinson. Red Schoendienst loved to tell the story about how angry Frank would get if you threw at him. But Frank wouldn't fight, he wouldn't charge the mound. Instead, he'd wear out that pitching staff for the rest of the series. And Robinson stood right on the plate so it was easy to hit him accidentally, and all the more so on purpose. At some point Schoendienst called a meeting and told his pitchers he'd fine them one hundred bucks for hitting Frank Robinson. Leave him alone. We want to win these games. There are some batters around today you don't want to make mad, either. We'll meet one of them in the New York–Detroit game. Kirk Gibson. Throw at him and you'll have a Tiger by the tail, literally.

After showing his displeasure over the pitch at his feet, Lenny Dykstra settles in for the next pitch, a curve on the outside corner, or so Dana DeMuth says. There you have Smith's three basic pitches to left-handers—fastball, curve, change-up. I emphasize left-handers because Smith featured a harder slider to right-hand-hitting Pete Incaviglia. This may be his preference: sliders to the right-handed batters, curves to the left-handed. We'll see as the game goes on. If it turns out to be the case, it's not unusual. Many, maybe most, pitchers who throw both breaking balls are more comfortable with the curve against hitters on the opposite side of the plate. They're not confident they can get the slider in on the hands. But I'm sure there are pitchers practicing today who have just the opposite bias. It all comes down to what selection gives them the most confidence, and you can watch for some kind of pattern with pitchers who throw both the slider and curve.

On 1-2, Pete nibbles with a fastball, ball two, and change-up, ball three, before coming in with something unidentifiable that Dykstra hits hard but right at Otis Nixon in center field.

Mickey Morandini steps up for the Phillies. Like Otis Nixon against Danny Jackson, Morandini hasn't demonstrated that he can handle Pete Smith's fastball. This second time around, Smith will challenge him again. I think. That's what I predicted when Jackson faced Nixon the second time, but Danny fiddled around with other pitches before walking Otis. But this time I'm right and Pete Smith throws five fastballs in a row, the last one down the middle, but Morandini lifts it to Nixon in center for the out.

All those fastballs were good strategy against Morandini, who has zero power, but I don't imagine Pete Smith thinks he can get away with a similar approach against John Kruk. However, after a strike with the curve, Smith does follow with two fastballs. One Kruk fouls straight back (careful now, Pete! Kruk was on that pitch), and the next one is low. Now a change-up misses, and so does a fastball. Nibbling with the count 0-2. You hate to see it, but Smith does not intend to throw one down the middle to Kruk, not with two outs and the bases empty. You might think that doesn't show a lot of aggressiveness on Pete's part, but that's not really the case. It's common sense, intelligent pitching. Over the past six years with Atlanta, Pete is 26-40, with a 4.05 ERA. But he also had injuries for three years, and in '92 he was 7-0 with a low, low 2.05 ERA in twelve games. This tells you that Pete knows how to pitch and how to win when he's healthy and on his game.

What will he do with the count full against Kruk? He got Dykstra on a sinking fastball, one that he takes a little off of, trying to spot it away from the hitter. He could try that pitch against Kruk, or he could choose the straight fastball he throws over the top, a good weapon against left-handers that seems to have about four or five more miles on it— miles per hour, that is; eighty-nine or ninety, say, versus eighty-six. Rick Reuschel of the Cubs, Giants, and Pirates was a master of using two different fastballs. There was even less difference between them than "five miles," but it was just enough to throw the batter off stride. But, as I emphasized earlier, changing speeds over the middle of the plate can get you clobbered. If you have a little sinker that you use as a semi-off-speed pitch, you've got to keep it outside and low. This is true of any pitch with sinking action; the higher it is in the zone, the less it sinks.

Smith can live with a walk here to John Kruk, but he doesn't really want to concede the base with Daulton coming up. He wants a pitch on a corner somewhere. After one breaking ball, one change-up, and three fastballs, the selection is…the backdoor curveball, right on the outside edge at the knees. Called strike three! Side retired. Kruk just salutes and walks away. Great pitch, Pete! But John is also saying to himself, "Do that again with the bases loaded, I dare you. Let's see if your butt tightens a little." Because if that pitch misses a fraction to the outside, it's a ball and a walk; a little to the inside, it's right over the plate, sitting pretty. These pep talks help the hitter stay in a positive mode as he heads back to the dugout, stick in hand.

To say a guy throws a fastball says nothing. What kind of fastball? Tailing? Sinking? Rising? Cut? Straight? Danny Jackson throws the tailing and the cut fastball, Pete Smith throws a couple of varieties, at least, most pitchers do, and the differences between them mean everything. After three innings in Philadelphia, I want to lay this out clearly.

The tailing fastball moves laterally or "flat" a few inches—to his left, in the case of a left-hander, to his right, with right-handers. The sinking fastball, known usually as simply "the sinker," moves laterally in the direction of the tailing fastball and also downward. The rising fastball is the opposite of the sinker. It appears to rise as it approaches the plate. The rising fastball is the product of pure power. Tom Seaver and Don Gullett had nasty rising fastballs. The tailing fastball can sometimes rise, too. Ryan's is an example. And many pitchers' fastballs have a rising action when they're up in the strike zone or even higher.

While the rising fastball always has great velocity, the sinking fastball has the least velocity of any fastball. Usually. Kevin Brown of the Texas Rangers throws his sinker ball very hard, and he's therefore about as tough to hit as anyone when he has control of the pitch. That's the catch. The ball's explosive movement downward can take it out of the strike zone. Brown's sinker ball—Roger McDowell's, too, and Bill Swift's—can have so much downward action it might be mistaken for the screwball except that no screwball could be thrown so hard. The sinker also bears a resemblance to the split-finger. When I faced Bruce Sutter, who gets a lot of the credit for developing the split-finger, I just thought of him as a sinker baller in order not to get psyched out.

Perhaps more common than the hard sinker ballers are pitchers like the former Padre Randy Jones, a left-hander with a sinker that traveled in the low eighties—not hard at all, really, but that pitch broke late and sharply and killed the league. Right-handed batters lost patience, chased after it, and missed it every time. Finally some manager had the bright idea of going against book by stacking his lineup with left-handed hitters to go against the left-hander Jones. Unheard of! But the sinker broke into their favorite hitting zone. Jones retaliated against left-handed batters with a good, sharp slider that he could break over the outside corner. Randy was a terrific craftsman who won the Cy Young Award in 1976, but I don't believe he ever got the respect he deserved.

It's easy to see the sinking action of a sinker baller when you're watching on television, harder at the ballpark. One giveaway that the pitcher is probably throwing a sinking fastball is when he records mostly ground-ball outs. Rick Reuschel must have averaged at least two or three grounders for every fly ball. Classic sinker baller.

The tailing, sinking, or rising action of a fastball is the natural action for a given pitcher. The cut fastball, on the other hand, is a pitch that's developed and thrown differently. The cut fastball has a small amount of movement in the opposite direction of the tailing fastball. You could think of it as a flat slider that doesn't break much. Thus Danny Jackson tries to cut his fastball inside to the right-handed batters. Better yet would be the straight fastball, which is dead ahead with no movement, and the pitch of choice for coming high and tight to the batter on the opposite side of the plate. Probably the best combination for a right-hander, say, is the hard sinker, which comes down and in to the right-handed batters, and the straight fastball, which bores up and in to left-handed batters. Kevin Brown has that combination.

It might help to visualize these various fastballs as they appear on the face of a clock. Think about standing on the mound, with a large clock the size of the strike zone set up at home plate. The right-hander's straight fastball will move straight at the middle of the face. The rising fastball moves (or seems to move) toward high noon, the tailing, rising fastball toward two o'clock, the tailing pitch toward three o'clock, the sinking pitch toward four or five o'clock, and the cut fastball toward nine o'clock. For lefties, the movement is just the reverse. Their rising, tailing fastball moves toward ten o'clock, and so forth.

I have not forgotten the split-finger fastball in this discussion, but I don't put it in with the others because the split-finger is not really a fastball. It serves as a change-up for most pitchers who throw it. It's thrown harder than the standard change-up, but still a little slower than the pitcher's fastball, eighty-seven mph versus ninety mph, perhaps, while the standard change-up might be eighty-two versus ninety. The split-finger is actually a variation of the fork ball, which was developed years earlier. With the fork ball, the fingers are farther apart on the baseball, almost on the sides of the ball, so it can't be thrown as hard as the split-finger.

To the batter, the seams on the fork ball have a very slow, over-the-top roll almost like a knuckler, but the split-finger has no telltale spin at all. The same is true of the fastball (with one exception; the seams on the cut fastball form a tiny dot smaller than a dime). The main reason the split-finger is so devastating is that its spin doesn't differentiate it from the fastball. You have to pick up the difference in velocity. If the batter does this, he knows he shouldn't swing unless the pitch appears to be coming in at mid-thigh level. Anything lower and the pitch will break out of the strike zone. The batter must make the pitcher get the split-finger up; lay off the low one. But this is not easy to do against a guy like Kevin Appier with Kansas City. If he's sharp and you're not, you're in big trouble against his split-finger.

The split-fingered fastball was the big pitch of the eighties, and some experts wondered whether it had altered the delicate balance between pitcher and batter. Batters wondered, too, when they were facing Mike Scott, who threw his doctored version of the split-finger at ninety mph (more on that later) and it seemed even harder. But the split-finger has three drawbacks. Throwing it is a strain on the elbow; it's easy to throw in the dirt in clutch situations when the pitcher is trying to get a lot on it; conversely, if the pitcher gets nothing on it, the ball sits on a T for the batter, just like the knuckler that doesn't knuckle, the curve that doesn't curve, and the change-up that doesn't change.

The split-finger doesn't seem as prominent as it was just five years ago, but I don't think it endangered the balance of power at the plate, even though it's a great pitch. If that balance has been altered at all in the modern era, it was right after World War II, when the slider became popular. This is the pitch that changed baseball. Ask Ted Williams. The early version of that pitch had a big, flat break, what we might call a "slurve" today, but when Williams saw even this embryonic slider he realized instantly that hitting had become more difficult. The reason is that this was the first breaking ball that was not significantly slower than the fastball. The seams on the standard curve have an easily identifiable spin (like a moon orbiting from one o'clock to seven o'clock, in the case of a lefty's curve, or from eleven o'clock to five o'clock from a right-hander), but even without that spin the curve is unmistakable. The velocity is slower than the fastball, it can be timed, and the break begins the moment the ball leaves the pitcher's hand.

The slider, on the other hand, doesn't break as much as the curve, but it breaks late and it's coming in a lot faster, almost as fast as the fastball. Like the curve, it has its own unique spin (the red stitches form a circle about the size of a half dollar in the center of the ball). The batter can identify

the pitch, but the speed and the late break still made it difficult on the generation that learned how to hit facing only
the fastball and the curve. The slider is also easier than the
curve or the split-finger for most pitchers to throw for a
strike. J. R. Richard's slider had such a big break (so did
Steve Carlton's, as big as the normal curve's break) and was
thrown so hard (over 90 mph) that left-handed batters,
including myself, would take J. R.'s slider if it was near the
inside corner at the knees. It was not hittable, and I am not
exaggerating. So take it. Maybe the ump would call it a ball.

After about fifteen years of experimentation, pitchers
and pitching coaches finally perfected the slider in the late
sixties. They did a beautiful job refining that pitch. In fact,
all pitching is more refined these days. Twenty years ago,
who could have believed that the split-finger would be
developed? The way they throw that pitch just amazes me,
with the thumb ending up clenched between the first finger
and the index finger. The slider and the split-finger: the two
greatest bait pitches ever. And I have no doubt they'll come
up with another one in twenty more years.

I know the physicists say I'm wrong about that much
break on any pitch. They say that a rising fastball doesn't
really rise and that any pitch breaks four inches at the most.
I agree about the rising fastball, but I can't accept that
pitches don't break more than four inches. J. R.'s slider
broke from the outside corner to the inside corner. Ask anyone who had to face him. Besides, physicists (or maybe oph-
thalmologists) also say it's impossible for the human eye to
see the bat hit the ball. Well, not only did I see the bat hit
the ball, when I was red-hot, I saw the bat recoil. I know
what I saw. On the other hand, I never smelled the smoke
from a foul tip, as some guys claim they do.

CHAPTER 4

After three innings in Philadelphia, where do we stand? This is a good time to glance over the scorebook for a quick, preliminary assessment. Danny Jackson has allowed the Braves two runs on four hits, with two walks and no strikeouts. I show him with forty-nine pitches, almost evenly divided between fastballs and sliders, with a couple of changes thrown in and with a majority of the strikes recorded with the fastball. He has struggled, leaving a lot of pitches over the heart of the plate. Pete Smith has given the Phillies one run on just two hits, with one walk (Dykstra to lead off the first inning) and four strikeouts. I have forty-seven pitches for Pete, mostly fastballs. By the way, this important statistic is not revealed by counting up all the balls and strikes on your scorebook because that total misses foul balls with two strikes. If you really feel like getting into this, you have three choices: Come up with a scheme to mark those two-strike fouls somewhere in the box for each at-bat, or keep a chart of all the pitches for each at-bat as they do in the dugout, or keep a running count of pitches in a blank space somewhere. Your choice.

Pete Smith, with five straight losses coming into the game, is more than holding his own against Jackson, who came in with the better record. When Pete gets that slightly off-speed sinker away for strikes against left-handers and throws enough fastballs hard and in, he can be very effective. He's doing that well tonight. He has made good pitches when he needed them, including a couple of deadly back-door breaking balls, and only one bad pitch that really hurt him, the wild pitch scoring Kruk in the first. All in all, he's off to a good start.

Smith's battery mate, Damon Berryhill, leads off the fourth for the Braves. Berryhill looked bad his previous at-bat trying to hit the ball to right field to advance the runner to third with nobody out. Look for some better cuts this time. After a couple of sliders that miss, he gets a grooved fastball down the middle as Danny Jackson's third offering but fails to hit it well, but then Phillies shortstop Kim Batiste fails to field the grounder and Damon is safe on first. We could see the error coming from the stands. Batiste was back on his heels when he tried to field the in-between hop.

A basic principle in fielding—at least my basic princi-ple—is that you have to be moving aggressively toward the ball to make the play. Of course, this doesn't pertain on the bullet hit directly at the first or third baseman, when he only has time to react and lunge. On artificial turf, the middle infielders should never make a fielding error (as opposed to a throwing error) unless the turf is wet and the ball is skid-ding out of control.

If you have good fundamentals and natural ability, field-ing is easy. In spring training, that part of the job comes back after just a couple of days. It's the hitting and the pitch-ing that require six weeks or more to get in shape. Hitting especially. Pitchers have been throwing during the off sea-son; otherwise they'd blow out their arms on the first day. Plus they get to camp a week earlier than the hitters, so by the first spring games they're throwing decent stuff. Hitters show up more or less cold. I never swung a bat in the off season, and that's true of most guys unless they play winter ball. I would think the most interesting thing for a fan to watch over a period of games in the spring is the develop-ment of the hitters. It's dramatic over the first three weeks. I always thought a hitter wants to round into shape about the twentieth spring game. If you're sharp too early you may be due for your first slump right around Opening Day. Bad

timing. In fact, I'm betting the stats prove this. I'm betting that a comprehensive analysis of batting averages in the first ten days of spring training games versus the first ten days of the season show, on average, what we ballplayers call an inverse correlation: bad to good, good to bad. If any snowbird has the time and interest to compile this data, the clubs themselves might find it interesting reading. You might revolutionize spring training theory. You might even get a reward—or at least a couple of free tickets.

But the subject here is fielding. Kim Batiste just made that error. Fielding is relatively easy if you can do it, but there's still good technique required and I wonder if it's being taught effectively these days. I hear that there's more instruction than ever in the minor leagues today, but that might be offset by the fact that players spend less time in the minors. A lot of these kids just haven't spent enough time playing baseball, period. Plus a lot of basic habits are already in place, and hard to change, by the time a player is drafted.

When assessing an infielder's fundamentals, check out his position before the pitch. Specifically, where does he hold his glove? He should be crouched with his glove open in front of him toward the plate and almost on the ground. Everyone knows that on grounders, you want to bring the glove from down to up in order to make the play. You never want to be moving the glove up to down. Why not? You can move the hands up more quickly. It's easy to verify this standing in the living room, with or without a glove. The upward movement is quicker, and it feels more smooth and controlled. Or think about the bad hops you've seen on the infield dirt. Which ones are caught more often? The high hops, grabbed with the glove going up. The ones that skip lower than expected are much more likely to skid right under the glove, between the fielder's legs. You cannot react as quickly going down for the ball. Also, if you're bringing the glove up for the ball, you might knock it into your body if the play is not made cleanly, while moving the glove down probably ticks the ball, if it touches it at all. However, you can bring the glove up *too quickly*. We call this opening the floodgates.

Doesn't it make sense that the best way to assure that

77

the glove will be moving up with the ball is if it is held near the ground when the pitch is delivered? If the glove is held at the knees or even higher, the fielder has to lower it into position, then lift it to make the play. This requires extra milliseconds, and milliseconds are costly, especially on artificial turf. Many infielders today hold their gloves too high before the pitch. One who does hold his glove almost on the ground is Chuck Knoblauch, second baseman for the Minnesota Twins, and it's not coincidental that his father was a minor leaguer in the old days and a high school baseball coach from the old school. Another is Don Mattingly, the best-fielding first baseman in baseball today, in my opinion, and as good a fielder as any who ever played the position. Check Don's glove before each pitch. Right near the dirt.

Infielders today often don't show the greatest form, but outfielders make them look like purists by comparison. The snappy snare à la Barry Bonds is *de rigueur* today, even though every coach who ever taught Bonds—including his father, Bobby, I'm willing to bet—knows this is not the safe way to catch a fly ball. Kirby Puckett still uses two hands on almost every routine catch, and he's considered a throwback. Maybe so, but my kind of player.

Still, most balls—grounders or flies—are fielded cleanly, especially on artificial turf, and I don't think that fielding errors, per se, are as costly to a team over the long haul of the 162-game season as the mental errors of missing the cutoff man, throwing to the wrong base, failing to move the runner or get down the sacrifice bunt, or base-running blunders. You do have to be strong up the middle defensively (catcher, second base, shortstop, and center field) to win. That cliché is certainly true. In fact, the Phillies' main problem this year may be the absence of a solid, steady shortstop. Mariano Duncan is hurt tonight. Kim Batiste is unproved.

In any event, Batiste boots this grounder from Damon Berryhill and the Braves have their leadoff batter on first base with a pretty good bat-handler coming up in Mark Lemke, nobody out. Bunt? Why bother? Lemke is batting eighth. He moves the runner over, the pitcher Pete Smith is probably good for an out, leaving just Otis Nixon with a chance to drive Berryhill in. So the bunt is out of the question. Braves manager Bobby Cox might hit-and-run, hoping that Lemke can poke the ball through a hole in the infield and set up Smith to bunt Lemke to second base with Berryhill probably holding at third. In my discussion of the hit-and-run I noted that this play makes sense, but only with nobody out, never with one out, unless you pinch-hit for the pitcher, which Cox wouldn't do here.

It's good practice for us to analyze all these situations in depth, but I don't think Bobby Cox spends two seconds thinking about this one in the top of the fourth. He'll probably play things straight up and see what happens. Cox does play it straight up, and Lemke hits the second pitch to Dykstra in center field.

Pete Smith comes to the plate with one out and he'll try to bunt, that's a given, but this is not a cinch with Berryhill running. But Smith lays down a classic, and even the Braves' catcher can chug into second as Danny Jackson fields the ball and throws to Morandini covering first. Kruk and Jeff Manto were charging toward the plate from first and third bases, respectively. Ideal in the classic sacrifice bunt is to make the first baseman field the ball because he has to hold the runner on, and therefore he won't be as close to the plate as the pitcher or the third baseman, who can camp thirty feet away. However, with runners on first and second base, the first baseman is relieved of his obligation to hold the runner on, so he's charging, too, and the bunt should then be directed at the third baseman, who would have his back to the play for the lead runner going into third. Ideally, the bunt never goes back to the pitcher, because he should have the best (closest) fielding position. But steering the bunt away from the pitcher means steering it closer to the foul lines, and I guess that's why pitchers end up fielding a lot of bunts. People say bunting is rapidly becoming another of the many lost arts. Maybe so. I know it's inexcusable when a pitcher can't lay one down.

By the way, this bunt scenario is one standard demonstration why there are no left-handed third basemen in the major leagues, or shortstops, or second basemen, and why the ideal first baseman is left-handed (if I do say so). It all has to do with the throws required from each position. The left-handed third baseman and shortstop would never get anybody at first base on the play down the line or in the hole because they'd have to catch the ball, stop, turn, then throw. No way. Right-handed, they're ideally set to make all the throws to their left. The shortstop and second baseman do sometimes have to throw to their right, but their basic play to first makes the right-handed throw advantageous—no, mandatory. Although it's not ideal, first basemen can get away with being right-handed because the throw to second base is shorter than a throw from all the way across the infield. The reason catchers are right-handed is a little more subtle. Their main throw to second base gives no advantage to either hand except that most hitters are right-handed. Thus the left-handed catcher would be impeded more often on his throw to second. Plus he'd have a bad angle for the less common but critical throw to third base. So, no frontline left-handed catchers. The situation in the outfield isn't so important. The only rule is that the right fielder have a strong arm because he has the longest throw, to third base.

Damon Berryhill on second, two outs for the Braves. Jackson has to go after Otis Nixon. No fancy sliders on the 3-1 count, like last time. No 3-1 count at all! Jackson doesn't want the dangerous Jeff Blauser coming up with two men on. And again, the outfield alignment seems cockeyed to me. Jim Eisenreich in right field is playing way over toward the line where he should be, but look at the gap in left-center field. Pete Incaviglia is playing over toward *that* line. Either the charts prove me dead wrong or this is ridiculous. Get Pete in the gap, and I'm not referring to your local clothing store! Give Otis Nixon the lines! With his speed, he's going to get a double anyway on anything near the line. I just do not believe in these big gaps in the outfield. Against most hitters, bunch the fielders. But be your own judge. Check the out-fielders before each batter steps in. If they're leaving big gaps in left and/or right field, see whether the positioning pays off or backfires. And keep track for a whole season, not

just for one game.

In this at-bat, Jackson starts Nixon off with yet another fastball down the middle and Otis can only foul it into the stands behind first base. Late again. Now Jackson comes inside with the slider for a ball and follows with another fastball outside that gets the call from Dana DeMuth for strike two. With the count 1-2, Jackson can throw anything he wants, and he selects the slider. Oh! Bad pitch. This ball is right over the plate, and up, too. A healthy, sharp Otis Nixon wears out that pitch, but tonight he fouls it to the right. Now what's likely? Anything. Darren Daulton slides inside after he flashes the sign. This location should make us suspect this will be the slider because that's the pitch he has come inside with the whole game. Jackson checks Berryhill at second and delivers. Fastball, Danny's cutter, and he could have gotten that call but it's ball two. Close pitch. Nice try. I think this is the only fastball Jackson has thrown all the way inside all night.

With the count 2-2, Jackson has Nixon set up for anything, selects the fastball away, and puts it on the mark. On the corner. And he threw it hard, too. Mark down a "K" and turn the page. That was an outstanding sequence of pitches for Danny with the exception of the hanging slider on 1-2.

In the first inning, Darren Daulton pulled Pete Smith's first pitch, a fastball over the outer half, against the wall in right. In the Phillies' half of the fourth, Smith comes right after Daulton with fastballs, mainly, before getting him on the 2-2 count going to left field with that low, sinking, slightly off-speed fastball. Daulton was a little out in front of this version of the pitch, the one that's slightly slower than his over-the-top variety. Once Darren had committed just a fraction early, he had the right idea of hanging back with his body and hands and taking the ball to the opposite field—left-center field, in his case. He hit it hard but right at Ron Gant. Good pitching and good hitting, too. I wasn't thinking of this at-bat when I said in my preamble that the putout marked "F7" often doesn't tell the whole story of an at-bat, but this is an example. That was a tough pitch, and Darren went with it nicely. And credit the positioning of the outfield. Ron Gant was pulled into the gap in left-center, where he should have been, not straight up or down the line.

Pete Incaviglia at the plate. Pete Smith will probably throw him about the same as last time, with a heavy emphasis on that slider on the outside black. If the count goes long enough, you can bet that Smith will try to make the same pitch to Incaviglia in the same location in the same at-bat because that's the batter's weakness....There's the first breaking ball, a swinging strike. The second one, outside. Ohh! This is a high fastball over the middle, and Incaviglia fouls it straight back. After all I've said about pitching Incaviglia on the corners with breaking stuff, I understand why Pete threw this fastball, and I like the selection. You cannot absolutely live in one zone or the other. Even against a dead-pull hitter (Incaviglia doesn't qualify; he can drive the ball to right), you do have to come inside occasionally. After all, the pull hitters know they're pull hitters, and they know how they'll be pitched to, by and large. Incaviglia has to be expecting mostly curves or sliders outside, sliders, probably. Shock him now and then with the fastball in. Plus this pitch was so high—intentionally, I'm sure—that it would have been tough for Inky to climb all the way up there with his swing. He came close, but that was the whole idea with that pitch. It's easy to foul off for a strike, difficult to drive for a double. With the count 1-2, Smith is now in a comfortable driver's seat. Best bet is that he'll try to polish off Incaviglia with the trusty slider off the plate. This would be the good bait pitch to follow the previous bait pitch, the high fastball. And so it is, and the big slugger swings and misses. Have a seat, Pete. Grab some pine, as restaurateur Rusty Staub used to say.

The other Pete in this ball game, Pete Smith, is throwing what I call a refined game tonight for the Braves. More so than Danny Jackson, but then Jackson has never been that kind of pitcher. Smith is primarily throwing that little sinker away, living on the outside corner, coming inside on occasion, returning to the outside. And it's working so far against Jim Fregosi's predominately left-handed lineup. That was Smith's fifth strikeout in four innings, and he's not a strikeout pitcher. He usually records about one every two innings. Tonight, he's sharp.

He'll have to be against Jim Eisenreich, up next for the Phillies, because Jim is no dummy as a hitter. He's been watching how Smith has been pitching the other left-handers and has to believe that the same plan will be operative in his case. He won't rely on the evidence of his own first at-bat, when Smith made a mistake with a fastball over the heart of the plate. Jim will be looking away. After the first pitch, a fastball, is high for a ball, Jim reaps his reward on a change-up that dips perfectly down and away. Eisenreich is waiting for that location and drives a little liner inside the left-field line for the double. This hit is testimony to Eisenreich's "take it up the middle" approach, which is a balance between driving almost everything to the opposite field, like Wade Boggs, and pulling everything, like Ron Gant. Eisenreich's approach uses the whole field. It requires discipline and a good eye. There was nothing wrong with that pitch from Pete Smith. It was just trumped by better hitting.

In Kim Batiste's first try against Pete Smith, he struck out on four pitches, but he comes out hacking here in the fourth inning and hits a bloop into short left-center on the first pitch. Ron Gant makes a diving try on the ball but can't hold it when his glove hits the floor. (Yes, there's a floor beneath the artificial turf, along with some padding. Now there's padding. When they first laid the rug in Philadelphia, and when they had one at Candlestick Park for a couple of years, it was laid directly on concrete. You'd leave town after a series in either of those stadiums with throbbing legs. It was terrible. I remember my reaction to hearing that O. J. Simpson was going to play in San Francisco late in his career. On that surface! It must have been brutal for The Juice.)

Jim Eisenreich scores easily from second base on Batiste's bloop, but only because with two outs he was running at the crack of the bat. Otherwise, he would have had to make certain the ball wasn't caught, and he wouldn't have scored. That's an often overlooked advantage of these two-out rallies: The runners are running on anything and there-fore get an extra base on almost any hit. Score tied, 2-2.

With two outs and the moderately quick Batiste at first base, do you ask him to steal? With Jeff Manto at the plate, the situation says yes—if Batiste is thrown out, Manto will lead off the next inning, which is better than the pitcher lead-ing off—but the personnel involved say no. Checking the stat sheet, we learn that Batiste has twenty-seven hits and one walk. (One walk! A free swinger.) Subtract doubles, triples, and homers, and Batiste has been on first base twenty times, by my count. We don't know how many of those times were reasonable stealing situations, but we do know that he hasn't attempted even one. I'm willing to conclude that Batiste is not a base stealer at this early stage of his career. Plus Manto has power. He drove Ron Gant to the wall back in the second inning. The bottom line is that the steal isn't likely.

A somewhat related question: Why are steals in the National League down in recent years? In 1992, there were 1,560 successful steals in 2,301 attempts. Five years earlier, in 1987, there were 1,851 steals in 2,608 attempts. That's a drop of almost 12 percent in attempts and 15 percent in suc-cesses. Credit often goes to the pitchers for holding runners on better and to the managers for calling shrewd pitchouts or having the reputation of calling such pitchouts. Maybe so, but another factor may be that with all the money in the game now, players may not want to wear themselves out and risk cutting a few lucrative years off their careers. The skep-tic exclaims, "Wait a minute! Running an extra ninety feet every game or two is going to shorten a career?" It does sound ridiculous, but Lou Brock, one of the best base steal-ers ever, will tell you that his legs had had it by the end of a season, not so much because of the running as the sliding and the dives back into first base on pickoff attempts. I can cite my own experience. In 1982, I had nineteen stolen bases by mid-August. Then I was thrown out four times in a row after getting good jumps. My legs were dog-tired. So I do think that year after year of heavy-duty base stealing might well wear a guy out and cost him a year or two of effectiveness and that high salary. It's just a thought, and I could be talked out of it. The big problem with this hypothesis is that steals are *not* down in the American League. Attempts are actually up a fraction, from 2,506 in 1991 to 2,564. And the fellows enjoy high salaries in that league, too.

In Philadelphia, Pete Smith takes his stretch, checks the runner at first, Batiste holds, and Smith locates a curve on the outside corner for a strike. The next breaking pitch isn't so sharp, hangs over the plate, and Manto shoots it foul down the third-base line. Two strikes now, batter in a hole, so the possibility of a steal goes way up, even if Batiste isn't much of a stealer. The logic of the two-strike, two-out steal is simple: If the steal is successful, great; if it's not, the two strikes against Manto are wiped off the slate and he starts with a fresh at-bat the next inning, and the pitcher does not start the inning. Berryhill peers into his dugout, flashes a sign, Smith takes his stretch and Batiste...holds at first base. The pitch is a fastball inside. Ball one, and I like that pitch selection. To me, it's dubious to get two strikes with pitches away and then waste a pitch for ball one also away. No! Waste inside after you've gotten strikes outside. If you do waste outside after outside strikes, at least come inside immediately with the next pitch. Sometimes you'll hear announcers declare that the point of this inside pitch is to "drive the batter off the plate." Not really. The batter's not going to set up differently for the next pitch. The difference is going to be in his mind. You make him aware inside. To repeat, if you can get the batter concerned inside, you can get him out outside.

The odds are good now that Smith will go back outside with the curve or slider for the kill. He's been throwing that pitch for a strike all night....Yes, but the ball is fouled off. Same pitch again? Could be, but instead Pete switches to the inside fastball. Challenge the guy! Successfully, too, because Manto is jammed. The only problem is that Jeff Blauser at shortstop boots the ground ball.

How will the pitcher react? One run has already scored on a blooper following a two-out poke down the left-field line on a good pitch. Now we have this error in the infield. Pitchers get rattled, as we all know. It's Smith's good fortune here that the opposing pitcher is coming to the plate, and a weak hitter at that. Jackson really looks pathetic up there, but I'm sure he doesn't care. Smith will probably go to a breaking ball for the first pitch, and for the same reason I explained when the tables were turned and Danny Jackson was throwing to Smith with Francisco Cabrera on third base. Here it is, strike one. Slider, ball one. Strike two swinging on a high fastball! But the pitcher is at the plate, remember. He's more likely to swing at a high fastball because it looks a little more hittable than the others, even though it's not, especially for pitchers. And Smith threw it hard. Now it's back to the slider, I think, and Jackson hits the ball back to the mound for the easy out. Pete Smith throws the ball to Cabrera at first base with a little extra juice on it: Frustration and anger with the Mickey Mouse run, plus the error by Blauser with two outs allowed the pitcher to make the third out, so Lenny Dykstra, not Danny Jackson, will lead off the fifth. Pitchers think about this kind of thing. So did I. Game tied, 2-2.

We already know what I (and many others) think of the strategy that advises pitchers to work batters the same the first two at-bats, then switch to a new approach in the third at-bat. It makes sense in theory but that's about all. But we can check it out here in the fifth and following innings as both lineups come up for the third time in the game. We have already seen how Danny Jackson worked the Braves leadoff hitter Otis Nixon differently in his second at-bat, and to his regret, as he walked him with sliders. Leading off for the Braves in the fifth is Jeff Blauser, who has shown every indication of having a good bead on Danny Jackson's offerings, with two doubles, one of them misplayed into a triple. Even if this were not his third at-bat, you might figure on something a little different from Jackson because Blauser has worn him out. Watch for Danny to try to set that right this time.

Indeed, he spots the fastball precisely on the inside corner for strike one. That was the cutter, and a good one, but Jackson proceeds to miss with a pitch aimed inside that ends up in the dirt at the batter's feet—we don't know what that was intended to be—and two more pitches outside, one a fastball, one a slider. This is bad for Jackson because he's down in the count and Blauser owns him tonight. Now Jeff will sit "dead-red"—fastball—because what's the pitcher's choice? He doesn't want to walk Blauser leading off. But he does walk him because the fastball is low. Oh, well, Danny will set that experience aside as a bad set of pitches and try his luck with Terry Pendleton, who's having a rough night. Twice the Braves number three hitter has gone after first pitches with runners in scoring position, and twice he hasn't hit the ball hard. What to do this time up? Would Bobby Cox make it easier or harder on his hitter by calling for the hit-and-run? The situation for the play is ideal, in the abstract, because the game is getting on in innings, the score is tied, you have decent speed on the base path, although Jeff also has some kind of leg injury. Open things up! Get it going! I'm betting Blauser is off on the hit-and-run. So what if Pendleton hasn't had good swings tonight? He's a pro. He can handle the bat. The hit-and-run will help him bear down. He'll put some wood on the ball. And don't wait for the "ideal" 2-1 count, in my opinion. Do the deed on the first pitch. Make it happen. Apply the pressure.

Darren Daulton looks into his dugout. Does Jim Fregosi want the pitchout? That's the hitch with the obvious hit-and-run situation. Everyone in the park, and definitely the opposing manager, knows it's a good possibility. So Bobby Cox is standing in his dugout thinking that Fregosi knows that I know that he knows…what we ballplayers call an infinite regression. Was it Napoléon or U. S. Grant who didn't like calling a war council with his generals before battles because if he listened to all their differing opinions he'd never go to battle? One of the two. At some point, both the general and the baseball manager have to take responsibility and roll the bones, flip the coin, whatever. I'm flipping hit-and-run here, first pitch.

Jeff Blauser takes his lead. A throw over from Jackson wouldn't be a surprise; but it wouldn't be that valuable, either. Blauser is not a big base stealer. This would be the hit-and-run, and Jeff is not going to get picked off. Daulton flashes the sign and slides outside. Jackson takes his stretch, checks Blauser, who does break for second as Jackson delivers home. The fastball is right on Daulton's mitt—good pitch—and Pendleton fouls it down the first-base line. Blauser returns to first base. With one strike, the hit-and-run is off, of course, and it's off for the rest of the at-bat after Jackson comes inside with another fastball and Pendleton fouls this one down the left-field line. Really strong pitches from Danny Jackson. They have to be to come inside against the right-handed batters. I can't stress that enough. The tailing fastball has to start out three inches inside and then tail back over the inside corner. The cut fastball is in serious trouble if it doesn't cut enough. There's almost no margin for error with either one, so give Jackson credit when he pulls it off. That last one was the cutter.

With two strikes, all Pendleton can do is bear down and protect the plate. The interesting question is whether Jackson will now nibble around for one or two pitches or go after the batter....Oh, the backdoor slider, and close enough that Pendleton has to protect the plate by fouling it off. Next is a fastball outside, also close enough to require a swing that produces another foul. And now a fastball back inside. The pitch may be low but Pendleton can't be sure, and all he can do is fight it off with a weird hopper to shortstop, which Kim Batiste takes on a difficult in-between hop while back-stepping (justified, in this instance, because of the weird hops) and flips to Morandini for the force on Blauser, no play at first.

What we just saw was strong pitching, Jackson's best sequence of pitches in the game, without a doubt. He got Pendleton in the hole early, made the pitches to keep him there, then buried him for good with the fastball inside. These pitches could rev him up for the rest of the game.

One out but another tough batter steps in. Ron Gant can hit. Okay, what about the hit-and-run with one out? Cox tried it with Pendleton batting, but with Pendleton on first and one out, I doubt it here. Swing the bat, in my opinion, mainly because of Gant's power. But if you did have a more ideal hit-and-run man at the plate, you'd still have to have second thoughts about putting on the play on the first pitch because you just did that with Pendleton. You're risking the pitchout. On the other hand, you could figure that the other manager is also thinking, "Well, he just tried it on the first pitch. He won't do it again with this batter." So you *do* try it. Cat and mouse. I've seen managers call hit-and-runs on consecutive pitches.

Gant takes a slider low, ball one. Then he pops the fastball sky-high right over the plate. Note Darren Daulton's fundamentals on the play. He jerks off the mask but doesn't toss it down until he finds the ball and tracks it, finally discarding the mask at almost the last moment, in a safe direction. It's pretty bad for the catcher to toss the mask only to trip over it a couple of seconds later. But in the majors, you'll never see that. That's one fundamental that hasn't deteriorated. And the pitch? The high fastball, not quite in where Daulton had set up, but inside enough and, more important, up enough.

With two outs, Brian Hunter will take his cuts with Terry Pendleton still on first. Pendleton could take this opportunity to try to steal second base, but he hasn't been doing so all year, and the odds are against it this time, too. Hunter has seen an assortment of Jackson's pitches, but most have been either low or high-ish and outside. The one he hit for a single was a low fastball. Nevertheless, Jackson starts him off with a low fastball, then a high and outside fastball. On 2-0, he needs a strike in the worst way and Hunter can sit on the fastball if he wants to. If he does, he adjusts nicely because the pitch is the slider, not the heater, over the outer half, that Brian lines hard to deep left-center field. But Dykstra, one of the best in the business getting the jump on the ball, gets back and makes a running, stretching one-handed catch at the edge of the warning track for the third out. As I noted regarding Lenny's stealing prowess, it isn't based on speed. The same goes for his outfielding. He gets a great jump offensively and defensively.

That was an interesting sequence of at-bats for Jackson.

He couldn't locate the pitches well against Blauser or Hunter, but he was right on the nose with Pendleton and Gant. He has also been a little lucky on some hard-hit balls right at the fielders, but I have no problem with relying on the fielders. Sometimes, it's better be lucky than good. Most of the time, however, I'd prefer to be good. Tonight, right now, Jackson is both.

This bottom of the fifth is an especially important one for Pete Smith for a reason that's easily overlooked. Because this is the National League, this may very likely be the last time he faces the top and the heart of the Phillies order if the ball game remains tied. Even if he goes through the Atlanta lineup without incident, Bobby Cox may pinch-hit for him in the sixth or seventh inning. So Pete Smith wants to do his job while he still has the opportunity and hope that his team scores so he can stay in the game.

For the third time tonight, the leadoff hitter Lenny Dykstra actually leads off an inning for the Phillies. It doesn't usually work out this way, but when it does it's great for the offense. I can't stress this enough. The fielders come into the dugout saying, "Hey, top of the order, guys, let's go!" Believe me, it ain't the same when the pitcher's due up.

Dykstra will probably be taking a pitch. In fact, he'll probably take pitches until he gets a strike. That's book in this situation for Dykstra, but the pitcher can't be absolutely sure. He can't just throw a nothing fastball down the middle. Lenny has a reputation for taking a lot of pitches, then lying in the weeds in the later at-bats, ready to jump all over the first pitch if it's a fastball in the zone he's looking for. Any good batter has to do this once in a while so he doesn't start off 0-1 almost automatically. In the Monday-night game, for example, the Phillies were already down 6-0 when Lenny came up in the fourth inning. Take a pitch, you say. Work the walk. But the dude swung at the fastball on the first pitch and lined it hard—right at the shortstop. That was smart, even given the big deficit on the scoreboard. It was still only the fourth inning. In the sixth inning, he took the first-pitch strike. In the eighth inning of that game John Kruk swung at

the first pitch, a fastball, with Morandini on first base and
two out. Kruk was out 4-3, but it was still correct to swing at
that pitch against a pitcher like Greg Maddux. Greg had just
walked Morandini, but he wasn't going to give another batter
the free pass. He's too good for that. Kruk knew it, and he
knew that first-pitch fastball would be the best pitch he
would see in the at-bat. So take a rip even down 8-1. He'd
have been more likely to take it down three or four runs.

One of the things about baseball I've always liked is that
it's transparent. There are no secret moves, no trick plays,
no offensive set used for the first time in the season. Major
league managers never trick other major league managers.
Someone tells you that, don't believe them for a moment. In
any given situation, there's no option that the manager of
the offense is mulling that the manager of the defense is
unaware of. Not one. Likewise, the defense can't pull a single trick that the offense hasn't thought about. The pitcher
can fool the hitter, but this isn't because the pitcher has
pulled a brand-new pitch out of the hat. Dykstra knows Pete
Smith might try to slip one in for a quick strike in this situation, and Smith knows that Dykstra knows this. It's cat-and-
mouse out there, not hide-and-seek. Chess, not poker.

And I don't think anybody loves this part of the game
more than Dykstra. He loves to work the count deep, and
that's because he doesn't mind hitting with two strikes. He's
been hard to strike out his whole career, with that short
swing and small strike zone and great eye, and this year he
has only 22 strikeouts in 280 at-bats (an up-to-the-moment
figure). That statistic gives a player real confidence and a
tremendous edge over free swingers with a strikeout touch.
Nobody in the league takes a close pitch with more flair
than Dykstra as he looks the ball right into the catcher's
mitt, waits dramatically for the ump's call that will surely
verify his own decision that the pitch missed by half an inch,
and then struts around in triumph. Pitchers might not like
the show. I always loved it. The dude is in the game.

The last at-bat, remember, Pete Smith started Dykstra
off in unorthodox fashion, with the change-up. He could do
it again if he wanted. Something for a strike would be my

PUREBASEBALL

91

idea, but he has to be careful putting that fastball right down the middle. Then again, if you're Pete Smith you can't let the possibility that Dykstra is looking for the fastball keep you from throwing it. Just locate it well. Indeed, he does try the fastball to begin things with Dykstra, but misses down and in. Next, the slowest breaking ball of the evening, I think, but it arcs into the strike zone, so the count is 1-1 and Dykstra is ready to hit. Another fastball is high, but the next one catches the outside corner at the knees. Dykstra isn't sure about Dana DeMuth's call but doesn't say a word. He just spins out of the batter's box and goes off to think about it. The count is 2-2. Smith makes a good pitch with the curve—down in the zone, maybe even low—that Dykstra fouls off, then comes in with a fastball way high and way outside. Damon Berryhill couldn't even catch it. Not a good pitch. On that 2-2 count the pitcher wants to throw something that the batter might swing at, but this pitch never had a chance of finding the strike zone. Pete was probably overthrowing here.

With the count now full, it looks to me like the sinking fastball Smith has employed against left-handed batters all night would be the call. Then again, that's the pitch he used against Lenny in the third inning when the count was also full. Curve! Confidence! Dykstra lofts a fly to left field. That's a typical Dykstra at-bat, making the pitcher work, giving everyone in the stands his or her money's worth. Lenny is 0-for-2 for the night with one walk, but the more important statistic might be that he has forced Pete Smith to throw eighteen pitches in those three at-bats. Dykstra swung at no pitches the first time, one the second, two this time around. That's what often happens when a leadoff batter with a great eye and discipline faces a pitcher who tends to nibble.

Mickey Morandini now, and on the first pitch he beats out an infield grounder to short. Maybe something brewing. Does Jim Fregosi want to put on a play with one out and Kruk at the plate? He might, but I don't think he wants anything but a powerful cut from this guy. What about having Morandini steal? He's quick, he just beat out the infield hit, and he's seven for seven in steals this year. All true, but absolutely no steal, no matter how fast Morandini is, and I know a lot of fans don't understand why: You want the first baseman to hold the runner on because this leaves a big hole between first and second. Kruk drives the ball to all fields, but he can also pull the pitch—inside or outside—through that hole. Even if Kruk were a dead-pull hitter, second baseman Lemke could not move way to his left to fill the hole because of the possibility of the double play. In order to be able to turn it, the middle infielders have to play a little more up the middle than usual and a little shallower—"double-play depth"—because they have to be able to beat the runner to second with sufficient time to make the pivot and the throw without getting blasted and with enough time to get the runner at first.

When the first baseman has to hold the runner on with less than two outs, the result is a hole on the right side of the infield that the left-handed batter could drive a panzer division through. I know. I made a good living in this situation. This does not mean, however, that Francisco Cabrera would play *behind* the runner at first and almost give Morandini second base just in order to plug the hole. Of course not. The offense may not want to try to steal second base for strategic reasons, but it will take the free base as a gift. Kruk wants to hit with that hole on the right side, but nothing says he'll be able to hit the ball through it, so the defense in a tight game would never sacrifice a base in order to plug the hole.

This big hole on the right side is the chief advantage that left-handed hitters throughout the lineup have over their teammates who hit from the right side. The third baseman never has to hold the runner on. It's also one reason a lot of good number three hitters bat from the left side, and it's an even better reason for the number two hitter to bat left-handed. For the hit-and-run, he has that hole between first and second. For the steal, he blocks the catcher's view of the runner breaking for second.

Traditionally and because it makes sense, the third hitter is your best all-round hitter, a combination average- and RBI-man, a line-drive and doubles hitter with moderate power, and a quality "situation hitter," which means he's willing and able to hit-and-run, hit the ball behind the runner, all without excessive K's.

Why, then, do Barry Bonds and John Olerud bat fifth? Both of them hit for power and average; neither strikes out excessively. In Bonds's case, the Giants already have Will Clark, who is the perfect number three hitter, and Matt Williams has obviously benefited from hitting in front of Barry. Presto! Bonds hits fifth in San Francisco. In Olerud's case, well, he'll end up hitting third in Toronto, just watch.

On the evening of June 22, 1993—tonight—almost half of the number three hitters in the two leagues are positioned to take advantage of that hole on the right side (eight left-handed batters and five switch-hitters). John Kruk bats left-handed. The historically minded will interrupt to remind me right now that among the greatest number three hitters of all time were Tommy Davis, Roberto Clemente, and Willie Mays, all right-handed batters. Gotcha! But not really, because these great hitters were superb at driving the ball to the opposite field. Right field! They could take advantage of that hole between first and second as well as any left-handed pull hitter, or they could drive the ball into the gap in right-center. Or Hank Aaron. Early in his career in Milwaukee Hank hit third in front of Eddie Matthews, and he drove many a shot to right field. Hank learned to pull the ball later in his career. I don't believe you can name any great number three hitter who did not take advantage of the hole on the right side opened up because the first baseman was holding the runner on base.

Therefore I repeat: Mickey Morandini will not attempt a steal here.

If a drawn-in infield with a runner on third base turns a .300 hitter into a .400 hitter, what does that gaping hole on the right side do for John Kruk's average? A lot. But he has a problem. Pete Smith has handled him nicely all evening, starting him off with breaking balls, coming back with fastballs, then catching him, in the third, with that nasty backdoor breaking ball. If the idea about changing a pitching pattern in the third at-bat is going to mean anything here, Smith will start Kruk off with a fastball or two, then switch to the slider. But Kruk can't count on this. He can't over-think up there.

Fastball over the outer half, swinging strike one. So this is new. Now Smith throws over to first base. And again. Well, keep him honest, but I still say Morandini is not stealing. Smith returns his attention to the plate and fires a fastball high and outside, bringing the count even at 1-1. Now he needs a strike but doesn't get one with a lazy breaking ball outside. The count is 2-1, ideal for the hit-and-run, but it's not going to happen with Kruk here. Let him swing. Smith fires to first base, Morandini dives back. I must say, he's got a big lead over there....Oh, that's a good fastball, good tailing movement, outside edge. Pete threw that ball hard, too. He threw it right past Kruk, who steps out and mutters to himself after the swing.

On 2-2, Mickey Morandini stuns the crowd (or maybe just me) as he breaks with the pitch! It's the change-up, a good selection after that previous pitch, and Kruk can only reach out to bounce it to Pendleton at third base, who moves to his left to take it on the short hop and peg to first. Playing heads-up ball behind him, shortstop Jeff Blauser runs to cover third because Pendleton wound up closer to the mound than to that base after he made his throw, and Morandini, who reached second base easily, might have tried to run for the open base. In this situation, the shortstop must cover third. He's headed that way anyway to back up the third baseman on the grounder.

But what about Morandini's attempted steal on the play? It was a straight steal, of course, with two strikes on Kruk. Is there egg on my face? As I explain, you decide. With two strikes on the left-handed batter Kruk, he's much less likely to pull the ball with authority. He has to protect the plate. Jim Fregosi may have decided that the hole on the right side is not going to be valuable to this batter with two strikes. He may have also decided to ignore the common wisdom of holding the runner on 2-2 in the hope of getting the more advantageous 3-2 count. Or maybe Morandini has a green light and lulled Pete Smith to sleep. We don't know. In any event, that steal was a surprising, aggressive play.

I was probably assuming too much in my initial thinking on that situation. You know the Johnny McNamara story about assuming too much…you don't? Well, the umpire—I don't know who—called McNamara's man out at first, and when Johnny ran out to argue, the umpire said, "I assumed he was safe." Johnny told the ump, "You know about 'assume,' don't you? You just made an *ass* out of *you* and *me*." I was the first baseman, so I heard all this. McNamara winked at me. I thought this exchange was hilarious, but maybe you had to be there.

In Philadelphia, Atlanta manager Bobby Cox ambles to the mound. With nobody warming up, the subject of the discussion is obvious. First base is now open, two outs, and the left-handed hitter Darren Daulton is coming up, followed by the right-handed Incaviglia. Daulton slammed an easy fastball for a double and then hit a good pitch pretty hard to the opposite field. Meanwhile, Incaviglia is hitting a solid .368 with men in scoring position, but he has yet to prove tonight that he can handle Smith.

So: Do we put Daulton on intentionally? Various managers handle these discussions at the mound differently. Most managers usually don't even go out there. They just flash the four fingers from the dugout, and that's that. If they go to the mound they may want the pitcher's opinion, the catcher's, too, regarding which batter they want to pitch to. Or the manager may tell them what to do and deliver a little pep talk at the same time. Cox can tell Pete Smith to put Daulton on, pitch to him very carefully, or go after him full-bore.

I always like to observe the manager as he walks away from this meeting. I think some managers do like to hear that the pitcher wants to go after this batter. Damn the consequences; full speed ahead. Show no respect. The decision here is quick, and Cox is clapping his hands as he crosses the third-base line. This might mean his pitcher said he wanted to pitch to Daulton, and Cox liked this aggressive posture. Pure speculation on my part....Wrong, too, because Berryhill walks back to the plate and stands with his arm outstretched to the left. They're putting Daulton on. A no-brainer, really, given the strengths and weaknesses of Darren Daulton and Pete Incaviglia. It's the percentage move, and managers are rarely faulted for playing the percentages.

On the other hand, I've had a beef with the intentional walk for years. Why not opt instead for the quasi-intentional walk that's not such an obvious insult to the next batter? I've seen it happen too many times. The next batter accepts the challenge and makes the pitcher pay. Why don't the manager and his pitcher avoid this with four careful pitches to the batter they want to walk? The standard answer is that four careful pitches, all thrown for balls, might have a dangerous impact on the pitcher's command of the strike zone. In this regard, better to throw four fastballs nowhere near the plate. That makes some sense, but I've seen a lot of quasi-intentional walks that didn't affect the pitcher's control. It's a moot point in Veterans Stadium tonight. Daulton is given a free pass, his eighth intentional walk of the year, the most of any Phillie. (Kruk is next on the team with five. Mark Lemke is leading the Braves with six. Strange? In the American League, yes, but not here. Lemke bats eighth, in front of the pitcher.)

By the way, observe that Smith throws these four pitches correctly, meaning fairly hard. He doesn't lob the ball to the catcher. A lob is a half-throw, and you can't control the half-throw as well as a full delivery. I've seen a few botched intentional passes and a lot of close calls, with catchers leaping and lunging all over the place to catch the pitches. The fans groan. The manager winces. It looks terrible.

So the intentional pass is no surprise, but why doesn't Bobby Cox have a left-hander up in the bullpen, warming as fast as he can just in case Smith walks Incaviglia, loading the bases for the left-handed-hitting Jim Eisenreich? Would Cox be happy with Smith versus Eisenreich? Jim already has two hits tonight. The fifth inning isn't too early for a reliever in what we call a game situation—a turning point. But the

Braves' pen is empty. I guess Bobby isn't concerned about this scenario. Or maybe he thinks Jim Fregosi would just counter a left-hander from the pen with a right-handed pinch hitter, since Eisenreich is a specialist against right-handers. But Wes Chamberlain, the right-handed batter who platoons with Eisenreich, is injured. His replacement, switch-hitting Ruben Amaro, is just up from the minors and I don't think Fregosi is likely to replace Eisenreich with Amaro just for purposes of a righty–lefty matchup. And if Fregosi employed infielder Ricky Jordan to bat, with Amaro going in for defense, that's depleting the bench fairly early in the game. Unlikely, so the bottom line is that Cox could put in a lefty against Eisenreich and Jim would probably have to bat. If he didn't, Cox should be happy with Amaro over him. But no lefty is even warming up. Cox must prefer Eisenreich against Pete Smith. But I find that hard to believe. Eisenreich can hit.

With Morandini on second and Daulton on first, Pete Incaviglia steps into the batter's box and he's not happy with Bobby Cox and Pete Smith. He knows he's being challenged. "The guy has trouble with right-handers." Inky has heard this complaint his entire career, but if you look up his stats, they're not as one-sided as you might guess. In 1992 he hit .282 against left-handers, .251 against righties. Seven homers versus four, twenty-seven RBIs versus seventeen. This year, .316 versus lefties, .273 against right-handers. I've seen a lot worse discrepancies than that, and Incaviglia's strikeout ratio is essentially the same. So Pete is not helpless against right-handers by any means, and he has one advantage here, in a way. He knows that he's going to see breaking balls outside from Pete Smith. That's what he saw in the first inning, that's what he saw in the fourth, and Pete Smith is not about to follow some formula about changing the approach in the third at-bat. He wants to vary his selection, but that will not prevent him from going back again and again to the batter's weakness.

If Incaviglia isn't following this reasoning, too, if he isn't setting up for the outside pitch, then he's just not thinking at the plate. But I'm sure he is. He's all business in this situation.

Slider away, ball one. Well, that's not ideal for Pete Smith, but it's not fatal, either. But a strike is required on this next pitch. Should the count get to 2-0, the guy in the on-deck circle will suddenly loom large in Smith's perspective because there are many batters you'd rather face with three runners on base than Jim Eisenreich, who gives Incaviglia plenty of protection in this situation. There's pressure on the pitcher as well as on the batter. Berryhill slides outside, the slider misses the target to the inside, but it breaks sharply and low, and Incaviglia waves and misses. Now the fastball misses outside, way beyond the strike zone. All of a sudden, Smith is having a little trouble spotting his pitches. Hey, it's *tougher* now. Tie game in the balance. The fans feel that way, anyway. With the count an advantageous 2-1 for their favorite at the plate, they're stomping on the metal floor beneath the box seats and clapping and yelling, and they want Incaviglia to do something good. He's done it all year, why not on this beautiful night? Berryhill flashes the sign, sets up outside…

Gone! GONE! Oh, Smith deserves that. Terrible error. Slider right over the middle, belt-high. But give Incaviglia credit. He still had to hit the ball, and he did, all the way over the left-field fence. He races around the bases, pumping his fist, yelling something to somebody. Himself, probably. He's pumped. Phillies 5, Braves 2. Pete Smith has thrown a good game, but now he has bad numbers to show for it. One bad mistake, that's all, but as I've said, it's harder to put the pitch where you want it when the game is on the line. Still, the top pitchers seldom make that mistake. Almost never. That's no rap on Pete Smith; it's just a fact. Tom Seaver, Jim Palmer, pitchers of that caliber said they only threw three to five bad pitches a game when they were sharp. That's amazing, but I believe them because what they really mean is three to five bad mistakes over the heart of the plate. The great ones all make bad pitches, but they don't make them where they can get killed. If they miss inside, they miss inside. If they miss outside, they miss outside. And if a pitcher like Catfish Hunter gave up a home run—and he did, lots of them—it was with the bases empty

K
E
I
T
H

H
E
R
N
A
N
D
E
Z

nine times out of ten. They were solos. You can look that up.

Damon Berryhill was set up on the outside edge for that pitch, but Smith missed toward the middle of the plate because he had fallen behind in the count. He knew where he wanted to locate the pitch, but he hung it because he needed a strike. And when he hung it he got clobbered because Pete Incaviglia is an excellent representative of the "mistake" hitter. These guys are also called "cripple" hitters, and that's the term I prefer. Incaviglia is a dangerous cripple hitter. He has "holes," as pitchers say, he can be pitched to, he can be retired most of the time if pitched to carefully and properly, especially by right-handers, but throw him just one mistake, one cripple, and he'll hurt you bad. Frank Howard was a famous cripple hitter from another era. Frank had a lot of trouble with the breaking ball. Why, then, would a pitcher ever throw him anything but curveballs? Trying to be cute? Could be. Frank told me the story about the game in which he had struck out three times on a total of nine or ten pitches, all breaking balls, looking just terrible at the plate. In his fourth at-bat he was down two strikes, curves, of course. Then the pitcher tried to sneak a fastball past him and, as Frank put it, he "turned on the fan and wrapped that ball around the flagpole." "Turned on the fan" is his lingo for getting the barrel of the bat out in front and generating some serious power. Frank had a big fan. That's the perfect story to illustrate perfect cripple hitting. Dave Kingman was another dangerous cripple hitter. Dave could look terrible on breaking balls and fastballs in good locations, but make one mistake…

For the record, cripple hitters are usually thought of as big power guys, but there's another kind, the weak hitter without power. When any kind of hit—the blooper, the bleeder, the squib—can kill you, this cripple hitter can become as dangerous as Dave Kingman. Take a look at the "old" Ozzie Smith, the best number eight hitter you ever saw back in '82, '83 with St. Louis. Two outs, Ozzie needed to get on base to bring up the pitcher? He could do it. He found a way. Or late in the game with the threat of a good pinch hitter to follow? The number eight man in the National League will see some hittable pitches if he's patient. Ozzie came through

100

in this situation with regularity. Maybe this was the early sign that he would eventually develop into a fine hitter, period.

Pete Incaviglia is the other kind of cripple hitter—the guy who can blast one—and he just proved it in what was a fascinating at-bat from many perspectives. Unless TBS is your favorite network and you live and die with the Atlanta Braves, you have to feel good for Incaviglia. The intentional walk was a challenge, and, as so often happens, he made the Braves pay.

And definitely don't forget Mickey Morandini's contribution to that three-run inning. His surprising steal took away the possiblity of the double play on Kruk's ground ball. Maybe Pete Smith wouldn't have made the same pitch if Morandini had remained on first base, but he might have, and if so, the double play would have ended the inning. Neither Daulton nor Incaviglia would have come to the plate.

The 40,000 fans at Veterans Stadium are still buzzing—loudly—when Jim Eisenreich steps into the box, and he hits Pete Smith's second offering for another sharp hit—three in a row for Eisenreich. This gets Bobby Cox's attention, and Kent Mercker, the Braves' ace left-handed middle reliever, starts throwing in the pen beyond the left-field fence, where Incaviglia's home run ended up, in fact.

Pitchers can lose it in a flash. I was a batter, but I have great respect for the ability of the great pitchers to maintain total concentration. That requires terrific toughness. Pete Smith is going to have to get tough right now, and Bobby Cox will have to start planning ahead in case he doesn't. This is the time in the game when the manager in the National League has to be sure he's on top of things. Smith will be the fourth batter in the top of the sixth inning; if he comes up, a pinch hitter will definitely be required, down three runs. Cox does not want to take him out in this fifth inning, only to have to pinch-hit for the reliever who will have faced only a batter or two. But he might have to, before the game gets totally out of hand. In the pen, Mercker throws for all he's worth. It'll take about five minutes to get ready, and Bobby Cox can't come to the mound to stall. He's already made his one free trip this inning. If he returns, Smith is gone.

KEITH HERNANDEZ

In the American League, forget most of these considerations. I know that AL managers sometimes claim that their job handling the pitchers is actually more difficult because they don't have the luxury of the mandatory pinch-hitting situations. Their decisions on pitching changes are related to the pitching only. They claim that this somehow makes the decisions tougher, but their logic defies me. Managers in the National League have to make all the "pure" decisions on the status of the pitcher plus decisions on when he's coming to bat in future innings. They have to wonder whether they can, indeed, squeeze a few more decent pitches out of their man so they can avoid a situation such as Cox might face in this game: a pitcher on the ropes but scheduled to bat fourth in the upcoming inning.

Then there's the consideration of the double switch. Say Bobby Cox feels he must take Pete Smith out, can't wait, no choice. One option is also to take out Brian Hunter, whose at-bat just finished the Braves' half of the fifth inning. Whoever replaces Hunter in the outfield—Deion Sanders—is put into the pitcher's spot in the batting order—ninth—and the reliever is put into Hunter's position, the fifth hole, so he probably won't come to the plate for two or three innings. The ins and outs of the double switch can get complicated when the manager is weighing offense versus defense. Plus if Bobby Cox starts double-switching in the middle innings, he may run out of players later on. I'm not pretending all this is rocket science, but which version of baseball—with or without the designated hitter—gives the manager and the fan more to think about? Correct. Jeff Torborg acknowledged as much when he came over from Chicago in the American League to manage the Mets. Much tougher job in the National League, he said, even setting aside the fact that he had taken over the Mets

In the ball game tonight, Pete Smith rebounds against Kim Batiste, gets him on a pop to first base, and saves Bobby Cox the decision of taking him out. If Pete comes up to bat in the sixth, he'll be removed from the game; if he doesn't, he'll be back on the mound for one more inning. Score 5-2, Phillies, end of five.

102

CHAPTER 5

Danny Jackson has to throw a goose egg this inning. You can ask any ballplayer, nothing is more discouraging than a big inning immediately nullified by a big inning for the other team. You've got 'em down, keep 'em down. Another tennis analogy is fair: When you've just broken serve, you must hold your own, too. Otherwise, the opponent gets the big lift. In fact, John McEnroe told me that it isn't even really a break until you've held your own serve. In baseball, the fielders want to see their pitcher, who has just been blessed with a three-run lead in the bottom of the fifth, go right after the other guys in the top of the sixth. No messing around, please. Jackson has been doing that nicely over the last two innings. As reported, he threw forty-nine pitches in the first three innings; in the fourth and the fifth, he needed only twenty-three, an even mix of fastballs and sliders, few change-ups, with excellent control of the fast-ball, even inside.

In the sixth inning, Jackson follows orders by coming right after Francisco Cabrera with two fastballs for strikes, one of them at least half a foot wide of the plate—a generous gift from Dana DeMuth—the other the cutter or maybe a slider inside that Cabrera rips hard, but pulls way foul. And it had to be foul. The crowd often ooohs and ahhhs after these blasts, but the players know that you can't get hurt on the pitch six inches inside. If that location was Jackson's intention, and I think it was, it was a successful bait pitch because the only place to hit that ball is foul. What happens is that when the hitter realizes the pitch is staying inside the only way he can get the barrel of the bat on the ball is to step slightly in the bucket and rip the bat through the hitting zone. This generates a lot of power, but never to any avail. It's practically impossible to hit that pitch fair with the sweet spot of the bat. Don't be fooled or impressed by the long, long drives that are sixty feet foul. They might as well be tipped at the plate.

But now, a Jackson mistake. Daulton sets up inside, but the slider misses out over the plate. Cabrera turns on this sweetheart like John Daly on a golf ball and hits it about as far as Daly drives the ball. Oh, wow! What a shot, and they soon announce that this is only the thirty-eighth home run into the upper deck at the Vet in twenty-two years. I saw Greg Luzinski hit two of those. It takes a monster blow. I should note here that Danny Jackson throws what batters and therefore broadcasters call a "heavy" ball. Tom Henke, formerly the closer for the Blue Jays, now with the Rangers, throws an exceptionally heavy ball. Physicists will say this is impossible, I'm sure, and I certainly have no idea what makes these pitches heavy, but it's a fact that you have to hit them in the sweetest part of the sweet spot to get any results. Otherwise, it's "bees in the hands." Ask Francisco Cabrera. He'll tell you he just hit that ball perfectly.

Want to know what the fielders and everyone on the Phillies bench are thinking right now? "%#&°$%#" or something even ruder. And on an 0-2 pitch, too. There's just no excuse, but it happens all the time. And when it does, no one is more pissed than the pitcher himself.

Knuckle down. That's all you can do. Let it serve as a wake-up call. Jackson still has a two-run lead with the bottom of the order coming up, represented first by Damon Berryhill. (Pete Smith just headed for the locker room. His ninth spot in the batting order will now come up this inning; pinch hitter.) Jackson starts Berryhill off with a fastball—blowing off some steam?—that's outside for a ball. Another fastball, another ball, low this time. Now we're getting into a spot of trouble. Daulton suggests another fastball, Jackson says okay, and gets a big break when Berryhill swings at ball three up in his eyes. That's undisciplined hitting. If the Braves go on to lose the game, the Wednesday-morning quarterback could declare with some plausibility that this one pitch was possibly a turning point. If the count had gone to 3-0, as it should have, the odds are decent that Berryhill would have gotten on base by either walking or getting a good pitch to hit. With the count 2-1, he's still ahead, but now he has swung at a bad pitch and given a big lift to Jackson. The pitcher takes advantage, throws a pretty good fastball on or near the outside corner at the belt, and Berryhill obliges by grounding out short to first.

This is a different kind of botched fundamental that you don't hear about, but nothing is more fundamental than making sure you get a good swing when you're down on the scoreboard, up in the count, and the pitcher might be a little shaken after a big home run. You could argue that I overemphasize selectivity at the plate because that's the kind of hitter I was. True enough, I wasn't a hacker. But I still say that in certain situations any major league batter must be disciplined and selective at the plate without losing aggressiveness. This was one of them.

Now Mark Lemke lifts a high pop to Kruk at first base and pinch hitter Bill Pecota takes one ball before grounding to John Kruk for the unassisted putout. It's easy to say, but I relate these two lackluster at-bats to Berryhill's swinging at what should have been ball three. This may sound harsh, but that kind of thing can change the complexion of a game. The homer was a lift, the next at-bat a downer. But we'll see what happens. The Braves could come back with seven runs in the seventh. You never know. Long way to go.

As expected, left-hander Kent Mercker comes in to pitch for the Braves. This choice of relievers by Bobby Cox is basic baseball because of all the left-handed hitters in the Phillies' lineup, even though the new kid, Jeff Manto, leads off the Phillies' sixth inning batting from the right side, followed by Danny Jackson, who also bats right-handed. Manto flies out immediately to Brian Hunter in right field, Danny Jackson strikes out on four pitches, and that leaves it to Lenny Dykstra to make Mercker do a little work this inning and also to give his pitcher a quick breather on the bench (not that Jackson put out all that much effort batting). The dude takes a fastball right down the middle for strike one. That will probably be the best pitch to hit he'll see from Mercker. Taking into account the dude's stalling tactics after the pitch, you could conclude that Dykstra took the fastball mainly to give his pitcher a little time on the bench. Dude takes heat for being cocky, but he knows the game. Now he strikes up a conversation with Dana DeMuth about something, running a few more seconds off the clock. Suddenly he has a problem with his chaw and works with it for a moment. Valuable time wasted. If you wish, you could compare the Monday-night game, when another cocky center fielder, Deion Sanders, was hitting for the Braves. After his pitcher Greg Maddux made the second out in the sixth inning (a strikeout), Sanders strode immediately to the plate and swung at the first pitch he saw, fouling it off, then made an out on the second pitch. A little thing? Maybe, but still not smart.

Mercker follows the fastball with a big slow curve for a ball, then three fastballs for three more balls and the walk. Those fastballs, by the way, look to be pretty straight, little if any tail in any direction. Mercker throws hard, too, noticeably harder than Pete Smith. He's got some pop, but he also has a problem: thirteen walks in nineteen innings, and that ratio is not good for a reliever. Bad enough with a starter, worse for a reliever. Managers fume over airmailed cutoff throws, but they see red when a reliever can't find the plate. With a manager like Whitey Herzog, you were gone—not just from the game, from the team—if you didn't come in and throw strikes with men on base.

With two outs, will Dykstra be running? This would make sense except for one thing. As a left-hander, Mercker should be able to hold him fairly close, and if Lenny is thrown out, Mickey Morandini will be leading off the eighth, and he's not the strongest hitter in the lineup. So I don't look for Lenny to go.

On the fourth pitch of the sequence, I'm proved wrong, but you can now probably tell me the main reason Lenny felt free to take off, the same reason Morandini took off with John Kruk batting in the fifth inning. In both cases, the batter had gotten behind in the count with two strikes. If Dykstra is thrown out here, at least Morandini gets to start the Phillies' next inning with a clean slate.

But he's not thrown out. It didn't look like Lenny got a great jump off Mercker, and the pitch was a high fastball, perfect for Berryhill to catch and throw, but the dude is still safe and now in scoring position. Morandini proceeds to do himself proud by fouling off two good pitches from Mercker, who's tough on left-handed batters. The next pitch, a fastball, is over the inner half of the plate, and Morandini times this one perfectly, sending a shot to deep right field that twists Brian Hunter this way and that before he finally makes a nice running catch over his head—a great catch considering that Brian is making his second start in the outfield in over a year. The first one was last night. That play is pure athletic talent. The man on the street wouldn't come close to that ball. Side retired but a great at-bat for Morandini, who was driving the interstates against left-handers last year. His average was in the .100s, a buck and change.

In the top of the seventh inning, Nixon, Blauser, and Pendleton are retired by Danny Jackson on a total of eight pitches, six of them fastballs. Mow 'em down, why don't you? No reason to go into a lot of detail on these at-bats. Simply put, the air seems to have leaked almost completely out of the Braves' balloon, as Nixon swings at a high pitch for strike three (Daulton had set up low and inside), Blauser lifts the second pitch to Incaviglia in left, and Pendleton completes a rough evening by sending a routine fly to Dykstra in center on a fastball down the middle. After the previous inning, highlighted by the Berryhill episode on the 2-0 count, I said it looked bad for the boys from Atlanta, but who knows, they might come back. One inning later, they still might, but they don't have much pulse at the moment.

In the bottom half of the inning, Kent Mercker features high fastballs and a few slow curves in getting Kruk and Daulton, and that brings Pete Incaviglia to the plate to a rousing round of applause. This could be interesting because Inky has what amounts to some free swings here against his favorite opponent, a left-hander. Two out, nobody on, team ahead, he's the hero. Let 'er rip, I'll bet. Mercker must be in a combative mood because he comes after Pete with three hard fastballs, high, high, and high. Of course, Incaviglia has the hit sign on 3-0 in this situation. Again, the trick here for the batter is to be disciplined. Look for the pitch "middle-in" and lay off anything else, even a pitch you could probably handle if you were protecting the whole plate. If the bases were loaded, you might look for the pitch outside, but not here. Middle-in. The fastball is outside and high for what should be ball one, but Incaviglia swings anyway. This tells the manager that he might not want to give Pete the green light on 3-0 most of the time. You want a good swing on a good pitch to hit on 3-0. Inky waved at that one. He just had to scratch that itch, I guess. Some hitters, good hitters, too, tend to get overanxious on that count, and their managers know it and have them take. They should get something just about as good to hit on 3-1, a count they approach with a much more disciplined frame of mind.

Hitting ahead in the count is a real challenge. It's your best opportunity to look for one zone or the other—in or out—but if you're a smart hitter and have set up mentally for the pitch inside, you have to take the pitch on the outside black. If you have set up for something outside, you have to take inside black. You may well get the bat on the inside pitch, but will it be the meat of the bat? No. So you cannot swing if you don't get the pitch you're looking for. Cannot! Wait. You're still ahead in the count. But a lot of patience and confidence are required to hit like this. (This declaration assumes that the pitcher throws fairly hard. Against a real slow pitcher—Fred Norman, who pitched for Cincinnati and other teams, springs to mind—you could cover the whole plate no matter where you were looking.)

On 3-1, we have the same program for both protagonists. Incaviglia can pick a spot, and Mercker will go for the outside corner, where he shouldn't get hurt too badly if he's on target. He is, and Pete swings and misses again. Full count, and the sixth and final fastball is way high but Incaviglia takes a mighty cut and misses the ball by a mile, and the fans love this, too. Side retired. Inky just got swept away by his emotions in this at-bat. I don't want to preach, but you do have to harness those emotions if you want to reach your full potential.

Note: The following afternoon, in the third game of this series, Bobby Cox once again ordered an intentional walk to Darren Daulton with Pete in the on-deck circle. Fifth inning, bases loaded, one out. The hard-throwing right-hander John Smoltz was pitching for the Braves, and he had already struck out Inky twice on a total of eight pitches, primarily those hard sliders outside. In his third at-bat Pete had the opportunity for a repeat of the previous night's heroics, but what were the odds? Strike one, strike two, ball one, strike three. Sliders. Over the two games, Pete struck out in five of six consecutive at-bats, but in the other one he hit a three-run blast. That's the definition of a dangerous cripple hitter who took advantage of a pitcher's fatal mistake.

Tonight, thanks to Incaviglia, the Atlanta Braves are down to their last six outs. As I said, it doesn't look good, it doesn't *feel* good for them. Six consecutive batters have gone timidly, and Danny Jackson is throwing strikes. This eighth inning is the big one. This is the meat of the order. Danny throws a fastball to Ron Gant, who lifts an easy fly to medium-short right field. However, second baseman Mickey Morandini catches the ball. I swear, Morandini is just short of being in medium right field, way too far out. That's Eisenreich's ball. The two fielders are laughing about the play. They're laughing because the ball was caught and they're winning.

In the bullpens we find Mark Wohlers, a right-hander, up for Atlanta, and Larry Anderson and David West up for Philadelphia. Wohlers is up because he's coming into the game to face the Phillies in the eighth. Kent Mercker has thrown two innings. In twenty-three previous appearances, he has thrown a total of nineteen innings, so he's on his quota. He's already enjoying his shower. Wohlers is a right-hander because Bobby Cox has no choice, regardless of who might be coming up for Philadelphia. He only has one other left-hander in the bullpen, and that's his closer, Mike Stanton, who won't be brought into the game when the Braves are behind.

Anderson and West are throwing for Philadelphia because you never know. Jackson is cruising now, but he has averaged a little under seven innings per start and he could give up a single and a double on two pitches and be in big trouble in a flash. The Braves seem flat right now, but I've seen such an instantaneous turnaround too many times to count. Fregosi has to have his pen ready. Playing it safe, he has two guys, a lefty and a righty, ready for all contingencies. The downside of this sensible strategy is that a manager can wear out his bullpen just warming them up game after game, month after month. You have to pick your spots, rotate the job. To me, handling the bullpen would be one of the most challenging parts of the manager's job, with considerations not only about whom to bring in, but whom to warm up in these situations in which they probably won't get into the game. Of course, the pitching coach is key here, too. He has to know his guys. And many times this part of the game is more interesting in a losing cause, especially in the National League with the pitcher batting.

Take Monday night, when Fregosi found his team down 6-0 after three innings, 7-0 after five. However, the game was by no means out of reach at that point, and in the seventh inning the Phillies scored a run, then loaded the bases with one out. Fregosi sent Ricky Jordan to bat for Joe Millette in the number eight slot, with another pinch hitter ready for the pitcher's slot, and with two relievers warming in the pen just in case. Behind by six runs, Jim was managing for all he was worth. He ended up using three relievers and three pinch hitters trying to come back. Tonight's game, shaping up now as a victory, is a no-brainer in comparison. Fans love to speculate about how important all these managerial decisions really are. How many games does the manager win or lose? I don't know, but I do believe that the blunders will help lose more games than genius will win. And these blunders often involve maneuvers with the relief pitchers, bringing to mind Whitey Herzog's quip, "I'm as good as my bullpen." And Whitey has worn out many a pen.

As it happens, this eighth inning becomes one of those situations in which the relievers aren't necessary because Jackson follows up on the quick putout of Gant with equally quick work on Brian Hunter and Francisco Cabrera for the final two outs. Good fastballs, good sinkers. As the Phillies come in to take their cuts in the bottom of the eighth, Anderson and West sit down in their bullpen, and Mitch Williams, the Wild Thing, gets up. Fregosi has a choice. He can either start Jackson in the ninth, with Williams ready, or he can begin the inning with his closer. The modern style is to bring the closer in to start the inning, but the Phillies starters do have seventeen complete games in seventy-one starts, a high percentage by today's standards. But Jackson has only one of those complete games, and he has thrown 101 pitches tonight, more than a moderate number for him. Another consideration is whether Wild Thing needs the work. We'll just have to see.

First Mark Wohlers, the new man for the Braves, has to stop the Phillies from further scoring. Wohlers, a raw twenty-three-year-old right-hander, is a strikeout ace but sometimes also a base-on-balls ace, and that's why he's been down at Triple-A until earlier in the month. However, he's doing something right since his return because he has eight Ks and no walks in six innings. This appearance tonight gives him a chance to get in some work and perhaps build some confidence in what is probably, but by no means necessarily, a losing cause. He throws hard, which becomes obvious with his first pitch to Jim Eisenreich, but he may not have any idea where his big curve is going to wind up. At any rate, he doesn't throw the curve for a strike to either Eisenreich, Kim Batiste, or Jeff Manto, but he doesn't have to. Eisenreich grounds out, and Batiste and Manto each take called third strikes—all on the fastball. That was power pitching.

Ninth inning, and we have our answer to the big mystery about who will pitch for the Phillies. Mitch Williams is the man, and Jim Fregosi also makes some defensive changes behind him. Kim Batiste moves from shortstop to third, his better position, and Joe Millette, another kid, comes in at shortstop. He's your classic no-hit, all-glove specialty player, as we saw on Monday night, when he started the game and had three feeble at-bats. But the fans aren't worried about these guys. They're watching Wild Thing, who has had a checkered career, first with Texas, then with the Cubs, now with Philadelphia. His story is about the same as the younger Mark Wohlers's: lots of walks, lots of strikeouts. In fact, almost as many walks as strikeouts throughout Mitch's career. Otherwise, neither Texas nor the Cubs would have let him get away.

This year with the Phillies, Williams has kept his walks way down—only nine—while still striking out twenty-five in twenty-four innings. And he has thrown only two wild pitches and hit only one guy. Nevertheless, these Phillies fans have long memories, and they're primed to get upset if he comes in throwing high and outside. But right now Mitch is on a roll on a winning team, and Berryhill, Lemke, and whoever pinch-hits for Mark Wohlers cannot be all that excited about their prospects. Williams, by the way, is a left-hander and the Braves will send right-handed batters to the plate, but the manager with a strong closer doesn't play lefty-lefty, righty-righty matchups. The closer is the guy who is supposed to get out everyone for one inning, two at the most.

The outfield is playing deep. Incaviglia in left field is practically back at the warning track. The idea here is to prevent the double over his head. For the same reason, Kim

Batiste, now at third base, also plays closer to the line, although he's not right on top of it. This is not book. They must feel Berryhill has a decent chance of pulling Williams. Standard defensive strategy says that the first and third basemen guard the line to protect against the double only if the tying or winning run is on base or at the plate in the seventh inning or later. Two runs down in Philadelphia, the Braves do not yet have the tying run at the plate. Therefore, don't guard the line on the leadoff batter.

The formula is simple, but there's also the fine print: Don't guard the line if the single *also* wins the game. Think about the bases-loaded situation with a one-run lead. Do not guard the line because the single scores two runs and wins the game. But with a two-run lead, you must guard the line because the single ties the game while the double wins it, scoring the runner from first base. The same logic reveals itself in the distinction between runners on second and third, as opposed to runners on first and third, with a one-run lead. With runners on second and third, don't guard the line because the single scores both runs, but with runners on first and third you must guard the line because the single does not score both runs, while the double does.

Clear? I thought so. In Philadelphia, they do things a little differently, anyway. In a lot of other towns, too. If you watch closely over the course of a season, I guarantee you'll see these basic principles sometimes rigidly observed, sometimes scandalously ignored for an assortment of reasons, good or bad. Baseball people love to debate this whole subject. Announcers can be counted on to add their opinions to the mix. Whitey Herzog didn't like to guard the lines—but sometimes he did it. He felt you get beat more often in the holes than down the line, just as he felt the outfield gets beat in the gaps more often than in the corners. I concur, and when I did guard the first-base line, I wasn't three feet from it. I'd measure the distance I could cover with one quick step and a lunge. Even at this greater distance—eight to ten feet—I got burned more often in the hole than down the line. With no outs, you would guard the line a little closer because you don't want the leadoff double followed by the bunt that moves the runner to third with one out. Also, know your hitters. Gant, Daulton, Barry Bonds, Gregg Jefferies, Dave Kingman: with these pull hitters, guard the "pull" line if you must, but forget the off-field line. With Gary Carter, third basemen used to hug the left-field line because Gary pulled more hard shots right on the chalk than just about anyone I've ever seen. When he played with the Expos, however, I did not guard the first-base line—after checking with the manager, of course.

We're ready on defense. Wild Thing winds and fires his first fastball to Berryhill inside, ball one. Good pitch. Get the batter's attention. Characteristically for him, Mitch has to use his right arm to keep from falling down on his follow-through. This does not result in what you would call ideal fielding position. Another falling-down fastball catches the inside corner for a strike. Compare Williams's fastball to that of his predecessor on the mound, Danny Jackson. Both are left-handers, but Jackson's regular fastball had that little tail away from the right-handed batters, making it tough for him to come inside with it. He relied on the cut fastball and the slider, neither thrown quite as hard and both capable of hanging up over the middle. With these first two pitches, Mitch Williams informs the batters that things have now changed. He throws a straight fastball that he can direct inside with velocity. But the hitters already know this.

Now that this pitch has been established to his satisfaction, Williams shifts outside and Berryhill pulls the ball to Incaviglia in left field. One away. Mark Lemke also sees fastballs, and on the 1-2 count he pulls an inside pitch to Kim Batiste at third, whose strong throw pulls Kruk off the bag. That's an error but scored a single. Funny how the ball sometimes finds the weak link. Batiste made a fielding error in the fourth inning while playing shortstop, now he makes a bad throw from third. This can rattle a pitcher.

Bobby Cox selects Greg Olson, his other catcher, to pinch-hit in the ninth position. Olson is hitting .208 this year, but he's more like a .240 hitter. Anyway, he's the best

Cox can do. One of his regulars, David Justice, is back in Atlanta on personal business, and the other regular who's not starting tonight, Sid Bream, is a left-handed batter, and Cox probably has stats showing that Olson has just as good a chance against Mitch Williams, plus Olson might have more pinch-hitting experience. The second catcher on the team sometimes does. You'd like for Olson to be fast in this double-play situation, but he isn't. Anyway, Olson it is, and now the defensive alignment is by the book. Batiste guards the line, Kruk plays behind Lemke at first base, and near the line. If Lemke were the tying run, or were a big-time base stealer, Kruk would have to hold him on.

Let's also think ahead for a moment. What if Olson hits a double? The defense should let Mark Lemke score rather than risk letting Olson reach third on a throw to the plate. On third, Olson could score the tying run on a sacrifice fly. The defense has to keep him at second, even if it means letting Lemke score without a play. However, Lemke will not even try to score unless he can be absolutely sure of the play, only if he scores standing up. Atlanta needs two runs, not just one. If he stopped at third, leaving runners at second and third, whatever hit scores Olson or a pinch runner from second as the tying run also scores Lemke. So both offense and defense in this situation have the same idea: Safety first.

One on, one out, tying run at the plate. Time to invoke what I think of as the Gene Tenace rule. Tenace was the veteran catcher for the Oakland A's in their heyday, and he strongly advised against pitching inside in the late innings to veteran power hitters. Olson is barely a veteran and not a power hitter, but the advice is good for most batters. The best—or worst—example in my experience of how pitching inside late in the game can kill you was the fourth game of the National League playoffs in 1988. We—the Mets—led the Dodgers two games to one, and we had a 4-2 lead in the ninth inning of the fourth game. Mike Scioscia was at the plate against Doc Gooden, one guy on. Scioscia is definitely a veteran but not a power hitter at all. He had had only three homers all year. Nevertheless, when I saw Gary Carter set up inside against Mike for the first pitch, I yelped to myself, "Oh no!" Gary called as good a game as any catcher, maybe better, an aggressive "inside" game, and there's no doubt that he made our pitchers better than they knew they could be. But Gary could also get what I call "happy" inside. The late innings of a close game are not the time to do that when a homer beats you. Scioscia was lying in the weeds. He lifted Doc's low, inside pitch over the fence for the home run that broke our backs. We never recovered. You can't tell me that if Scioscia makes an out there, the Mets don't play Oakland in the Series.

With the game in the balance here in Philly, Daulton sets up squarely behind the plate—not inside. He wants a hard, low fastball, and he gets it for strike one. Now he slides to the outside, and the fastball is right on the money. Olson hits it crisply but directly to the new shortstop, Joe Millette, and he and Morandini have plenty of time to execute a careful toss and pivot and throw to Kruk at first base for the double play. Wild Thing shouts something as he strides off the mound with his twenty-second save, and Danny Jackson must be delighted in the dugout with his seventh win of the year. And the fans are ecstatic, of course, yelling and screaming with their forty-ninth victory. And it only took two hours and twenty-eight minutes to record it. The players' favorite kind of game. The fans' favorite, too. We all like quick, crisp ball games, don't we?

CHAPTER 6

Looking is not guessing. There's a crucial difference between the two. All veteran hitters look for certain pitches or for a certain zone—inside or outside—or both in certain situations. I talked about a number of these opportunities in the course of the Phillies-Braves game, and I'll do so again in this Yankees-Tigers game. The 3-0 count is the obvious place to look for your pitch. Some hitters may also look for a particular zone on other advantageous counts when they know the pitcher, when they feel good at the plate—or maybe even when in a slump as a way to break out of it—and when they're prepared to take the pitch if it's elsewhere. You must be prepared to do this, and that's where the discipline comes in. Looking zone, you always gear for the fastball, ready to adjust to the breaking ball or the change-up. There are also situations against certain pitchers when you can feel pretty confident looking for the fastball, wherever it's thrown. The pitcher needs a strike badly, and this is the only pitch he has been able to throw for one. Still, you're not dead if the pitcher does throw the curve. You can adjust. Looking is not an all-or-nothing proposition for the batter. It's not even that risky because you're ahead in the count.

With two strikes, forget any kind of looking. Bear down and cover the plate, or try to. Likewise, you can't look for a pitch or for a zone on *every* advantageous count. You have to know your pitchers and pick your spots. Throughout the two games covered in this book, I point out where the hitter could look for a pitch or zone if he chooses. But he won't always choose to. I'm trying to show you how to think about situations so you're able to call the pitch with reasonable accuracy, but the batter would go crazy if he tried to do it every time it was possible.

If the hitter tried pure *guessing* very often, he'd be looking for another job because guessing, unlike looking, *is* all-or-nothing, and good hitters rarely guess at the plate. If you set up mentally for the breaking ball or the change-up but the fastball comes instead, you're dead. However, some productive hitters take this approach on occasion because they have had to. While most hitters can gear for the fastball and adjust for the breaking ball or off-speed stuff, some just can't do it. If they're going to hit the good curve, they have to be ready for it. One of these guys is Howard Johnson, the proverbial dead fastball hitter. You cannot throw the fastball past HoJo when he's hot. Pitchers try—it's a macho thing—and pitchers fail. But the downside for Johnson is that he can't adjust to the breaking ball very well. And this is not a state secret around the league. If HoJo is going to hit the curve, he has to look for it. It's hard to hit .300 with this approach, but it's smart in its way. Johnson has adjusted his approach to suit his abilities, and with success, obviously.

If you set up for one zone on two strikes and the pitch comes into the other zone, that's guessing and that's dumb, because you can't take that pitch. You have to protect the entire plate and you're not likely to get the meat of the bat on the ball. Another type of guess is when you're so confident of a zone that you alter your stance radically in preparation. If it works, you're brilliant; if it doesn't, you're wiped out. I learned this trick back in the days of ABC's "Monday Night Baseball," with Al Michaels and Howard Cosell. I played for the Cards then and was watching the Dodgers play Montreal from the comfort of a hotel room somewhere. Stan Bahnsen was pitching for the Expos. Steve Garvey was batting. I forget the inning but remember what happened clearly: Exactly when Bahnsen checked the runner on first base, Garvey took one quick step away from the plate. Amazing. I sat straight up. I'd never seen anyone do this after the pitcher had taken his stretch, and the timing was so perfect Bahnsen didn't see Garvey do it, either. This step away from the plate could mean only one thing. Garvey was looking fastball inside, and the step away would bring that inside pitch right into his power zone. He got that pitch and pounded a two-run homer. Not long after that we played the Dodgers. When I saw Steve I said, "You sly dog." He just looked at me. I added, "I saw you on TV against Bahnsen." Then he knew I knew, and laughed.

I decided to try this maneuver myself. We were in Atlanta facing sinker baller Rick Camp. The count was 3-1, and I decided to go all out and pull the hard sinker away with power. This was more than looking; this was close to guessing because just as Rick went into his stretch, I stepped right up to the plate—one inch away. I guessed correctly, the pitch was on the outside corner black, knee-high, but with my adjusted position in the box this was, in effect, over the middle of the plate. I pulled that sinker over the right-center-field wall. The next time I came up to bat Bruce Benedict, the Braves' catcher, said, "That was pretty sly."

"I learned it from Garvey."

This is such a good a way to hurt a pitcher that a batter should only do it late in the game, big RBI situation, perfect count, real confidence. It comes with experience. Do this very often and you're running the risk of being double-crossed. You guess correctly as the catcher sets up outside, but the pitcher sees your last-moment adjustment and intentionally misses the target inside. Or the catcher could call an instantaneous time-out if he has any idea you might do this. So, as a fan, don't hold your breath waiting to see this trick. On the other hand, you can sometimes observe how a batter positions himself differently for different pitchers and on different counts. He's not trying to fool anyone. He's just adapting to that particular pitcher. Lou Brock worked with me a lot when I came up with St. Louis on "zoning" against lefties, and he also suggested I move closer to the plate against them and dare them to throw me inside. At the same time, Ken Boyer was having me move off the plate against right-handers because I was having so much trouble with their hard sliders inside. I followed both sets of advice, which meant that, in effect, I had to learn two different strike zones since my distance from the plate varied by a foot at least. Still, it's not as hard as it sounds. And against tough sinker ballers or a split-fingered specialist like Bruce Sutter, I moved way forward in the box, toward the pitcher, with the idea of swinging at those pitches before the sharp break. I think it helped, and I don't really understand why more veterans don't take the same approach. One guy who does is Frank Thomas, first baseman and resident slugger for the Chicago White Sox, and at age twenty-five, he's not even a veteran. But The Big Hurt, as they call Frank in the Windy City, is an amazingly mature, disciplined hitter, moving in or out four or five inches on particular counts against particular pitches.

The best way for the fan to watch for this kind of strategy is to pick a seasoned hitter and note his position in the box against a pitcher with one particularly effective pitch, perhaps a left-hander's big sweeping curve or Kevin Brown's hard sinker ball. Then if this pitcher gives way to a reliever with a different repertoire, or one who throws from the other side, check to see whether the veteran hitter sets up in a different location. And follow the hitter for a series of games. You might spot some maneuvering.

Shift the scene to Yankee Stadium. Lou Whitaker is at the plate for the Detroit Tigers in the first inning of their game against the Yankees, one week after the game in Philadelphia. The count is 3-1, best in the world for the hitter. Lou is the sweet-swinging veteran second baseman, batting second in the lineup tonight for Sparky Anderson. Ahead of him, leadoff man and left fielder Tony Phillips has started the game with a blooper off Yanks right-hander Scott Kamieniecki—a bad break for Kamieniecki, at that, because he had pitched Phillips great, getting ahead in the count with two fastballs and a curve before coming with a 1-2 fastball up and in, paying a visit to Phillips's kitchen, but Tony fought off the pitch, hit it in on his hands, and lifted a flare to left field. If you're the hitter you say to yourself, "Thank you!" If you're the pitcher you say, "That was good pitching. They won't get many hits off that stuff and that location."

Kamieniecki will try every trick to stay positive in this game. He's recently back from Triple-A ball in Columbus, after beginning the season in the Yankees' starting rotation, then being shifted to the bullpen. All in all, he's 2-2 with one save and a 4.61 ERA for the big club in '93, and he could use an impressive game tonight. So could his team. For the first time in a decade the Yankees look as if they might be true contenders in the AL East. Tonight, they're in a virtual tie with these Tigers for second place, three games behind Toronto. We know the defending World Champions are for real, but what about New York and Detroit? Can they hang in? If the pitching keeps up, yes, because any team with good pitching can hang in. This is one baseball cliché that holds up every time. My guess at this juncture is that neither of these teams has the pitching to win the Eastern Division, but only time will tell that. And the Blue Jays are having pitching woes of their own.

Twenty-nine-year-old Scott Kamieniecki is a battler who will give everything he's got on the mound. This guy is intense, that's obvious. He should be because pitching in the major leagues is unbelievably demanding. Pitching successfully, that is. And the same goes for hitting. Is the pressure worse on the pitcher because he's out there batter after batter, inning after inning, or on the batter, who only has four or five opportunities to prove himself? Tough call. I can see it both ways. But when Lou Whitaker steps to the plate against Kamieniecki with Tony Phillips on first, I have to figure the unproved pitcher has a little more on the line. Whitaker has been hitting against major league pitchers for seventeen seasons.

Lou bats from the left side so he's a low-ball hitter, naturally, and an excellent bat-handler, and Kamieniecki starts him off with a sinker away for a ball. The sinking action on this Kamieniecki fastball is unmistakable, but, like Greg Maddux of Atlanta, he also employs a straighter fastball that he can throw inside to these left-handed batters—a fastball that comes inside and stays inside. That's what he jammed Tony Phillips with just a moment ago. Now Yankees catcher Jim Leyritz flashes the sign and eases toward the outside corner...sinker, low, ball two. Now Kamieniecki is getting his butt in trouble. He follows with what I consider strictly American League pitch selection—the change-up—for yet another ball. But as I've said, that's the style these days—in both leagues.

On 3-0, Kamieniecki has to try to throw the sinking fastball for a strike, and Whitaker has to let him do it. Lou is not Cecil Fielder, after all, and a main job of the number two hitter is to get on base, especially with Detroit's power waiting to bat. I say Lou "has to" take. There's no law, of course, but the odds are great that Sparky gives him the take sign. Later in the game, left-handed batter, the famous short porch down the right-field line in Yankee Stadium waiting for the line-drive homer, Sparky Anderson will be more likely to let Whitaker swing. Probably not here...Strike one, Whitaker taking all the way.

Here's that 3-1 count, and I'm betting that Whitaker is going to be looking for the sinker on the outside half of the plate. He's not going to step up almost to the edge of the plate the way I did in Atlanta, but he's thinking along with me here, I'm almost certain. You know when you're facing a sinker baller, especially as a left-handed batter facing a right-hander with men on base and less than two outs and ahead in the count, that the pitcher wants not only a strike but, ideally, a double play. The fastball is the best pitch to throw for a strike, and the sinking fastball, if you throw one, is the best pitch to throw for a ground ball. That's two good reasons for Kamieniecki to throw his sinker. Where's he going to throw the sinker to a left-handed batter? Down and away, of course. So the batter should know this, sit on that pitch, drive it the other way. This is the intellectual process of hitting.

Why is Kamieniecki going to throw this sinker anyway? Because the count is 3-1. He can't afford to throw ball four. He's got to try to get Whitaker to hit the ball on the ground. This does not contradict my observation that throwing breaking balls behind in the count is popular strategy these days. It's popular when the pitcher has established that he *can* throw the breaking ball for a strike. Kamieniecki hasn't done that yet. Plus it's early. He's trying to get settled in. The odds are excellent he'll go with the pitch he's most comfortable with, his sinker. But if Kamieniecki does throw a nasty breaking ball here, Whitaker could take the pitch, tip his cap, and dare Scott to do it again on a full count. But I'm wagering he throws the sinker because that's his pitch, and you can't blame him for throwing it when he's behind in the count. Maybe he also hopes that Lou is having visions of hitting a homer on this ideal hitter's count. Maybe Lou is thinking big. The Tigers have been struggling, to say the least. They've lost the first seven games of this road trip. If Lou tries to be the first-inning hero by pulling a sinking fastball, he'll probably pull it on the ground for the double play.

Leyritz eases toward the outside corner; Kamieniecki checks Phillips at first and delivers the pitch we believe will be the trustworthy sinker down and away…and it is…and Whitaker drills it into the gap in left-center field for the double, scoring Tony Phillips. The fans pouring into the park haven't found their seats and the Tigers already lead, 1-0.

Really, you have to admire that hitting. Lou Whitaker was all over that pitch. That's just good, seasoned hitting. I made a living off right-handed sinker ballers who needed a double play, and I'm sure Lou does, too. They think they can get the ground ball on their sinker, but if you're smart you'll drive that ball in the gap to the opposite field. And the key in this at-bat was that Kamieniecki got behind in the count, reduced his options, and Whitaker knew how to take advantage. I remember one game when the Mets were playing Pittsburgh and facing Rick Reuschel, a terrific sinker baller. When the count went to 3-1, I sat on that pitch, got it, and drilled a double to left-center. Back in the dugout Rusty Staub told me, "Good hitting. You took what he gave you." That's the perfect phrase to describe the hitter's perfect approach at the plate. In this last at-bat, Lou Whitaker took what Kamieniecki gave him. He didn't try to pull that sinker for a homer. On the other hand, Pete Incaviglia did not take what Kent Mercker tried to give him in his last at-bat in Philadelphia—pitches away—and instead tried to pull for the fences on each of them.

Said it before, I'll say it again. This give-and-take at the plate is the heart and soul of baseball.

With Whitaker posted on second, young Travis Fryman steps in. He's the shortstop for the foreseeable future with Detroit and in his two full years has demonstrated good power—twenty homers a year—and good RBI totals—ninety or so. Ball one. Kamieniecki is getting behind on everyone. You just can't pitch that way, but it's early and the pitcher is trying to get his rhythm. Let's see what Fryman does to get the runner over, and let's see where Kamieniecki pitches him. Fastball, pretty much down the middle, and Fryman rips a bullet to shortstop. He wasn't even trying to move Whitaker over with a ball to the right side, and I don't believe you can fault that in this case. Remember when Atlanta's Damon Berryhill sacrificed his at-bat trying unsuccessfully to move the runner to third, and Ron Gant, too, in the preceding game? This is one "fundamental" that's not always a good idea, in my opinion, especially early in the game. Besides, the American League has always had the reputation of featuring station-to-station baseball, even though the statistics on steals I cited earlier don't really verify this impression (183 attempts per team in 1992 in the AL, 191 per team in the NL, not that big a difference). But the Tigers are the preeminent slugging team in the game. On this Tuesday evening they lead the American League and therefore all of baseball in home runs and runs scored. (They also lead in home runs given up.) The Yankees are third scoring runs, behind Toronto.

Cecil Fielder steps to the plate. No need to introduce this mammoth individual who has led the majors in RBIs three consecutive years. If he does it again in '93—and I say, what will stop him, he's leading the way in late June—Cecil will become the only man in baseball history to lead the majors in RBIs four consecutive years, and that's a lot of history and a lot of great run-producers, including George Herman Ruth, who accomplished the feat in 1919, '20, and '21. Computers make it possible for statisticians to come up with a lot of dubious "first man" declarations—first man to hit .280, slug fifteen homers, twenty-five doubles, five triples, drive in seventy-five runners, steal twenty bases, walk one hundred times, strike out fewer than fifty times, and have twenty outfield assists (that's the ringer)—but four straight RBI crowns would be one of the truly great records in baseball. And since it appears that John Olerud or Frank Thomas will probably be Most Valuable Player in the American League in 1993, this might make the fourth straight year Cecil Fielder does not win that award. You can't blame the MVP voters—the winners all had great years, too, and for winning teams—but it's terrible luck for the Detroit first baseman.

Kamieniecki's first pitch to Cecil is a big-breaking curve for a ball, and his second offering is a big-breaking curve for a strike, and already we have reaped a reward from watching this game on television. In the stands, you have to have the right seats and be watching carefully to see that Yankees catcher Jim Leyritz gives the sign and slides inside, then back outside just as Kamieniecki goes into his delivery. Leyritz is not the steady catcher—Mike Stanley is getting the night off before tomorrow's day game, and Matt Nokes is on the disabled list—and this may just be the way he works behind the plate, but it could also mean that Cecil Fielder has the reputation of sneaking a peek at the catcher's location now and then, and this is a way to cross him up. He peeks, you're set up inside, he focuses on the pitcher, you shift outside. Clever. Some hitters have this reputation of peeking, sometimes it's merited, sometimes it's probably not. I have no idea regarding Cecil, nor do I care. Maybe I say this because I peeked myself, now and then, not too often.

In my case, the rumor started that I was peeking when I looked at my hands gripping the bat to make certain the knuckles were lined up properly. That was a blasphemous lie because I checked those knuckles before the catcher settled in. I believe Orel Hershiser started this rumor. No, no, no, Orel. I like to believe I was a little more clever than you suggest. And, anyway, with you on the mound, I didn't need to! I picked my spots for peeking, usually facing left-handers in late-game, tight-game RBI situations, and here's how I did it. The pitcher takes his stretch. *Precisely* when he glances toward the runner at first base, I shift my eyes backward *without* moving my head. This is the critical point, obviously. The head cannot move because the catcher would pick this up. With my quick motionless glance backward, if I could glimpse the catcher, he was set up outside. If I could not see him, he was inside. Dennis Martinez caught me doing this one time and got mad. He stepped off the mound, glared in, and shouted, "Don't you &%#$@ peek!" He caught Ray Knight, too, and maybe a lot of other guys, I don't know.

When I played with the Cardinals, Steve Carlton threw me (and most batters) 95 percent sliders. It was a great pitch, as good as J. R. Richard's, but he had even better control of it than Richard. Carlton threw the slider like an automaton: outside corner black, at the knees, every time. And Carlton beat the Cards like a drum—payback, I guess, for when Augie Busch wouldn't pay him $100,000 (!) and traded him instead to the Phillies for Rick Wise. That was 1972. In any event, I peeked on Steve a few times. I glanced back one game, didn't see Tim McCarver, and concluded this was one of Carlton's rare pitches inside to me. I hit that pitch against the scoreboard. The next day Tony Taylor, the Phillies' first-base coach, accused me of peeking. He wrapped an arm around my shoulders and said, "After all those sliders, he throws one fastball inside and you hit it for a homer? No, no. I don't believe that. You were peeking."

What could I say? Deny. Deny. Deny. Another time I pulled off the same trick against Carlton—another homer—and this time he confronted McCarver in the dugout after the inning: "You see? Forget the fastball!"

McCarver defended himself, and they had quite a tiff.

After one of these Hernandez homers—I forget which one—McCarver suggested from behind his mask that I was peeking. Furthermore, he suggested I cut it out. "You know," he said, "you can get hurt doing that."

Deny. Deny. Deny. But Tim was right. If you get caught peeking you deserve to get drilled. It's as simple as that. It's also simple for the pitcher to pull off. The catcher sets up outside, you peek and look outside, the pitcher ignores the target and fires it right at your heart or head. Nevertheless, a lot of guys peek in one way or another, but they must be very selective. Do it often and you'll get caught. Also, the pitcher often misses his target, so your advance knowledge can screw you up!

Is peeking cheating? Absolutely not. Poor sportsmanship? No more so than stealing signs or doctoring the ball. I consider all these tricks as part of the art and craft of playing baseball, not as cheating. Now, hitting with a corked bat, that is cheating because there's no way to catch this trick on the field. But if you can stand on the mound and somehow scuff the baseball in full view of the umpires and everyone else and not get caught, more power to you. I admire the guys like Mike Scott, Don Sutton, Rick Rhoden, who scuffed the ball with regularity and no one ever figured out how. (Or maybe their catchers did the deed for them. Rumor has it that Yogi Berra hid a razor blade in his shin guard to mark the ball for Whitey Ford. Yogi allegedly scraped the ball across the blade as he was retrieving it from his mitt for the return throw to the mound.)

Vern Hoscheit, the Mets' bullpen coach who had been around forever and seen it all in baseball, would spend the first several innings watching Mike Scott from the dugout whenever he started against us, and Vern never detected anything suspicious. But after nine innings of hard work against Scott, we had a bucket full of baseballs at Shea Stadium with the same scuff mark on the same part of the ball: three lines, like a chicken scratch. Coincidence?

Or Bob Forsch. He gave himself extensive manicures on his off days, working hard on his index and middle fingers. Sharpen, lacquer, sharpen, lacquer. Five days later, those nails were like razors. If the umps go out to check, where's the foreign object? Or Don Sutton. Lou Brock collected balls thrown by him, and many had what looked like *and were* razor-blade marks. But where was the blade, or whatever? Or the legendary Nolan Ryan. National Leaguers thought he scuffed the change-up, and I gather that some guys in the American League—Yankees manager Buck Showalter among them—also believe he doctored some pitches in this league. They said as much after he got in the big fight with Robin Ventura. I think Nolan doctored his change-up to make it drop like a split-fingered fastball. What was his technique? Well, a collection of balls thrown by Ryan had the same telltale chicken scratch as the bucket of balls collected after Mike Scott pitched. Nolan and Mike were teammates in Houston. Therefore…"Elementary, my dear Watson." Ask Mike Scott how Nolan Ryan doctored the baseball—or vice versa. The difference was that Mike used the trick to make his fastball move in or out, while Nolan used it to make his change-up sink inordinately sharp and late.

The way I look at it, any benefit I or any other batter might have gotten from peeking—and it wasn't that much, to be honest—is more than offset by doctored baseballs. But I say it's all an art! Hats off to all the old-time craftsmen who doctor the ball, peek, steal the catcher's and the third-base coach's signs—and deke the runners. "Deke." You know the term? Yes, surely, but just in case, it comes from football. The runner "dekes" the defender with a fake to the left, then cuts right. In baseball, fielders try to deke runners, and maybe I'm an admirer of this particular skill because I was the victim of the cleverest deke I have ever seen, much less been a part of, on any baseball field.

The Cardinals were playing the Reds in Cincinnati, and I was charging home from first base on a double. Ken Oberkfell scored in front of me, and I don't know whether Ken was signaling me to stand or to slide as I approached the plate. He may have been urgently signaling a slide, but I was too mesmerized by Johnny Bench's performance in front of the plate. Bench was standing there holding his mask in his throwing hand against his hip, watching lackadaisically but also with disgust as the ball was being kicked around by the other fielders. He had nothing to do on this play; that much was obvious to me. Then, at the last conceivable moment, Johnny threw down his mask, took one giant step back directly onto home plate and directly beneath my foot as I tried to plant it on the plate, took the throw, and swiped me with the tag. I was stunned at how instantly the play had gone from a ho-hum score to "You're out!" Johnny's teammates hadn't been kicking the ball around after all. He had known all along he had a shot at me *if* I didn't slide, so for my benefit he put on a show Olivier would have been proud of. He saw where my foot was going to land and got his directly underneath it. I never touched the plate and I knew it, but I yelled and screamed at umpire Ed Vargo anyway. George Hendrick, who saw it all from the on-deck circle, told me bluntly, "Keith, you were out." Of course I was out. I was just embarrassed. What a fabulous play by Bench. Nevertheless, I had to tell him the next time I came to bat that if he tried that again, I'd level him. He never did, but I don't believe the opportunity came up, either. You now see this kind of charade often when the third baseman, waiting for the throw from the right fielder, stands as if nothing is happening, then tries for the last-moment catch and tag. But it's overused and rarely works anymore. The rule: When in doubt, slide.

I don't know whether Cecil Fielder is considered a peeker, or whether he actually does peek, nor, as I've made clear, do I care. And I don't think you should, either. It's part of the game. If you do observe the catcher sliding back and forth or setting his target very late, you can try to pick up what the batter might be doing. No harm in that. Kamieniecki's third offering to Cecil in this first inning is a big-breaking curve, ball two, and his fourth delivery is yet another curve hit sharply over the shortstop's head for a single and, yes, another RBI, Cecil's sixty-fifth of the campaign. Detroit up, 2-0. To me, that's not intelligent pitching. You can't throw curve, curve, curve to these Detroit hitters just because they might be dead fastball hitters. Or if you do, you'd better have great command of it and put it on the black every time. And who can do that?! The fourth curve to Cecil was hanging right over the middle, as big in his eyes as a full moon. As I've said, that's the problem with the curve. Hang it and you're hurt, and you do make a mistake with the curve far easier than with the fastball, no matter where you're trying to throw it. I'll stick with my analogy of the rifle shot and the mortar lob. In Cecil Fielder's next at-bat, Kamieniecki will come inside with some hard stuff. You can count on that. He won't wait for the third at-bat to change his approach.

The next batter, left-handed-hitting Kirk Gibson, is no bargain with that short porch in right. Doesn't everyone know that Kirk Gibson loves to drill the low ball down the line? The Gibson home run everyone remembers was the two-strike, two-out, two-run pinch hit he golfed out of Chavez Ravine in the ninth inning to win the first game of the '88 World Series. A week earlier, Gibson's homer in the twelfth inning had won the fourth game of the playoffs against the Mets, the one Scioscia tied with the homer off Gooden in the ninth.

In the Series, Dennis Eckersley was on the mound. Kirk's legs were shot by then. He could barely move, and he couldn't turn through the pitches at all. This homer would be his only at-bat of the Series. Eckersley had thrown fastballs right past Kirk, who was fortunate to get a piece of the ball and hang in. They were pitiful swings; Kirk was crippled at the plate. Then Eck came back with a slider, giving Kirk just a little more time to get the bat head through the ball. Granted, it was supposed to be a backdoor slider, catching the outside edge, but it caught too much of the plate. Gibson hit that ball with one hand, literally.

For what it's worth, that pitch struck me as one of the worst pitch selections I've ever seen. Throw another fastball to a guy who can barely walk!

If you throw the ball low to Kirk Gibson, make very sure it's on the outside edge or beyond; if you come inside, make very sure it's belt-high or higher. This is the standard approach for most left-handed hitters. Wisely, Kamieniecki starts Gibson with a high fastball, which Kirk fouls into the left-field stands. Scott threw it by him. Kirk takes a second strike on the outside corner at the knees and swings feebly for strike three on a fastball low and outside. Terrible swing. The change or the fastball? If the difference in the speed of the two pitches is not great (and it doesn't have to be for them to be effective) you can't always tell from the stands, or even on television, but many times—like this one with Gibson—you can tell because the batter is obviously out in front, most of his weight on his front foot, even letting go of the bat with the left hand. To no avail. That was Kamieniecki's circle-change, I think—the pitch perfected by Frank Viola.

I don't know which stance is odder, John Kruk's or that of the next Detroit batter, Mickey Tettleton. This one, I think. Kruk at least looked ready to hit, while the Tiger catcher stands completely relaxed, the bat almost resting on his shoulder. There's no sense at all that he's poised for action. He could be studying a shelf in the library. And he seems to be perfectly still, which is unusual. Almost all hitters are moving some part of the body at all times before the pitch, to keep from freezing up. The most notable exception to my knowledge was Rusty Staub. He was a statue prior to the pitch. My father could never understand how Rusty did this. He even asked him once. Rusty understood the wisdom behind the question, but he just smiled.

Whatever Mickey Tettleton looks like before the pitch, he gears up as the pitcher winds and he hits with power. Anyone batting sixth for the Tigers has to do so with power.

Jim Leyritz sets up inside for the first pitch. With no count on the switch-hitting Tettleton, this location does not tell you which pitch it will be, but it does tell you which of two pitches it will be: either the curve or the fastball. The change-up is never purposefully thrown inside. Never. The reason is simple: If the change does what it's designed to do and gets the hitter off stride, about all he can do with the pitch over the outside part of the plate is to hit it weakly toward the end of the bat. But even if he is off stride he can still get the head of the bat on the inside change-up and pull it with power, sometimes with one arm. The pitcher who throws an inside change-up runs a major risk that he will soon be, in the immortal words of George Hendrick, "rubbing up a new one." (The same goes for the pitcher who telegraphs his change-up. That's Western Union. Ben Rivera, the Phillies' pitcher in the third game of the Atlanta series at Veterans Stadium, gave away his change-up a couple of times with noticeably slower arm speed. He's young, and he's going to have to correct this if he wants to stay in the big leagues.)

The pitch here is the fastball for a strike, and after two more pitches inside, the count on Tettleton is 2-1. The book says Kamieniecki goes away this time. Oh, a fastball right down the pipe, but Tettleton misses it. Well, he hits it fairly hard, but on the ground to Don Mattingly at first base. Again, there's my point: You have a better chance of getting away with a fastball in a bad location. That pitch was a mistake the pitcher got away with. If you're counting, that's two for him. The hanging curve to Fielder hurt him, this fastball to Tettleton doesn't.

The Tigers take the lead in the first inning, 2-0.

Center fielder Bernie Williams leads off the bottom of the first for the Yanks, and two pitches—both fastballs—from the Tigers' Mark Leiter are enough to give you the lay of the land. Leiter is a right-hander, and because he throws between three-quarters and sidearm, his fastball runs away from left-handed batters, rather than sinking down and away, like Scott Kamieniecki's. This is the flat tailing fastball, just about the same as Danny Jackson's in Philadelphia. I suppose it's clear that, all other things being equal, the sinker is the better pitch against hitters on the opposite side of the plate. (With Nolan Ryan, all other things were not the same. He threw his tailing fastball harder than anyone else, and it rose, too.) The pitcher with the flat tailing fastball can be meat-and-potatoes for the batters on the opposite side of the plate if he doesn't establish a good breaking ball he can break off on the batter's hands and a straight fastball he can bust them with up and in. We saw time and again in the Phillies game how Jackson, a lefty, relied on his slider and a few cut fastballs to come inside to right-handed batters. Now we'll see what pitch the right-hander Leiter uses inside against Buck Showalter's lineup, which includes seven left-handed batters, including the switch-hitters. As a last resort, Leiter can just have excellent control of that running fastball, making certain that it starts four or five inches off the plate inside and runs onto the inside corner. But a sure sign that he has had trouble establishing the inside pitch is the batting average posted against him last year by left-handed batters: .312. So far this year, Leiter is 6-4, with a 4.20 ERA, but he's had three rocky outings in a row, and in two of them he didn't get out of the third inning.

Bernie Williams lines the second pitch—that tailing fastball over the middle of the plate—hard to right field, where it's caught by Rob Deer for out one.

Wade Boggs steps in. Boggs, of course, has come over to the Yankees in the off season as a free agent, and he has the highest career batting average of any active major leaguer—the highest by far, .338 coming into the season, with five batting titles. Last year was a disaster for Wade with the Red Sox, when he hit only .259, but nobody in baseball thought that meant that Boggs was finished just because he's now thirty-five years old. Other things were going on. Wade could hit from the day he was born, I'm sure, and he'll be hitting until the day he dies. His main idea at the plate is contact, and this is apparent from his stance. He holds his hands more in front of him than way behind his body. He isn't standing there with a stance that radiates power. I think this is obvious even to the untrained eye. Playing his whole career before this season in Boston, Wade perfected the inside-out stroke that drove ball after ball against the Green Monster in left field at Fenway, or down the line, or into the gap toward left-center. Watching Boggs bat is as close as you can come to watching a scientist at the plate. He isn't afraid to take a fastball down the middle. He isn't afraid to hit with two strikes. He's one of the best at fighting off inside pitches for fouls down the left-field line. About every fourth day Wade will strike out. My only quibble with Wade—and I'm not alone here, by any means—is that I think he should pull the ball more often, especially with that short porch in Yankee Stadium. His new park is exactly the opposite of his old one. A veteran like him should be able to make this adjustment.

In a way, and by way of contradiction, Boggs's ability with the bat can make things easier on the pitcher and the defense. You know you're not likely to strike him out, you know he wants to take the ball to left field, you know he has the bat control to fight off the inside pitch time after time, so you just make your pitches, play the outfield around to left field, and let the chips fall. One theory suggests that with the guy who likes to go away with the pitch, you might as well pitch him out there, play him that way in the outfield, and rely on catching the ball three out of ten times. "Pitch away, play away." Otherwise you'll just wear yourself out trying to get these batters out inside. This strategy makes even greater sense in Yankee Stadium, where there's a lot of room out in left field and with the fast outfielders that the Yanks and almost every team now feature. With most left-handed hitters in Yankee Stadium, you have to be a little worried about coming inside, you have to be very careful, but you're not as worried with Wade. When the Mets played Boston in the '86 World Series, we dared him to pull the ball. I played farther off the line at first against him than against any left-handed batter I played against in my entire career. I was over where the second baseman would be against a pull left-handed hitter. Sometimes I was so far over I had to remind the fielders to give me time to race to the bag to take their throws. At the same time, Wally Backman at second base played almost up the middle, six or seven feet from second base. In effect, we gave Boggs two holes on that side of the infield, one to my left and one to my right, but he refused to try to take advantage of it. In the sixth game of that Series, when the Sox were ahead in the early innings, Wade had an opportunity to take the ball to the right side and advance the runner to third with nobody out. But he didn't do it. I've mentioned times when this fundamental might not be a good idea, but in my opinion, it is a good idea in the sixth game of the World Series when your team has the lead.

With Boggs, some pitchers refuse to go along with the "pitch away, play away" strategy. Mark Leiter, we soon learn, is one of them. He starts Wade off with a fastball on the inside corner, strike one. It's a given, of course, that Wade will not swing at the first pitch he sees in the game. I'll bet he can count the exceptions to that policy on one hand— and that covers over 1,600 baseball games. That first pitch is a free strike for the pitcher against Boggs, and he should take advantage of it. Now Leiter follows with another fastball inside for a ball, and that pitch was straight. Little if any movement on that fastball, so we know that Leiter, unlike Danny Jackson, does have a straight fastball to locate up and in against left-handers. That's good news for him. Boggs knew this, of course, because he knows Leiter, but if he had never seen him before tonight, he would log this in as an important fact. Now he looks at a slider in the dirt and a fastball high. On 3-1, what is Wade looking for? He might be looking for something inside because Leiter obviously wants to establish control in there, but he's ready for anything outside, too. He's probably looking fastball anywhere. There it is, the fastball over the inside half of the plate, but not over the corner, and Boggs, predictably, fouls the ball down the left-field line. (In timely fashion, we read on the screen that Wade has a total of 9 base hits to right field this year, 9 out of 83.) And something instructive now happens on the field. Someone in the Tigers dugout waves center fielder Alan Trammell even more into left-center field. Watching on TV, you normally wouldn't know this, but the sharp crew working this game catches it. The reason for the maneuver should be clear: With two strikes on him, any disciplined batter will be more likely to take the outside pitch to the opposite field. And with a careful hitter like Boggs who goes that way anyway, this is practically guaranteed. Trammell is not a center fielder by trade. He was the Tigers' shortstop until Travis Fryman got the job, so Alan now starts mostly at third base. When he's in the outfield, they'll position him from the dugout, waving towels, and they have him where he belongs now. Rob Deer, however, remains in right field, leaving a huge gap in right-center field. You should know by now my reasons for doubting that alignment.

Important note: Infielders also shift positions against a batter, but with the pitch selection, not with the count. If you want to catch this you'll have to watch the fielders on the "pull" side of the infield, who will shift on the middle infielder's quick command just as the pitch is delivered. And this command has to be *last-moment* because shifting too early would be a giveaway. If you as a left-handed batter are standing at the plate and see the first baseman and second baseman shift toward the line, you know the pitch is either a breaking ball or off-speed pitch, a pitch you're more likely to pull. So the shift has to be last-moment, when the hitter has to be focused totally on the pitch. It follows that the infielders can't shift unless they know the catcher's signs. This is why the middle infielders are informed by the catcher when he changes those signs, usually because a runner is on second base. The catcher does this with a series of gestures on his mask, chest protector, and shin guards. You see it all the time if you watch for it. In effect, this first sequence of signs tells the pitcher and the fielders how to interpret the next sequence. However, I think this signalling is often a meaningless decoy from the catcher!

Shifting by the infield is mandatory. When a left-handed

hitter is about to see the breaking ball or off-speed stuff, the first baseman and second baseman must shift a couple of quick steps to their left, toward the "pull" line. Likewise, the shortstop and third baseman should shift toward the third base line when a right-handed batter—Cecil Fielder, in this case—is going to see the breaking ball or off-speed pitch. Watching the infielders for nine innings will show you how this works. But try it at the stadium—watching on television will probably leave you in the dark.

With the count full on Wade Boggs, Mickey Tettleton behind the plate edges outside for the pitch, but the tailing fastball doesn't get out there, catches too much of the plate, and Boggs nails it into the narrow gap in left-center. A pitcher's mistake? Yes, you could say that, but it was even more the result of the batter's patience. In the outfield, the Tigers play the ball correctly: Tony Phillips goes for the catch on the warning track, and when he can't reach the ball Trammell is backing up for the carom off the wall.

At first glance, the Yankees' number three hitter, Don Mattingly, is a similar kind of hitter to Boggs. High average—.311 career coming into '93—line drives, few strikeouts (fewer even than Boggs). But Don is also what I call a disciplined free swinger, and there aren't many of those around: not many walks, not many strikeouts. He isn't afraid to pull the ball with power down the short right-field line at the stadium or into right-center field. A survey of the outfield tells us this much. Against Boggs, center fielder Alan Trammell was pushed over into left-center field. Against Mattingly, he's pulled around into right-center. Mattingly's numbers have been down some the last three seasons—injuries haven't helped matters—but at thirty-two years old, he's still a dangerous hitter, and this run for the roses by the Yankees after about a decade of futility and embarrassment seems to have rejuvenated my deep-sea fishing buddy. He proves the point on Mark Leiter's first pitch, a fastball that's tailing toward the outside corner. Before it gets there, Don rips it hard to center field.

What happens next is a comedy of errors. Remember,

Trammell is not by trade a center fielder. On this hard line drive, he fields the ball and without hesitation throws it to Lou Whitaker near second base. Trammell was assuming one of two things: that Boggs, who is not fast, would not try to score from second base, or that Boggs would automatically score. Indeed, Boggs should stop at third, but instead he runs through the hold sign from coach Clete Boyer and there's no play on him at the plate because of Trammell's mistake. In effect, Boggs's mental error—not picking up his coach—pays off because of Trammell's mental error. Trammell should have been thinking that Boggs isn't very fast at this stage of his career and that the defense might have a play on him should he try for home. Rickey Henderson, forget it, but Wade Boggs? From medium-short center field, throw home and hit the cutoff man near the mound! That's what Cecil Fielder is in position for. If there is a play at the plate, the cutoff man will let the ball through. If there isn't, he'll cut it off. But there's no throw to the cutoff man, no throw to the plate, and the Yankees have just cut the lead in half, 2-1.

This at-bat also demonstrates another difference between the Mattingly and the Boggs approach at the plate. Wade is taking that first pitch in his first at-bat ninety-nine times out of one hundred. Don will also often take the first pitch of a game—many, maybe most, batters will—but he's shrewd, too, and innately aggressive. Runner on second base, sneak attack, Pearl Harbor, sit on the fastball, drive in that run. The beauty of first-ball, fastball hitting (and not just in the first at-bat) is that it eliminates the pitcher's strategy in the at-bat. You step in, get a good swing on a good pitch, put the ball in play, and your chances are reasonable. The guy can't fool around with you for three or four pitches. Those pitches may put you ahead in the count, but they may also put you behind. The whole idea of working the count is to see a fastball in a good location (the hanging curve is perfectly acceptable, too). But if you see this good pitch to hit as the first offering, go to hacking! No use waiting!

Check out catcher Jim Leyritz as he steps to the plate.

Batting right-handed, Leyritz is extremely deep in the box and way off the plate. He's as deep as the Phillies' John Kruk and even farther off. Deeper or farther and he'd be in a different ballpark. You wonder how he can possibly reach the ball over the outside corner. The answer might be as simple as a long bat! Most hitters who take this stance are expert at diving into the pitch and hitting to the opposite field, but they are obviously in a good position to pull the inside pitch, too, so that pitch had better be really inside. Psychologically, I think they might present a problem for the pitcher because it seems as though it would be hard to pitch them inside because there is no inside, in a way. The key for these guys is, can they handle the pitch on the outside corner? Since they've made it to the major leagues, the answer, presumably, is yes. All in all, Leyritz's performance so far this year is a recommendation for his technique. He's hitting .350 as he steps in (about one hundred points above his lifetime average accumulated over three seasons of part-time play).

Perhaps the most successful modern-day hitter to set up so far away from the plate was Jack Clark, a well-traveled slugger now retired. Clark was a dead-pull hitter. With less than two strikes, he simply conceded the outside corner to the pitcher. The bait pitch slider that pitchers tried to throw on that corner would often be a ball anyway, but with two strikes, Jack had to swing at that pitch. He did strike out a lot (145 times with San Diego in 1989, his personal high), but he got a lot of walks, too (a league-leading 132 that same year). Conceding the outside quarter of the plate with less than two strikes is not as wacky a strategy as it sounds. The tough part is having the confidence to take sliders on or near the outside black that might be called strikes, being ready to battle down in the count two strikes. On occasion I did just about the same thing as Jack Clark, looking outside, taking the inside pitch, and a couple of times I did it even with two strikes. And once or twice I looked inside with two strikes. The first time was against Jerry Reuss, a left-hander who had always pounded me inside with his hard sinking fastball, which he threw around ninety-three mph. I didn't like that fastball in, I'll admit it, but I felt better when I asked Joe DiMaggio what his toughest pitch to hit had been. This was at the MVP banquet in 1979, when he was as gracious as he could be. Joe said the right-hander's sinker down and in. Since Joe batted right-handed, that was the equivalent of Reuss's sinker to me, and that may be the only aspect of hitting I had in common with the incomparable DiMaggio. One year—1980, I think, the year after that banquet—Reuss got me down in the count 0-2. I knew he was going to come inside because that's what he had always done on two strikes, and with success. By this point, I knew the pattern and I just decided to look fastball inside, and if he threw it outside, I was dead. Strike three. And I was already 0-for-3 for the day. I didn't take a step back from the plate like Steve Garvey did against Stan Bahnsen, but with two strikes, I was not looking, I was guessing. Correctly, as it turned out. Reuss threw the fastball inside and I lined a double. Never in my career, in my life, had I flat-out guessed with two strikes. My father would definitely not have approved, had he known. Another thing: Only a veteran can try this because he knows he'll be playing the next day. Jack Clark knew he was going to be in the lineup for the following game even if he struck out four times in this one.

As the pitcher facing Jack Clark, why not throw seventy-five consecutive sliders toward the outside corner? Mainly because you can't do it unless you're Steve Carlton or Larry Anderson. Your control of that breaking ball is far from perfect. You'll hang some of those sliders, which Jack would jump all over, and some would be outside. (This is another reason why pitchers didn't throw all curveballs to Frank Howard and why you can't expect to get away with four straight curves to Cecil Fielder.) In his heyday with St. Louis, Jack Clark was as intimidating as any hitter in baseball, proved by all the intentional walks he was given (13 in '87). He hit thirty-five homers for the Cardinals that year and he was the only power guy they had. His success is testimony to an approach at the plate that relied on discipline—and power.

At Yankee Stadium, a check of the outfield against Jim Leyritz shows Trammell moved a little into right-center field. That tells us that Leyritz likes to "dive" into the ball from that position way off the plate and drive it to the opposite field. Leiter's first pitch is a hanging slider, right over the plate for a strike. He follows with a fastball inside and another one high, and now on 2-1, a nothing pitch, maybe a slider that didn't slide, right down the middle that Leyritz could have—should have—jumped on, but watched instead. Maybe he was looking fastball. Although I've argued at length for the wisdom of gearing for the fastball and adjusting to the off-speed stuff, some hitters can't do it, and some who can do it get frozen anyway. That's when the announcers say, "He couldn't pull the trigger." The pitch just freezes you. It happens to everybody. Still, that's not as great a sin, in my opinion, as guessing curve and taking the fastball down the middle.

Leyritz now fouls off a slider and a change-up before failing to check his swing on a bad pitch in the dirt on a full count. This can happen to the best of batters once in a while, and more often than not—nine times out of ten, I would say—it's a hard breaking ball outside or in the dirt. The slider in the dirt is the pitch that makes more hitters look bad than any other. That's why I call it the pitcher's best bait pitch. In the stands you can practically hear the fans grumble when the guy swings at a pitch the catcher has to dive for in order to stop. Sometimes it happens a couple of times in the same at-bat. "Why is he swinging at those pitches?!" the cognoscenti demand to know. All I can say is, that sharp breaker is a tough pitch to hold up on.

Two down, Mattingly still on first base, Paul O'Neill gets his opportunity. Another left-handed batter. Only one of the Yankees' first six hitters—Leyritz—bats from the right side. O'Neill is a career .260 hitter over from Cincinnati in a trade for Roberto Kelly, responding to the change of scenery with a .329 batting average. Tonight, Paul swings at but misses a slider with a pretty good break, but then he moves ahead in the count on a fastball inside and a curve way high.

Leiter is too wild. He's already gone to the full count on two of the first four batters and he's behind now to O'Neill, and he has offered fastballs over the plate to the other two batters of the inning—Williams and Mattingly—and both hit those pitches hard. His breaking pitches have good snap sometimes, but more often they're hanging, like the nothing pitch on the 2-1 count that Jim Leyritz could have jumped all over. This is only the first inning, but the Yankees, and certainly the hitters in this inning, should realize that if they exercise some discipline at the plate and wait out this pitcher, they'll get a good pitch to hit, without a doubt. On the 2-1 count, Leiter serves up a slider at the knees, a little in from the middle of the plate—the left-handed batter's erogenous zone—and without much break on it. A hanging slider, in short, which you don't hear about as often as a hanging curve, but this is one of them.

Boom! O'Neill jerks this juicy offering against the facing of the upper deck for his eleventh homer of the campaign, and there goes the Tigers' one-run lead. A raw pitcher makes a mistake and a good hitter capitalizes. The fans go wild. George Steinbrenner has been complaining about poor attendance at the park and once again threatening to move his team to Delaware or thereabouts, but almost 40,000 rooters have come out on this weekday evening. That's not bad. The O'Neill fans seated in the first level in right field hold up their bull's-eye signs in honor of their hero, even though he missed their target high this time.

Ironically, Mark Leiter now gets left-fielder Dion James on a variety of pitches on the corners, his best work so far. But he has lost the lead.

Yanks 3, Tigers 2.

Are we getting into a slugfest here? Maybe, but I haven't given up hope yet. These two moundsmen could get it together in the next inning or two. Scott Kamieniecki gets off to a good start against the old pro Alan Trammell to begin the second inning with a curve that catches the outside corner and another one, really slow this time, that's hammered on the ground to Spike Owen at short for the first out.

Rob Deer comes up. He's the definition of a one-dimensional ballplayer and the kind of guy Detroit seems to specialize in. He's a nineties version of Dave Kingman, and both happen to be products of the San Francisco farm system. Rob is big and strong and has one thought in mind at the plate: Kill the ball to left field. A dead-pull hitter. Deer's approach to batting is fascinating, in a way. After all, he holds the modern-day record for lowest batting average recorded with at least four hundred at-bats: .179. That was 1991. And the preceding two years he managed all of .210 and .209. It's amazing he was still on the team in 1992, but he was and he responded by upping his average to a respectable .249, with thirty-two homers. And he got those in only 393 at-bats. That's power. However, all those blows produced only sixty-four RBIs. That seems almost impossibly low. So far this season, Rob is batting .214, with eleven homers. Topping off all of these intriguing numbers are Deer's strikeout totals: In his career, he has struck out in over one third of his official at-bats (walks not included), leading the American League in that category three times, and he has almost six times as many strikeouts as home runs.

For the fun of it, let's compare these high numbers with Cecil Fielder's. As we would expect, the figures demonstrate that the Tigers first baseman is not nearly so one-dimensional. Cecil strikes out in slightly over one fourth of his official at-bats, and he has fewer than four times as many strikeouts as home runs. Thus his RBI totals are much higher than Deer's.

As you know since you've followed baseball over the last decade, the game has become almost overwhelmed by statistics. Many are worthwhile, others are bogus. For a while back in the early and mid-eighties, the "game-winning RBI" became a focus of attention as the final word on clutch hitting, and I led that category for the half dozen or so years in which it was kept. In 1985 I set the major league record with twenty-three. But I was also among the first to state that the statistic was meaningless. Batting third on the Mets, a pretty good team at the time, I often got an RBI in the first inning, maybe in the third. If that run gave us a lead we never lost, which often happened with our excellent pitching staff, it was considered the game-winner. In '85, the record-setting game-winner came on a sacrifice fly in the first inning of a game against the Phillies we won 7-1. Absurd! Then, I believe, they—whoever "they" are— thought about limiting the statistic to those game-winners recorded in the last three innings. Better. Finally, they dropped that number, and good riddance.

Forget the GWRBI, but a lot of other baseball facts are instructive. The new "inherited runners" statistic for relievers is important, showing what percentage of these runners score. But do they score on bloopers or bullets? Are they on first base or third base when the reliever comes in, with no outs or two outs? A big difference, obviously, so it's hard to judge this statistic without knowing the habits of the manager, too. The numbers cannot be the whole story, but I still recommend you have a couple of stat books handy, along with the game notes from the media relations department I mentioned earlier. One thing about the books, you *can* get them. Book in hand, you don't have to take my own or anyone else's word that Rob Deer is a one-dimensional slugger. Your own calculations and comparisons can prove the point.

Back at the ball game, the bottom line with Rob Deer, from the pitcher's perspective, is that reasonably good pitches will get him out most of the time. Facing him is the opposite of facing, for example, Wade Boggs. Absolutely the opposite. In Deer's case, you're probably watching the pitcher dissect the hitter. In Boggs's case, you're probably watching the hitter dissect the pitcher.

The camera pans the defense. In the infield, Yankee second baseman Mike Gallego is playing almost behind second base against this right-handed hitter. That makes sense. In the outfield, Dion James and Bernie Williams are pulled way around in left field. Also sensible. But Paul O'Neill? Straightaway right field. Okay, the Yanks have their charts, but we fans are also entitled to ask why the second baseman is way over toward the bag while the right fielder is not in right-center field. There seems to be a contradiction here. Why wouldn't the second baseman and the right fielder be positioned with the same approach? I don't know. The Yankees have their reasons.

Kamieniecki starts Deer off with a slider for a swinging strike, then comes back with a fastball that's probably both high and outside, but it's called a strike nevertheless. With two strikes, next comes the wasted pitch outside. Leyritz slides outside for the 1-2 delivery, and the slider misses in that direction. Now what? Outside, you have to figure…but Leyritz slides inside and Kamieniecki puts the fastball right on the mitt. Strike three looking. Have a seat, big guy, and don't be bitter, because that was a great pitch. I thought the man on the mound was a pitch late throwing inside, but maybe throwing outside with the wasted pitch convinced Deer (as it convinced me) that Kamieniecki would stay outside with everything, so Deer was surprised. His valves locked on that fastball inside on 2-2. (On the curve, you're frozen. On the heater, your valves lock.)

Next, third baseman Scott Livingstone steps in against Kamieniecki, batting from the left side, and after a fastball away for a ball, Kamieniecki scores with two curves over the plate. These are better curves than in the first inning. These have some bite to them, as did one of them to Rob Deer. Ahead in the count, 1-2, Kamieniecki can do whatever he wants, and he chooses to come inside with the fastball. I like that even though the pitch is too inside, for ball two. Kamieniecki has shown a straight fastball that he can throw inside to the left-handers, one that doesn't run out over the plate. On 2-2, he throws another fastball on the inside corner, and Livingstone hits it hard down the line, but Mattingly makes a good backhanded catch. That was good, aggressive pitching, good hitting, and good fielding. Good baseball. Side retired. Score still 3-2.

       ❖   ❖   ❖

Mike Gallego is paid to field, and he does that beautifully. He's a journeyman hitter with a lifetime .234 average, but he hit better than that in an injury-riddled 1992 season, and this year he's banging away at a .340 clip. Everybody seems to be hitting for the Yankees this year. That's why they're in the race. But despite Gallego's prowess so far this year, Mark Leiter challenges him with one, two, three, four, five consecutive fastballs. Three are fouled off, yielding a 2-2 count to the little guy. Leiter switches to the breaking ball in the dirt, which Gallego chases and, of course, misses. All those fastballs set up the breaking ball, but Leiter also had another reason to throw them, and this is an important point, easily overlooked. The pitcher had a rough first inning, throwing a lot of balls. In this second inning he needs to find his rhythm. What's the best way for a pitcher to do this? By throwing fastballs. It often happens that a pitcher who is roughed up in the first inning, with six or seven guys coming to the plate, comes out the second inning throwing almost all fastballs to the seventh, eighth, and ninth hitters. You can see this time and again—the pitcher finding his rhythm with mostly fastballs in the second inning facing the bottom of the order, and that might be all she wrote for the offense for a while, and certainly so with the great pitchers. It's true that you have to get to them early, before they find their rhythm.

It should also be noted that on the last pitch, the slider to Gallego, Mickey Tettleton did something a little different behind the plate. In the first inning and on the preceding fastballs to Gallego, Tettleton was sitting squarely behind the plate. Generally, the catcher doesn't set up right down the middle because he doesn't want the pitch right down the middle. What does it mean when he does so, pitch after pitch, batter after batter? His guy on the mound is raw, a little wild, and his fastball has a lot of movement—usually sinking and/or tailing. A check of Leiter's record shows that control has indeed been a big part of his problem recently. In his last start he was rocked for four runs, five hits, and four walks in two innings. Over his last three starts, ten walks in ten innings. Looking even further back, Mark has had games with good control, but now he's in a wild streak. The attentive fan could pick this up not only from the stat sheet but also by observing that the catcher sets up down the middle on just about every pitch. Sid Fernandez is another guy for whom the catcher will set up down the middle. At least, Gary Carter used to do that with Sid, whose fastball had a ton of movement. Pat Borders is often right down the middle for Juan Guzman's fastball. The next time you see the catcher set up squarely behind the plate on almost every pitch, ask yourself why. The answer is probably that neither he nor the pitcher has a good idea where the pitch is going. The problem here is that the fastball doesn't always move. What happens if the catcher sets up down the middle but the pitch goes straight and therefore ends up down the middle? Trouble. I've heard this pitch called a hanging fastball, but I don't like the terminology.

On that pitch to Mike Gallego, Tettleton held the glove right down the middle, but his body was set up outside. He wanted to give the easiest target possible for his unrefined pitcher, but he also wanted to be ready to catch or block the slider in the dirt in case Gallego swung and missed for strike three. If that third strike got past Tettleton, Gallego might reach first base anyway. Really shrewd catching technique, it seems to me.

The backdoor slider for a strike on the outside corner against left-handed-batting Kevin Maas is a good, strong pitch, just about Mark Leiter's first one to a left-hander. Still, Maas should be thinking positively, "Okay, Leiter, that was a good pitch, but do it again. Bet you can't. The left-handers hit you in the first inning, I'll do so here and now." Don't panic, be patient. Working against Maas, however, is the fact that he isn't playing much and isn't hitting well. The Yankees were hoping this tall, strong guy with Rob Lowe looks would launch thirty or so homers into the right-field stands at the stadium every year. Add in a mere dozen on the road and you have a bona fide power hitter. But Kevin's highest HR total was twenty-three in five hundred at-bats in

1991, with only sixty-three RBIs and a .220 average. Twenty-three homers is twenty-three RBIs, and say Maas drove in fifteen other guys as well on those homers. That should be a close guess; they weren't all solo shots. That's about thirty-eight RBIs on the homers, leaving twenty-five others. Kevin had 110 hits in 1991; eighty-seven of them were not home runs. So he had about twenty-five RBIs on eighty-seven non-home run hits. That's not a lot, and that's an important breakdown on the raw stats.

Following up on the previous comparison of Rob Deer with Cecil Fielder, let's match up Maas, also something of a one-dimensional batter, against Fielder for a different kind of comparison. In 1991, Fielder had about sixty RBIs on his 119 non-home run hits. (Trust me on the math.) What does this mean? It means that one of baseball's two or three premier home run hitters also gets good production from his other hits, while Maas has much less to show for those hits. It's another sign that the Yankee outfielder is just not hitting major league pitching very well. Therefore he's no longer playing every day. He has also had some injuries. In short, Kevin just hasn't been able to get it going as a major league ballplayer. He doesn't play consistently, and this can be a vicious circle that players go through for years before somewhere, somehow, they get the opportunity for full-time work and it all comes together. A great case in point is in the park today, the Yankees' regular catcher, Mike Stanley, who's getting the game off. Stanley was the platooned catcher in Texas for five years and in 1992 with the Yankees. This year, at age thirty, he plays much more regularly and is killing the baseball. A .251 lifetime hitter, he's hitting .310 as of tonight. This might happen with Maas, who's still only twenty-eight years old.

But in this game, he doesn't handle Leiter's next delivery in the second inning, a hanging slider that he pops to shortstop. If he's hitting well, Maas creams that pitch somewhere. Mistake number three for Leiter, but the Yanks are only 1 for 3 in taking advantage of them.

Spike Owen, a switch-hitter, doesn't have Kevin Maas's

power, that's for sure, but he's a better all-round hitter, that's also for sure. Spike is a contact hitter. He had good years in Montreal in 1991 and '92. But here he is batting ninth for Buck Showalter. What about batting him eighth in front of Maas? One reason might be Maas's ego. A power hitter batting ninth? That might be tough on a guy who must be having trouble with his confidence anyway. Another reason in Showalter's thinking might be the idea that in the American League, the ninth hitter is like another leadoff hitter. In the National League, you want the first and second hitters to be good, pesky batsmen. In the American League, why not have one of these guys as your ninth hitter, too—three of them in a row, causing a lot of problems for the pitcher. I know Tony La Russa thinks this way, and he had Walt Weiss, a pesky hitter, batting ninth in some of the A's great years. In Baltimore, Johnny Oates has Harold Reynolds batting ninth quite a lot, and Reynolds is a pretty good hitter. Ozzie Guillen bats ninth for the Chicago White Sox. He can hit. His career average is .266. With him batting ninth and Tim Raines batting first, Gene Lamont has two solid leadoff hitters. Reynolds and Guillen would hit first or second in the NL.

I thought about this strategy later in the '93 season when Oakland traded Rickey Henderson to Toronto. Before that acquisition, Cito Gaston's standard batting lineup for the Jays was Devon White, Roberto Alomar, Paul Molitor, Joe Carter, and John Olerud, one through five. After the trade, Gaston put Henderson batting first, of course, and left the others in the same order except for Molitor, whom he dropped from third to sixth. An alternative would have been to move White from first to ninth, leaving Alomar batting second, his more natural slot, and keeping Molitor third. But this lineup might bring up the ego problem with Devon White. Cito would have to explain his thinking to Devon and to the fans. But with these quality players, any lineup is fine.

From where you sit, it's usually obvious why the first through the fifth spots in the batting order are as they are, but the other positions may give the manager more leeway, and it's instructive to look at the order, compare batting averages and power numbers, and try to understand what the manager has in mind. Kevin Maas and the Tigers' Rob Deer are similar one-dimensional hitters. Maas has had the majority of his at-bats this season in the seventh position, but tonight he's batting eighth. Deer also hits eighth for Sparky Anderson. There must be a reason.

Spike Owen at the plate for the Yankees, remember. Leiter starts him with a hard running fastball, strike one. Two more fastballs, one high and one fouled back, show that Leiter believes he can have success against Owen as he did against Gallego, with hard stuff, and it also verifies that he's working with the fastball to find his rhythm. Note that against Kevin Maas, a low-average hitter but also a power hitter, Leiter did not throw all fastballs. There are different kinds of low-average hitters, and they require totally different approaches by the pitcher. With guys like Gallego and Owen, who just don't have the power, you can challenge them with fastballs. With guys like Maas and Rob Deer, who can hit a mistake into the upper deck, you have to be more respectful of their power, using other pitches to compliment the fastball, as Kamieniecki did with Rob Deer, who then stood looking at the fastball over the inside corner in the top half of this inning.

Against Spike Owen, Leiter is ahead in the count 1-2 and throws a curve that gets away from him, way high. Those really wild pitches don't mean anything unless they happen more than once or twice in a game; then you start to wonder what's going on. This time, Leiter follows with a strong slider that Owen hits to the shortstop for the easy 6-3 putout. A much better inning for the Tigers pitcher, obviously, but then again this was the bottom of the Yankee order. The next inning could be a different story, and it will show whether Leiter is really getting his rhythm. The ease with which he got through this inning points out the importance of having some kind of hitting in the bottom three places in the lineup. You hear a lot about teams who have a solid first five hitters, maybe even six. With Rickey Henderson, the Blue Jays now go all the way through seven, where Tony Fernandez bats. That's a tremendous asset, as it was with the Mets in '86 when we had Ray Knight batting seventh much of the time. After the last really solid hitter, whether he's batting fifth or sixth or seventh, what are the final two or three or four guys doing? Do they give the opposing pitcher too much of a breather, too much opportunity to get his rhythm in the early innings, often the second inning? In another context I mentioned the value in the National League of a number eight hitter who can get on base in front of the pitcher in order to give him something to do—bunt—or at least to give the pitcher the opportunity to make the last out so the leadoff batter starts the next inning. The strategy in the American League is different, but American League managers still need hitters in the bottom of the lineup who can pester the pitcher.

CHAPTER 7

Top of the third, Yankees leading 3-2, Scott Kamieniecki facing Tony Phillips and the top of the Detroit lineup for the second time. He starts Phillips off with a breaking ball away for a strike, then three more breaking balls follow, two for strikes, and Kamieniecki finds himself in the catbird seat, ahead in the count 1-2. How to administer the coup de grace? The pitcher and his catcher have a disagreement. Watching at home on television, we have the perfect seat for seeing how this at-bat plays out. As I noted while explaining how Don Sutton called his own game from the mound, four fingers is the usual sign for the change-up. And the catcher usually wiggles these four fingers, too. On this 1-2 count to Tony Phillips, Jim Leyritz wiggles four fingers. Kamieniecki brushes off the pitch. He wants something else. Leyritz switches to the "1" and taps his right inner thigh—inside against the left-handed-batting Phillips. This is what Kamieniecki wants. He jammed Phillips with the inside fastball in the first inning, although Phillips looped it for a hit, and here in the third inning he throws the pitch perfectly again, starting it out two to four inches inside, letting it run naturally back toward the inside corner, on the black. Well, almost on the black. Maybe the pitch was a bit inside, but maybe not. Kamieniecki gets the called strike three on a good, aggressive pitch. This fastball had a little tailing action on it, not the sinking action of Kamieniecki's natural fastball, not the straight pitch he has used a few times inside to left-handed batters. Something a little different, it seems to me. Effective, too, and proving the point again that you do not have to throw ninety-five miles per hour to come inside to the hitters. You do not have to throw ninety-five miles per hour to break bats. What you have to do is locate inside with a pitch that is truly inside—on the black. Both leagues have a number of soft-throwing left-handers who get left- and right-handed batters out with eighty-five mph fastballs on the inside black.

At the ballpark, no matter where you're sitting, you could not have followed that give-and-take between Kamieniecki and his catcher. It's only open to your inspection watching on television, where you can often read the signs from the catcher, if they're not hidden in the shadow, and this is exactly the kind of point you should be looking for if you can't get out to the park. Read the sign, read the shake-off from the pitcher, if any, read the catcher's location. Shake-offs such as we just saw are especially important because they show a difference in approach between the pitcher and his catcher, and if a pattern sets in, these shake-offs allow you to judge whether the pitcher or the catcher seems to be calling the more aggressive game.

With Phillips retired for the first out, Lou Whitaker comes up for the second time. Recall how he worked Kamieniecki for a 3-1 count in the first inning with Tony Phillips on first. Lou had good reasons to look for the sinker outside, got that pitch, and hit the double to the wall in left-center field. That was a textbook example of looking area by a veteran hitter, and it's impossible for Kamieniecki to wipe out that memory. For Lou, who is so seasoned at the plate, that's not a memory; that's just knowledge. If Lou likes to pick a zone when the count is in his favor, and I'm sure he does to some extent, he'll consult his book on a pitcher he has faced over a period of games and seasons. He can hardly do this with Kamieniecki, who has less than two years in the big leagues, so Lou will place stock instead in his knowledge of how sinker ballers like to work, period. But when an experienced hitter like Lou faces for the umpteenth time a veteran pitcher like, say, Jimmy Key, now with the Yankees, the matchup will be full of memories for both of them. It's tough for you to be privy to these mind games unless you're totally gung-ho about charting the pitches year after year, but you can at least understand that they're going on. As a young hitter in the big leagues, I had always heard that hitting becomes easier as you face the same pitcher and pitches year after year, and this turned out to be true, as a rule. What happens is that pitchers develop a book on hitters, and the hitters develop a book on pitchers, and this book is based on the pitcher's book. In my case, the book said to pitch me inside. Late in the game, particularly in RBI situations, pitchers tend to rely on their book on a hitter. So late in the game, when pitchers got into trouble and needed an out, more often than not they pitched me inside. In selected situations, you can turn the tables. I started looking for this area, especially on the first pitch because pitchers like to get ahead in the count with an aggressive strike inside in big situations, and rightly so, especially if they feel this is the hitter's weakness. So I often looked in that area and I hurt the pitcher. If I didn't get the pitch inside, I took it.

Well, you ask, if I started getting hits inside, why didn't the book change? Because I looked area only on certain counts, not on every pitch of the at-bat. I got hits outside, too. Plus the book was essentially correct. When I was slumping the inside pitch was my greatest vulnerability. No doubt about it. (However, after four or five years of facing Bob Welch, I knew he wanted to pitch me away. Orel Hershiser, too. Early in my career I must have gotten some hits off a few of their inside pitches. In Orel's case, his decision to work me outside was fine with me because his sinker inside was one tough pitch.)

Experience against the pitchers makes all the difference. I probably hit against the Phillies' John Denny for four years before I realized I could pick up his palm ball before he threw it. You might think that batters would look forward to the arrival in September of all the young, unseasoned guys called up from the minors by the also-ran teams. A chance to fatten up the average for the contract drive. But in fact, most good hitters hate to face these unknown pitchers, who can give you more trouble than Randy Johnson and Juan Guzman do. One story proves the point. In 1979, I hit .340 or so almost all year, while Pete Rose was down around .295 in July before starting his late-season charge for the batting title. At one point in late September Pete got up to .336, I think, and after a head-to-head series between St. Louis and Philadelphia, his team at the time, I still had a four- or five-point lead over him with one series to go. The Cardinals went into Shea Stadium to meet the terrible Mets and a bunch of new pitchers I'd never heard of. Oh, the buzzard's luck! I thought. The first night was Roy Lee Jackson. Remember him? He was a pretty good reliever for five or six years, but in 1979, he was just starting out. I had to fight negative thoughts, but I must have done a pretty good job of it: I went 5-for-5 off Jackson and two relievers, including a three-run dinger off Roy. Rose went hitless that night, I jumped eight or ten points ahead of him, and that was all she wrote for the batting championship that year. I won. So far the story sounds as if it disproves my point, but move ahead to the following spring training, 1980. The Cardinals play the Phillies and Pete walks up to me with congratulations and then says, "Man, you go to Shea Stadium and go 5-for-5 off a guy who came up in September!"

Pete was surprised, too. You don't expect it, believe me. You'd rather face a guy with great stuff whom you know than a new man about whom you know almost nothing, whose motion to the plate you've never seen, whose patterns you don't know. Pitchers try to avoid patterns, but they still have them. I've pointed out several specific instances. (Catchers have patterns, too. Early in my career, Lou Brock taught me to know the catchers as well as the pitchers. For example, Ted Simmons, a dead fastball hitter, called for more breaking balls than just about any catcher I've seen.)

A strange thing about a batter's relationship with a

pitcher he has faced a lot is how subjective it is. I always thought John Candelaria was a tough guy for me. I really had to tighten my belt against him. When Davey Johnson, Mets manager at the time, got his computer up to speed and told me I had a career .345 average against Candelaria, I was shocked. So shocked I remember the exact average Davey quoted. Steve Carlton, same thing. Tough, tough pitcher for me, but I had a good average against him. One explanation for the discrepancy might be that against these guys I knew were tough, I really bore down. As a hitter, you're always trying your best, but there's no doubt that some situations get your attention better than others. Adrenaline, maybe, I don't know, but I do know that the best hitters are at their sharpest in big-game, RBI situations. That's what makes them the best hitters! Successfully or not, my father tried to instill this attitude in my brother, Gary, and me. Every day the two of us took alternating fifteen-minute sessions of batting practice from Dad until either the hitters or the pitcher were about to drop. Toward the end of each fifteen-minute segment Dad would look into the big bucket by his side and call out, "Last ten pitches, Keith. Bases loaded, two outs, tie game, bottom of the ninth, bear down."

With Lou Whitaker at the plate and with a fresh memory of the 3-1 sinker Lou nailed in his last at-bat, Scott Kamie-niecki chooses the curveball for his first pitch in the third inning and gets the called strike from home-plate umpire Rick Reed. He follows with a sinker outside for a ball, and he now comes inside with a fastball for a strike. This guy knows how to pitch! You can pitch inside at Yankee Stadium or anywhere else if you do it right. Do it wrong and you'll get killed here—or anywhere else. That said, I have to acknowledge that many left-handers do have trouble in Fenway Park because of the Green Monster in left field. The standard point is that right-handed batters take advantage of their inherent preference for left-handers by pulling double after double off the Green Monster. This is true, but *why* can they do this? The answer is important because it's another illustration of the necessity of pitching inside. As previously noted, a good percentage of left-handers live or die with their off-speed pitches—located outside, of course, to right-handed batters. However, they have to establish inside in order to keep the batters from sitting on the outside pitch, as explained earlier. In Fenway, many lefties are intimidated by that wall and tentative with their hard stuff inside. Therefore the right-handed hitters can concentrate "middle-out." Consider three left-handers who have been effective in Fenway. Bill Lee, Bruce Hurst, and Frank Viola were (and are, in Frank's case) fearless in locating a good fastball on the inside black. They weren't overpowering, by any means, but they had the pop to do it. And they weren't afraid to do it. Consider John Tudor, a good pitcher in Boston but a great pitcher for a couple of years in St. Louis. You have to believe John was a lot more comfortable with the Death Valley in left-center field at Busch Stadium.

Back at Yankee Stadium, another aggressive inside fastball from Kamieniecki is fouled back by Whitaker, the count is still 1-2, and Kamieniecki semiwastes another fastball high and tight. He's throwing with intelligence and confidence now. The batters must be able to sense this, too. Whitaker has to be ready for anything. Even though the count is now even, the at-bat more or less belongs to the pitcher. He's calling the shots. Oh! Fastball right down the middle, and Lou fouls it back. Just as I'm bragging about Kamieniecki's control, a bad mistake. But again, there's one of my main points throughout this book. Whitaker is hot right now. He's hitting .418 for his last twenty-three games. He got a pitch to hit. But he missed the fastball down Broadway by a fraction. The hanging curve, forget it.

With the count 2-2, Kamieniecki can still do anything he wants. After all the aggressive inside stuff, he might like to try the change-up or the fastball away. I'd throw the change-up...but Leyritz slides inside for the fastball. High and tight. Ball three.

Kamieniecki has decided to pound the inside zone,

hasn't he? Now he goes with the curve, leaves it over the middle of the plate, and Whitaker hammers it foul past first base. Another bad location. Now the change-up, proba- bly…but it's hard to tell because the pitch never gets off the ground, almost literally, and bounces in front of the plate. Now you have to suspect that the sinking fastball is the call. Leyritz slides outside, but the pitch—the fastball—comes in over the inner half of the plate. Not good for the pitcher, great for the hitter, and Whitaker drives the ball hard, but Don Mattingly makes a nice backhanded stop down the line and flips to Kamieniecki for the 3-1 putout.

Okay, Whitaker made the out, but look deeper into that at-bat. Kamieniecki had control of it and then lost control when he missed with two pitches and went to 3-2, and then he completely missed the outside target but got the out any- way. He's fortunate. I say the hitter won that exchange even though he made an out because he battled and was able to extend the count, and when you do that, you'll get a pitch or two to hit. And Lou had good swings at those pitches. That's all you can ask for. Lou feels better about that at-bat than Kamieniecki does, believe me. Then again, it's an out.

Travis Fryman takes his cuts. He lined out to shortstop in the first on a fastball down the heart of the plate. This time he sees a curve for strike one, but on the inside corner of the plate—precisely where Kamieniecki did not want to locate that pitch. Leyritz was set up over the middle. I've previously explained the backdoor breaking ball from a right-handed pitcher to a left-handed batter or vice versa, the pitch that starts off outside the strike zone but breaks late onto the outside corner for a strike. It never crosses the width of the plate. The equivalent pitch for a strike when a right-hander is facing a right-handed batter, or a lefty a left- handed batter, is the *backup* curve or slider. This backup breaking ball starts off three to six inches inside and breaks at the last split second to catch the inside corner. And it's always a mistake.

The right-handed pitcher facing the right-handed batter wants to throw the breaking ball on the *outside* corner. Why?

If any breaking ball misses the target, it's usually to the left, outside, as the right-handed pitcher sees the plate. Locating the breaking ball inside in this righty-righty matchup is even tougher psychologically because the pitcher has to aim almost behind the batter. So the tendency is even more to miss to the left. And if you aim at the inside corner but miss to the left, where does that leave the pitch? Over the inner half—the heart of the plate. If that pitch doesn't have a lot of action on it, it's a hanger.

No less a hurler than Bob Gibson said that the inadvertent—and I stress the inadvertent—backup slider was his most effective pitch. Too bad, he said, that he couldn't throw it there intentionally. If as great a pitcher as Bob Gibson couldn't throw the backup breaking pitch with any consistency, who can? Nobody. That's why it's never thrown intentionally. When you see it, mark it down as a mistake, even if it froze the batter for a strike. You heard it here first.

Given this fact, you are now in a position to amaze your friends by calling the pitch selection in this one situation, based only on the catcher's setup behind the plate. Here's the rule: When the catcher sets up over the inside corner in a righty-righty or lefty-lefty matchup, gasoline is on its way— cheese, cheddar, the fastball—because the catcher is not going to request either the change-up or the breaking pitch on the inside corner. You can bet the mortgage on that.

So by sheer bad luck, Travis Fryman finds himself down in the count after the backup breaking ball, and with Cecil Fielder hitting behind him, with two outs and nobody on, Fryman might expect Kamieniecki to try to keep the heat on with a fastball. He does, and Travis takes the pitch for strike two. Now he's in trouble, and Kamieniecki finishes him off with his best curve of the day, right on the black, and Fryman swings feebly, drops his bat, and walks off. He was beat on that at-bat, pure and simple. No reason to moan about it, and he doesn't.

Kamieniecki clearly has settled in against the Tigers. He handled the top of their order without a lot of sweat. He had the upper hand against Tony Phillips and Fryman and was finally able to get the tough Lou Whitaker. Will his counterpart, Mark Leiter, be able to do the same against the top of the Yankees' order in the third? This is the half inning that will tell us whether we have a good pitchers' duel taking shape. My own bias in this regard should be apparent by now, and my reasons should be apparent, too. If the heart of baseball is the contest of wills and talent between the pitcher and the hitter, you need both good pitching and good hitting to make a good ball game. And if you do have the best of both, the pitchers should dominate because they have the inherent advantage of surprise. Even as a kid growing up in San Francisco, I preferred the great pitching duels between Sandy Koufax and Juan Marichal to a slugfest. Twenty-five hits in a game does not signal good hitting as much as it signals bad pitching. It makes for a lot of excitement and runners tearing around the bases, but I still don't call it a great baseball game. If you follow a baseball game as closely as we're following the two games in this book, pitchers' duels are beautiful to watch. In my opinion, of course.

Mark Leiter threw a lot of fastballs in the second inning, working on establishing his rhythm. He appeared to succeed with this strategy, but he'll have to change his approach now, regardless. We won't see three, four, five fastballs in a row in this inning. Bernie Williams, Wade Boggs, and Don Mattingly will see more of a mix of pitches. This is immediately demonstrated with the first delivery to Bernie. Curve inside, ball one. Now another curve, outer half, strike one. If Tettleton calls for a third curve, he's getting a little happy with that pitch, I think. Either that or Williams is a dead fastball hitter. But even if he is, you can't give in like this. Leiter on the mound is ready for the sign...Tettleton does flash the "2." Curveball. Leiter shakes it off, and more power to him. We watch on television as Tettleton now flashes "1." This is what Leiter wants and the fastball is up in the zone, maybe out of the zone, and Williams fouls it on a bunt attempt. With the count 1-2, Tettleton throws down the "2" again. He wants another curve! Leiter stands and waits. Bernie

Williams waits, too, and finally gets tired and steps out of the box. Why is the catcher calling for curves while the pitcher obviously wants to throw fastballs? We are allowed to speculate. A lot of times catchers do call what they can't hit. The cliché is true, as I just illustrated with the Ted Simmons story. Maybe that's the case with Mickey Tettleton, or maybe the book on Williams is to throw him breaking pitches. Williams did hit the fastball hard in the first inning, but that doesn't mean you don't throw it the rest of the game! Nor does Leiter's desire to throw the fastball contradict my statement that against the top of the order he'll have to mix things up more than he did in the previous inning.

Williams returns to the box, Leiter peers in for his sign, and Tettleton finally flashes the "1" and taps his right thigh. Location: inside. The pitch is on the mark and jams Williams, who does a good job fighting it off with a foul down the line past third base as Livingstone and shortstop Fryman give chase. Happy with that result, Leiter jams Williams again with just about the identical pitch and Bernie pops it up again, this time in fair territory, and Fryman catches the ball for out one. Up-and-in fastballs: A new approach that at-bat against Williams, and it matches Kamieniecki's approach against Tony Phillips, the Tigers' leadoff batter in the top half of the inning.

Solid pitching by Leiter against Williams, and he'll need to keep it up because Mister Full-Count is at the plate. Wade Boggs. Leiter sends a fastball right down the middle. Boggs takes it without a second thought. Strike one. Now another fastball inside, ball one. Tettleton flashes "3." Leiter seems to have just one breaking ball, a slurve, it looks like, which has more break than the straight slider, less than the straight curve, and a spin rotation from ten o'clock to four o'clock, rather than the eleven o'clock to five o'clock spin of the regular curve from a right-hander. So this "3" must be Mark's off-speed pitch—but which one? I'm told that he throws both a straight change and a split-fingered fastball. They should be easy enough to distinguish, with the splitter breaking more sharply down while the straight change-up tails off to the right, but you can't always be certain. Whichever this will be, I think it's his first off-speed pitch of the game.

You can bet that Tettleton will slide to the outside for his target. He does, but Leiter misses the target completely low and inside, ball two. That was the splitter. The next pitch is the fastball and what we call an American League strike. It was high, but the umps give you that pitch in this league. In the National, it's a ball. This brings up a question: Why doesn't the bigger strike zone in the American League produce lower batting averages than in the National League? Two sure reasons—the smaller parks and the DH, which strengthens the whole lineup offensively because the pitcher doesn't get a break—and another likely one: The American League may have the better hitters right now. Let's face it, fans of the National League, the All-Star Games are starting to look like a mismatch. (Jumping ahead: The NL squad in '93 was the weakest in my memory.)

With the count now 2-2, Leiter could come inside, but as we know and have seen, Boggs will just fight off that pitch for a foul, all day, if necessary. I still say throw Boggs tough pitches away and let him hit them to left field. Leiter misses high and outside with the fastball. Another fastball, on the low side, fouled back. Here we go again with Wade. Foul after foul. Oh! Good pitch, slider on the inside corner at the knees that Boggs can only pull on the ground to second. Give Leiter credit for making a helluva pitch. The odds weren't that great he'd get the slider over with great location, but he did. It usually takes that kind of pitch to beat Boggs.

Now Don Mattingly. He hit the first pitch he saw in the first, and he might do it again in the third. This time, Leiter serves up a change-up down the middle and Mattingly drills it just wide of the bag at first. And look at Cecil Fielder at first base. The big guy goes sprawling after that ball; he's quicker than he looks. In fact, he was an All-State point guard in high school in Los Angeles. Effort is one part of a baseball game that any fan can spot: effort, or lack of it. Then again, don't get sucked in by meaningless, showboating efforts like the unnecessary slide, the runner's final lunge at first base even after he's already out by a mile. In St. Louis, Tito Landrum enjoyed timing his catch of a fly ball in the outfield so he'd make it on the dead run, even when he could have been camped under the ball. We called him Tito-Timer. Pete Rose had this reputation in the sixties, too, after he moved from second base to the outfield.

A breaking ball over the plate freezes Mattingly for strike two. Fooled him. On 0-2, Leiter wastes a pitch outside and follows with two more fastballs outside that move the count from the pitcher's advantage to full. Nibbling? Leiter doesn't know how! Wildness. And it cost him the advantage in this matchup against Mattingly. So what now? Leiter got Boggs on that good slider inside; he could try to get cute with Mattingly with a breaking ball. The change-up! The pitch is not a strike, sinking down and away, but it's a last-moment movement and Don swings and misses. Good pitch. Good inning. Leiter shows better command of his pitches against good hitters. We probably have ourselves a pitchers' duel. Probably. No guarantees in baseball.

In the first inning, Cecil Fielder saw four curves from Scott Kamieniecki, the last one hit hard for the RBI single. Kamieniecki will not wait until Cecil's third at-bat to change his approach. Indeed, he starts him off with a fastball, inside corner, too, for a strike. This sends an aggressive message to Fielder, "You don't scare me." All those curves in the first inning sent the opposite message. Leyritz flashes the "1" and sets up away this time. Fielder tries to pull the outside pitch and the result is a 6-3 putout, short to first. Like most power hitters, Cecil likes the ball out over the plate where he can extend his arms, but you can still pitch to him out there. You have to. Some pitchers might feel, "Oh, wow, Cecil Fielder. All I can throw outside to him is the breaking ball." This idea couldn't be more wrong. If you stay inside all day with your fastball against a batter of Cecil's ability, he'll adjust and crush you eventually. As I've said, pitching Fielder inside means five or six out of ten, maybe, not ten out of ten. When you locate the fastball away, just be sure it's on the outside edge and down, like this pitch, or misses the zone entirely.

With Kirk Gibson, the Tigers' next batter, you might—probably should—decide to work him outside, but seven out of ten pitches, not ten out of ten. Kamieniecki's first offering to Gibson is the change-up off the outside corner for a ball. Good pitch even though it was a ball. Next, Kirk swings and misses at a fastball over the middle of the plate at the knees. Pretty dangerous pitch, but the next one is even more dangerous against Kirk—the low, inside fastball—but the pitch misses the strike zone and Kamieniecki might be better off because it did. That's Kirk's erogenous zone. On 2-2, Kamieniecki throws a good slider that Gibson manages to top in the hole at deep short, and the old man beats it out. Hard-luck pitching, but amazing running by Gibson considering how many knee operations he's had. At thirty-six, he can still motor.

So if you're Sparky Anderson, what do you do now with Mickey Tettleton at the plate and a runner on first with one out? We can safely assume that the hit-and-run is not in the cards because Tettleton is not paid just to make contact, and he strikes out a lot. The steal is a possibility, and Kamieniecki must believe so, too, because he throws fastballs for his first two pitches, a ball and a strike. If he and Leyritz chose those pitches just because of the threat of the steal, I don't buy it. I'm on record in this regard, and so are many managers. They don't like it, either. Hold the base runner close—Kamieniecki throws over to Mattingly—but pitch your game. Nevertheless, Kamieniecki follows with two more fastballs for ball two and ball three. Now he's in a hole at 3-1 and doesn't look like the same pitcher...but give him credit. Just when Tettleton must be looking for the fastball with the count in his favor, Kamieniecki throws the curve over the plate for strike two. If the pitcher can do this consistently....

On the full count, should Mattingly play behind the runner? This is something to think about, but a lot of people never do. The move involves a trade-off. The first baseman who plays behind the runner and then drops back into regular fielding position covers more ground, but he also gives the runner an advantage. He may get a slightly bigger lead, and he will definitely get a better jump. It's not a huge advantage, but enough to make a difference on close plays on the bases.

The rules that determine when the first baseman plays behind the runner are simple enough. The first one states that he plays behind the runner when the runner is absolutely, positively running with the pitch: full count, two outs. There cannot be a steal on this play. The ball is either put into play with no jeopardy to the runner on a line drive, or the batter strikes out and the inning is over, or the pitch is ball four, in which case the runner advances to second base automatically. With the count full and nobody out, or one out, the first baseman has to hold all but the slowest runners in order to keep the possibility of a "strike 'em out, throw 'em out" double play. With runners on first and third, hold the man at first. But with runners on first and second or with the bases loaded, play behind the runner because he can't steal second base anyway.

Those are the basic situations, but there are a lot of gray areas, too. The situation is often a judgment call. With a slow man on first base and a left-handed pull hitter, check with the manager. He might choose the better defensive position over the smaller lead for the runner. Also check on a right-handed batter who drives the ball hard to the opposite field—right field. With a very slow man (Cecil Fielder would qualify, with zero stolen bases in his major league career, hard to believe, really) play behind him. Perhaps you say this business about holding the runner at first is just Hernandez's pet peeve because he was a first baseman. That's probably a factor, but if you pay attention, you see mistakes made all the time. But you see it done right, too. In the first game of the Phillies-Braves series, Atlanta had a 7-1 lead in the seventh inning, with Jim Eisenreich on first base and Milt Thompson batting from the left side against Greg Maddux. Sid Bream was correctly playing behind Eisenreich halfway. If you believe the situation regarding playing behind the runner at first base is a judgment call, watch the first baseman. He'll look into the dugout and cross his fore-arms one over the other, forming an X. This asks whether he should play behind the runner. The manager will tell him. One factor the manager has to take into account is that the decision to play behind the slower runner might entice the opposing manager into running this slower guy when he otherwise might not. With the better break he would get, he wouldn't be an automatic out at second in case of a strike-out.

When playing behind the runner, the first baseman stands just to his left and about three feet behind him. The faster the runner, the closer you get. When the pitcher com-mits to throw home, the first baseman should hustle back ten to fifteen feet, either straight back or angling toward his regular fielding position in the hole, depending on the bat-ter. I say "should" because not all first basemen make a great effort to get in the best position. Watch them. Does he take one halfhearted step, maybe two, or five fast ones? There's a big difference in how far they get back. Be your own judge. For that matter, also be your own judge when the first baseman does hold the runner close. When the pitch goes to the plate, does he scuttle as quickly as he can several yards off the line, or does he settle for one or two lazy steps? Watch. You'll see. I don't need to name names here. You'll have your own list after all the teams have come through town. A pet peeve? You bet it is. There are a lot of lazy first basemen. Now, sometimes the first baseman's dili-gence can hurt him. He gets quickly off the line, but the ball is smashed right down the line for a double into the corner. The lazy first baseman is still standing there and makes the play. I was burned that way, but more often the play will be made toward the hole, not down the line. You know my thinking on that subject.

When playing behind the runner I liked to tap my glove, a friendly reminder to him that I was close by and that the timing pickoff play was at least a remote possibility. Very remote. In practice it seldom works, and that's why it's seldom even put on. Nobody is fooled. And the runner has the first-base coach helping, too. This is the coach's main job at first, along with patting the batter on the rump as congratulations for getting there at all. The coach calls out, "Get another step...you're alright...careful...careful...back!"— some kind of sequence like that; the key word is "Back!" (The third-base coach provides the same service for the runner on second as the shortstop or second baseman jockeys behind him.)

You can watch a season's games and never see the pickoff tried, much less accomplished, when the first baseman plays behind the runner. For the record, however, here's how it's supposed to work. With a right-handed pitcher, the strategy is about the same as when the pitcher and the shortstop try to pick off the runner on second. On that play, the shortstop breaks to the bag and if the pitcher "sees daylight" between the shortstop and the runner, he wheels and throws. On the play at first, the first baseman breaks and the right-handed pitcher throws. With a left-hander on the mound, the play works differently. The first baseman keys off the lefty's first movement. When the pitcher lifts his right foot, the first baseman breaks.

I said nobody is fooled, but that's not quite right. The pickoff can work because once the pitcher takes his stretch, the runner can no longer look back for the first baseman who's playing behind him. He has to watch the pitcher and rely on his coach. I failed to do this one time. The first baseman was playing behind me, and I was stupidly keeping an eye on him. When the pitcher took his stretch I had to shift my glance from the fielder to him. At precisely that moment, the first baseman cut to first base. I was nailed. Stupid mistake and perfect timing for them.

For the sake of completeness, I should also explain the timing pickoff play of the runner on first with runners on first *and second*. You may never see this tried anymore, and that's a shame because I think it's a good play. We did it in St. Louis fairly often, with success. With runners on first and second the first baseman usually plays in his regular fielding position behind the runner, who can't steal because second base is occupied. This runner can fall asleep believing the pitcher is thinking only about the runner at second. There's a vulnerability here.

In order for the play at first to work, it has to be carefully set up by the preceding pitches to the plate. From his regular position with runners on first and second, the first baseman could never get to first base on a pickoff throw. It's too far to run, with too little time. Therefore he has to play somewhat closer behind the runner than usual on the first few pitches of the at-bat. By the fourth or fifth pitch of the at-bat, if it gets that far, the runner might expect you to be there. Then, on that fourth or fifth pitch, either the pitcher or the first baseman gives the prearranged signal, and the other player responds. The pickoff play is on. No response, no pickoff. If a right-hander is on the mound, he looks back toward second, checking that runner, while also peeking at the first baseman out of the corner of his eye. When the first baseman breaks toward first, the pitcher spins and throws to the bag. He keys off the first baseman; the timing has to be perfect. With a left-hander on the mound, the first baseman keys off the pitcher. When the pitcher lifts his foot to begin his delivery, the first baseman breaks. Again, timing is everything.

The situation is everything, too. I'd only try it against a right-handed pull hitter, not against a left-handed pull hitter, who might take advantage of the first baseman's somewhat drawn-in fielding position to drive the ball down the line. What's really ideal is when one batter is retired on a strikeout or pop fly, leaving the same two runners on the same two bases for a second batter. Several pitches into the count on this second batter, the runner on first isn't going to be thinking about a pickoff play, if he ever was. In this regard, he's probably sound asleep. Before the second batter steps in, I'd go to the mound for a regular-looking pep talk, but in fact I said, "Pickoff. Third pitch." This is better than flashing a sign because many times the pitcher doesn't see the first baseman's sign. He, too, has forgotten about the possibility of a pickoff at first! On the third pitch, if the count goes that far, if all goes well—bingo!

The best execution of this play I saw was with George Foster on first base for the Mets, Ricky Horton pitching for St. Louis. Ricky had just about the best pickoff move in the league anyway. On this play, he checked the runner at second base, Foster watched impassively, Ricky delivered—to first base! Jack Clark had the ball in his glove before George had moved one step. It was beautiful even though it was the Cardinals who pulled it off. As rare as this play is now, it's still a good play. But it's also a trick play, by any definition, and many managers hate it for that reason. In the first place, it requires a first baseman and a pitcher who really know what they're doing; I can think of guys at each position who shouldn't try it. Second, if the pitcher throws the ball away—a lot easier to do on this kind of timing play than on a straight pickoff to a stationary first baseman—the ball might roll all the way to the right-field corner. The runner on second walks home, the runner on first makes third easily, and the fast runner conceivably scores if the right fielder was playing way over in the gap.

Back to the ball game at Yankee Stadium. Watching on television you may never know what the first baseman is doing, but tonight's broadcast does verify that Mattingly is holding Kirk Gibson. He has to since Tettleton strikes out a lot. The Yanks could get the double play. Will Gibson be running on the pitch anyway? I hope so. That's the aggressive move, even though it's risky with Tettleton batting.

Gibson does break, and Tettleton barely tops the fastball foul. Let's do it again. Kamieniecki selects the breaking ball this time and locates it perfectly on the outside edge, and Tettleton can only lift a fly to left field. Gibson, off and running, retreats to first base.

Now let's see if Kamieniecki seems to be worried about Gibson stealing with Alan Trammell at the plate and two outs. Look at Gibson taking his lead. He crouches with his hands on his knees and doesn't look ready to run anywhere, but he gets great acceleration nevertheless. Kirk used to routinely steal about thirty bases and hit about that many homers when he played for the good Tiger teams in the mid-eighties, and he has a lifetime base-stealing average of 80 percent success. You can't tell when Kirk is going. You can't tell with any good base stealer, although various people have thought they spotted something. At some point, Rickey Henderson was supposed to have done something with his fingers while he was crouched. Others might dig in a fraction more. Sometimes I played a game with base stealers if I had a hunch they were going. Before the pitch was delivered I'd yell, "He might be runnin'!" This might put a negative thought in the runner's mind: "Is the pitcher going to throw over? Has Hernandez spotted something?" But I have no idea whether my bluff ever worked this way. I tried it some against the Cardinals but Vince Coleman, Tommy Herr, Willie McGee, Ozzie Smith—they stole us blind anyway.

Breaking ball away, strike one to Alan Trammell. Gibson holds at first, and Trammell bitches about the call. Trammell seldom does this, so we can figure that the ump is on shaky ground here. Leyritz flashes the sign and slides inside. Here we go! Even if we couldn't read the sign, we know this will not be the breaking ball or the change. It has to be the heater. It's a good one, too, right where Kamieniecki wants it, and the best Alan can do is fist it out to right field for the third out. Both pitchers are sharp now.

Jim Leyritz returns to the plate to lead off the Yankee fourth, and Mark Leiter starts him off with a slider down the middle, then a fastball high and inside, then a fastball in on the fists that jams Leyritz. All he can do is roll the ball back to the pitcher. So much for the theory that a guy who stands deep in the box and way off the plate cannot be jammed. Some of these fellows can be jammed because they stride *into* the pitch. And so much for the possibility that Leyritz concedes the outside corner, like Jack Clark. Of the ten pitches Leiter has thrown to him in these first two at-bats, only three were clearly aimed at the outside corner. The other seven were over the middle or inside. Leyritz probably likes the ball away, and, if anything, is vulnerable inside, even though he is a mile from the plate. The point here is that paying attention to pitch location against any batter, especially someone you're not familiar with, should tell you where his weaknesses are. If the pitchers more or less consistently pitch a batter in or out, up or down, that has to be considered that batter's weakness.

In the first, Paul O'Neill ripped a simple hanging slider right over the plate for a two-run homer. This time around in the fourth inning he doesn't have a chance at that pitch because Mark Leiter's first six pitches are a change-up followed by five consecutive fastballs. I believe they were fastballs. A couple of them didn't have much on them, but they didn't move like change-ups or split-fingers, either. The second pitch is six inches outside but called a strike. Horrible call. Not even close. O'Neill barks at Rick Reed.

You know my theory about the wide strike zone outside. I'll now offer two more observations on umpiring in recent years: One, it has gotten worse, even admitting that there are many excellent umpires. Two, it's worse still in the American League, although there are excellent umpires in this league, too. And I'll pinpoint the exact year in which I feel it deteriorated: 1979, when the umpires went out on strike and the ballplayers did not honor their picket lines. Minor league umpires were called up to handle our games. Scabs, in a word. That was a long time back, and many umpires have retired and new ones have come in (including some of those replacement umpires), but I still mark that date as the time when umpiring got a little less accurate. That's an opinion I cannot prove. But my second statement about the difference between AL and NL umps will be verified by just about any batter or pitcher who has switched leagues in recent years. Ask them. They'll tell you—if they know the strike zone, that is. There are good umps in this league, but when they're bad, they're pathetic. There are some astounding strike zones in the American League, many more than in the National League. The AL umps have a much more belligerent attitude, too. I don't know why.

Six pitches have yielded a full count to Paul O'Neill. This is an interesting call because Leiter has avoided the pitch—slider—that hurt him earlier. Will Leiter "dance with who brung him" in this at-bat and throw yet another fast-ball? The change might be a good pitch, but can Mark throw it for a strike? Mickey Tettleton behind the plate flashes the sign and slides to the outside edge. That location tells us nothing: could be the fastball, breaking ball, or change-up. All are appropriate on the outside edge. Leiter winds and the pitch is…the slider! But he misses the target toward the center of the plate. This is just about the pitch that O'Neill nailed for the homer in the first, and this time he hits it hard again, but only a single this time to center field. Leiter cannot trust the location on his breaking ball! That's his only problem in this game right now.

Runner on first, average speed, one out, fourth inning, moving into the bottom part of the Yankee lineup. Does Buck Showalter put on a play, either the hit-and-run or the steal? He could do either or neither, but the hit-and-run is more likely than the steal because O'Neill isn't much of a threat in this regard. On the other hand, Leiter has not shown a good move to first base, so O'Neill might be able to get a good jump and sneak a steal. Regarding the hit-and-run, Dion James is not a power hitter, and he's a good con-tact hitter who goes naturally the other way. Probably the biggest factor working against the play in Showalter's mind is Leiter's wildness. He might walk James. He might throw the hit-and-run pitch a foot outside.

All in all, it's the manager's prerogative here, and you can't second-guess Buck with any credibility. My personal guess is nothing's on. O'Neill talks with big Frank Howard, the Yankees' first-base coach. Then O'Neill and James check Clete Boyer's signs at third and Tettleton looks into his dugout to see whether Sparky has any special instructions. Leiter takes his stretch, does not throw over, O'Neill holds at first base, and Leiter delivers a curve low, ball one. No pitchout, and not even a fastball. This might tell you that the Tigers weren't concerned about a play, or it might tell you they follow my theory: Hold the runner, then pitch your game. Now Leiter throws over to first. Now one more time, even though the chances of a straight steal have gone down a little because Leiter needs to throw a strike and his best pitch for this purpose is the fastball and the fastball is the most effective pitch versus the steal. But for the same reasons, the hit-and-run might look a little better now to Showalter. James should get a pitch he can put the bat on.

You may recall that I mentioned earlier that it's not an ideal time to steal when the pitcher is ahead in the count, either, because then he has the luxury of a pitchout. The question comes up, when is a good time? The answer...anytime. Unlike the hit-and-run, which is closely regulated by the count, you'll see steals on *any* count even though some factors are working against it on *every* count. Speed has changed all the old thinking about base stealing. The quick guys have a permanent green light. When they get a jump, they can go.

I don't imagine Paul O'Neill is one of this green-light gang. He stole twenty bases for the Reds in 1988 but just six last year. With the count 1-0 tonight, Mickey Tettleton looks to his left into the Tiger dugout, flashes the signs, Leiter takes his stretch...holds the stretch...throws to first. Tettleton looks into the dugout again, flashes more signs, Leiter takes his stretch...holds his stretch....throws to first. It's significant to note with these two tosses to first base that Tettleton didn't even begin to adopt the poised crouch necessary to receive the pitch. You can't be certain, but this might mean that Tettleton knew there wasn't going to be a pitch to the plate and he knew this because his sign to Leiter was to throw to first base. The sign is the thumb pointed in that direction—the universal sign for hitchhiking. Right now, the

Tigers must think something is on. I still say the odds are against the hit-and-run.

I'm wrong. O'Neill breaks, the pitch is another breaking ball swung at and missed by James, but O'Neill is safe at second anyway, sliding in a cloud of dust as Travis Fryman tries to swipe him with the tag. We would expect Fryman to be covering, leaving second baseman Lou Whitaker in position against the left-handed batter. Who's to say this was a hit-and-run, not simply a steal on 1-0 on which Dion James has the option of swinging if he likes the pitch? All you can do is size up the situation and draw your own conclusion. Theoretically, as I've said, the runner can give you a clue if the play was a hit-and-run, in which case he's supposed to look back to the plate and find the ball, as O'Neill does on this play. On the steal, this is optional, and the true base stealer who knows his man at the plate will be taking a pitch or two on the runner's behalf will not look back at all. But a lot of guys do not look back on the hit-and-run, believe me, so this isn't a sure tip-off. But this was the hit-and-run. Good, aggressive baseball.

With the count 1-1 and a runner on second, Leiter will pitch very carefully...and, as it turns out, well. A backdoor slider nips the outside corner for a strike topped foul down the first-base line, and then a hard splitter is popped up by James for the second out. This leaves the inning up to Mike Gallego.

The camera shot shows a gap in right-center field, with Alan Trammell playing slightly toward left. The Tigers are playing Gallego to pull the ball. Intriguing. I think Mike's pretty much of a spray hitter. Leiter's first pitch is indeed the curve, but with nothing on it, a helicopter curve, as we say to break the monotony about the hanger, right over the middle of the plate, and Gallego slaps his thigh after he watches the ball float past for strike one. Another curve is low, and yet another is hit fairly sharply to Scott Livingstone at third base, who lobs it over to first. We can fairly conclude that Trammell was pulled around because of those curves. I should also note that this is another case in which the pitcher didn't wait until the third at-bat to change his approach to a batter. Leiter retired Gallego in the second inning on fastballs here in the fourth on breaking stuff. The switch was dictated by the situation, a runner in scoring position. Side retired. Score still Yanks, 3-2.

Remember the fastball on the inside corner that froze Rob Deer for strike three in the second inning? Scott Kamieniecki starts Deer off with the same pitch to lead off the fifth inning, but the pitch runs inside for ball one. Leyritz flashes the "1" and slides inside again. Same pitch. Be careful, really flirting with danger here. Oh! The pitch misses the target and comes in right over the plate and Deer pulls it foul, hard. That was a good swing, such a good swing that you have to be concerned about coming inside again in the immediate future. But Leyritz does flash the "1" and slides inside again. Three in a row! And, again, the pitch misses over the plate, and Deer pulls it hard on the ground to deep short. Spike Owen dives and makes a nice stop, but he has no play even against this not-so-fleet-footed Deer. All I can say about this pitch selection is that you have to come inside to these guys, but you can't get happy in there. You can and will get hurt. Three in a row is getting too happy. Kamieniecki, however, might try to use this entire at-bat to set up the next one against Deer. We'll watch and see what he does—assuming that Kamieniecki is still around in the seventh or eighth inning. He has a problem here in the fifth, tying run on, nobody out.

Kamieniecki throws over to Mattingly to hold Deer close. Why? Anybody's guess. Deer is not stealing. His combined steals in recent years number in the single digits. If Sparky has any play on, it's the hit-and-run, and the runner's lead and jump aren't a factor on the hit-and-run, as I've explained. Why is Don Mattingly even holding Rob Deer at the bag? Why isn't he playing behind him with a left-handed batter, Scott Livingstone, at the plate? With the count full, hold him at the bag to keep the strike 'em out, throw 'em out double play in order. But on these early pitches in the count? Deer is going nowhere. Play behind him! Is the dugout asleep? Did Don check on instructions? We don't know. Holding the runner at the bag should not be automatic, but if you watch closely throughout a series of games, you'll see some odd decisions in this regard, I guarantee you.

Kamieniecki throws to the plate and gets the strike on the fastball outside. Rick Reed is giving the pitchers at least three inches out there, maybe more. But the bottom line here is that Livingstone finds himself down a strike, never recovers, hits a belt-high change-up on the ground to second base, and Gallego and Spike Owen turn the double play. And this pitch illustrates the importance of location on the change: The ball was belt-high and without much movement, but it was on the outside corner, maybe beyond it. Just a fraction out in front, Livingstone pulled the ball to the right side. If that pitch had been toward the middle of the plate, real trouble.

It's obvious on instant replay that Rob Deer went way outside the base path in his attempt to break up the pivot, wasn't even close to making a legitimate slide into the base, and then he compounded the infraction by swinging his arm at Spike Owen making the throw. Really blatant interference, and, technically, the runner at first should be called out if he was otherwise safe, but that ruling is not often invoked. It's moot here because Livingstone was out at first base anyway. Sometimes managers storm out of the dugout to complain about the illegal slide, but it's usually in vain. When the play *is* called, the other manager has a legitimate complaint. Davey Johnson was thrown out of a game back in the eighties after he decided an umpiring crew had a vendetta against the Mets. What was his proof? One of the calls against us was interference at second base. This year, the mild-mannered Art Howe, skipper of the Astros at that time, was tossed after his man Steve Finley was called for interference. And Finley wasn't ten feet off the bag on his slide. He was on it. He grabbed it with his hand and never let go. He did roll up with his legs, but that's standard. Larry

Dierker, an old friend and one of Houston's broadcasters—the laid-back one—declared it was the worst call he had seen in three decades of playing and announcing major league baseball. That's quite an endorsement. I guess Art Howe should have gotten thrown out on that call.

Encouraged by the double play here in New York, Kamieniecki gets Tony Phillips to bounce back to the mound on the third pitch. Side retired. But wait a minute. That's the basic report on the at-bat, but we want to be watching this one closely because the previous two at-bats against Phillips had established that Kamieniecki could jam him successfully with fastballs. In this fifth inning, the first pitch was a fastball low and inside, and Phillips fouled it off, but we would be making a mistake to believe that Kamieniecki was trying to come inside and just happened to get the ball low. Television allows us to see clearly that Jim Leyritz set up outside for the pitch. Kamieniecki missed the target entirely. However, Tony Phillips does not know where Leyritz set up—presumably!—so Kamieniecki and Jim Leyritz will indeed count this pitch as a fastball inside in their attempt to mix things up. This is not a trivial point. As you watch the pitcher try to work the corners and vary his location in and out, remember that what matters for this purpose is where the pitch *ends up*, not where it was aimed. Pitchers miss their location all the time, but the batter doesn't know it.

The next pitch against Phillips is a curve away for ball one—a backdoor pitch that stayed in the backyard—and then a change-up down and away is tapped back to Scott Kamieniecki, who runs the ball to first base himself. Side retired. Good inning. Yanks still lead, 3-2.

In their half of the fifth, Kevin Maas once again proves himself to be a dead-pull hitter with a lot of holes, and Mark Leiter is shrewd enough to take advantage of the fact. After a slow curve drops in for strike one, Leiter comes inside with that straight fastball that works well against the left-handed batters, returns with another slow curve that drops over the outside edge for strike two, misses way outside with a change-up, maybe, then nails the hitter with a split-fingered pitch that really drops off the table. Tough pitch. A swing and a miss and out number one. Against Bernie Williams, the catcher kept trying to get Leiter to throw off-speed stuff, but the pitcher wanted to throw the fastball. Against Maas, Tettleton and Leiter agreed to show the fastball but get the batter with the off-speed stuff. Intelligent pitching, a good lesson for the discerning fan on reading the book on a hitter.

The league knows by now that it can get Maas out with good pitches. He's a fastball specialist at this stage of his career, but the pitchers won't give him one to hit when it really counts. Maas is a classic case of a hitter coming into the league with great potential but with weaknesses, too, and the pitchers find out about these weaknesses and capitalize on them. Now it's the hitter's turn to make adjustments and live up to his potential, or adios. What happens is this. When a new hitter comes into the league, I don't care if he's the Player of the Century in Triple-A, he'll be challenged with fastballs in most situations. If he proves he can handle big-league heat, the pitchers will start throwing their breaking stuff. I think this is a contributing factor to the sophomore jinx endured by many good hitters: It gets tougher when the pitchers employ their full repertoire.

Spike Owen steps in and Mark Leiter starts him off with a splitter for a ball, then gets him on a fastball that he flies to center field. Satisfied, Leiter tries the same tactic with lead-off batter Bernie Williams—a splitter (or is that a change-up?) on the first pitch—and Bernie swings and misses. The off-speed pitches are proving to be Mark's most effective stuff other than the fastball. He's showing command this inning, but what about next inning, next week, next year? Just as the minors are loaded with hitters who look great against fastballs, they're also loaded with pitchers with great raw stuff, but who can't control it consistently. In fact, that's the main difference between a run-of-the-mill pitcher and a winner in the big leagues: control of *all* his pitches. Mark Leiter has the stuff, but can he learn to control it?

Against Bernie Williams, he follows one splitter with another, this time low for a ball, and the stage is set for the fastball inside or outside. He's unlikely to throw three consecutive off-speed pitches. The fastball misses badly inside.

With the count 2-1, Leiter throws another fastball for a ball high. Nevertheless, that was the pitch to try; walk Bernie Williams and he may steal a base. A speedy guy is the runner you least want to walk with two outs, especially when he's followed by a bat-handler like Wade Boggs. We say that Bernie is "protected" by Boggs. That's a nice feeling. Ask Matt Williams in San Francisco how he feels about batting in front of Barry Bonds. When I was young, switch-hitting Ted Simmons was batting behind me and hitting .300 from both sides of the plate. On 2-1, 3-1, I got some pitches to hit. On this 2-1 count to Bernie Williams, he should get a pitch to hit, too, because this situation is the definition of a two-out rally in the works. You need a strike, throw the fastball, especially Leiter. What about the trend toward throwing off-speed when down in the count? Of course, I don't buy that anyway, but even if I did, it applies mainly with men on base. With nobody on, two out, and a fast man up, I believe you have to challenge the hitter with the fastball, and if the batter is thinking along with me and looking fastball—very possible—he still doesn't know where it's going to be, you have all those fielders out there, and this is Bernie Williams at the plate, not Ted Williams. I don't say that to show disrepect for Bernie, not at all, who may well become a big star for the Yankees. He's only twenty-four years old. But the pitcher has to know the hitter and the situation.

Leiter agrees with me—this time—and throws the fastball but misses outside, so the count is now 3-1 and logic would dictate the fastball again. The batter is licking his chops. Tettleton flashes the sign, Leiter just stands there. He wants a different one. More signs and now he winds and delivers. That slurve of his with a helluva big break! Swing and a miss, strike two. Well, that's what makes a horse race, right? But I was correct in one way. That pitch was not a strike; it was down and in. Bernie swung at ball four, and he knows it. In retrospect, we can say that was a surprising pitch selection that should have backfired but didn't because Bernie made a youthful error, showing no discipline. With the count full, will Leiter try again with the breaking ball? If you're going to throw it 3-1, you should be prepared to throw it 3-2. I've heard that philosophy. But are you prepared to throw a good one? In this case, the answer is no. Leiter throws his more dependable pitch—the high, rising cheddar—and Williams lifts it to Tony Phillips in left for the third out. Why wait until you're 3-2 to throw that pitch? If Williams hadn't swung at the curve, Leiter never would have reached this point in the count. He'd have a runner on first with Wade Boggs up. Pitchers and catchers can get too cute, in my opinion.

CHAPTER 8

Remarkable fact: After five complete innings, neither Mark Leiter nor Scott Kamieniecki has walked a batter, and this kind of control has been neither of their strong suits thus far in the season. It's also the reason both have pitched effectively since the shaky first inning. A quick check of the properly filled in scorebook reveals that only nine of the thirty-eight at-bats have reached three balls, six thrown by Leiter, three by Kamieniecki, verifying the subjective impression that Kamieniecki is showing slightly better control. Each has four strikeouts. I have Kamieniecki with a total of seventy pitches, forty-seven of them for strikes. And he has shown better control of his breaking stuff than of his fastball! Twenty-seven of the forty-three fastballs have been strikes, by my count, and seventeen of twenty-one breaking pitches. I show six change-ups, three for strikes. Overall, that's remarkable control, even considering that the batters can be counted on to swing at some pitches that would have been balls. Kamieniecki has also gotten away with some mistakes over the heart of the plate. His average of fourteen pitches per inning is a little high. Twelve is better; ten is great. Mark Leiter's average of sixteen—eighty-one total—is way too high, but he's had good control, with fifty-one strikes.

This accounting doesn't prove the point at all—the pitching is just about even—but all in all I think the chances are better that the Yankees will get to Leiter than that the Tigers will get to Kamieniecki. Or perhaps the Yankees will go on the offensive sooner than the Tigers do. Kamieniecki knows where he has to put the ball, he changes speeds, he's getting his breaking ball over, and he's facing a bombs-away team that has lost seven straight and will have a natural inclination to try to win the game with some of those bombs. That's a promising setup for a pitcher with excellent control.

Meanwhile, Mark Leiter has relieved more games than he has started in his brief three-year career in the majors, so you have to figure he's not going to finish this time around, especially since he's already thrown eighty-one pitches.

Again, the Tigers' number two hitter, Lou Whitaker, gets ahead of Scott Kamieniecki 3-0, and again he'll probably take a pitch down the middle. In the first inning, Tony Phillips had already reached base when Lou got the three-ball count. A walk would have given the Tigers two on, nobody out to open the game. So take the pitch. Now, in the sixth inning, the situation is different but the idea is the same. The Tigers are down a run. Whitaker is leading off this inning. Even if the 3-0 pitch is the expected sweetheart down the middle, nothing says that a hard smash won't be caught. Take the pitch. Detroit needs a base runner. Whitaker does take strike one, right down the middle. Nothing lost. If Lou is in a looking mood on 3-1, he has three reasonable choices. He could figure on the sinker ball away, just as in the first and third innings, even though he nailed it for the double on the 3-1 count. It's still a plausible pitch for Kamieniecki to throw because he needs a strike and that's his safest percentage pitch for that purpose. Kamieniecki has shown good control of his breaking stuff, but it hasn't been pinpoint control. The sinker would be a hard pitch for Lou to hit out of the park. So looking outside makes sense for Lou. Or he could look dead-red *inside* in the hopes of tying the game with the quick home run into the short seats in the porch. Lou's third option is to look fastball anywhere, a less restrictive approach.

Mind games: On the 3-1 count, they can make sense for the batter. Rarely does he go so far as what I now call the "Garvey approach," taking a big step toward or away from the plate while looking for a zone, but you can be certain that Whitaker is going to look for something on this advantageous count. As well as he's swinging the bat, I bet he looks fastball any zone. Pitcher and batter each have a choice here.

Kamieniecki winds and delivers...the sinker low and away, outside edge, and we know immediately that Lou is indeed sitting fastball because, once again, he's right on the pitch with his swing, but fouls it into the stands down the left-field line. Just a hair late on the swing. That's the way it goes sometimes. Now on the full count Lou has to protect the plate. Jim Leyritz puts down one finger and slides to the outside...Oops! The sinker misses the target, catches too much of the plate, and Whitaker rips a single past the second baseman into right field. That hit was the direct result of a good, red-hot, seasoned hitter—literally: seventeen seasons—who got ahead in the count, understood the situation, and went about his job accordingly.

Now this inning is shaping up as pivotal. It's fairly obvious but worth stating that the sixth inning often plays that role because what happens now will establish how the final innings will be played—aggressively or conservatively, with or without a lead. If the Tigers can push Whitaker across with the tying run, many of the decisions in the last three innings might be different. The first question is, does Sparky Anderson like the hit-and-run here, with the number three man, Travis Fryman, batting? No. This is a big-inning team. Will Whitaker try to steal? He could. Not likely. His best base-stealing days are behind him, and Sparky also knows that when Kirk Gibson was on first base in the fourth inning, Kamieniecki didn't throw a very effective set of pitches to Mickey Tettleton, even though he finally got him out. Whether it was pitching from the stretch or the threat of Gibson's speed or a combination, who knows. But Sparky will remember that at-bat and play this situation straight up and hope for Kamieniecki to give some good pitches to hit to Fryman or Fielder or both, preferably.

Everybody checks his signs, Kamieniecki winds and jams Fryman with a fastball, which he bloops to second base. I like that, pitching-wise. An aggressive delivery to open things up. I don't like that, hitting-wise, and neither does the batter nor his manager. If you decide to look for the fastball on the first pitch, you must be certain to get a good swing at it. If you can't handle it, take it, because you need to have something to show for swinging at that first pitch in this situation—a hard-hit ball, at the least, not a jammed pop-up.

With one out, Cecil Fielder gets his opportunity. You could safely bet that Cecil Fielder has never been asked to hit-and-run. The guy gets too many good swings, hits too many homers, drives in too many runs. And no steal by Whitaker, either. Leyritz flashes the "1" and slides inside for the first pitch. Coming inside! Challenge the big guy. And this is interesting: In his first at-bat, Cecil saw all curves, three out of four away, and hit the fourth one for a hard single; next time up, two fastballs, the first one on the inside black, the second away, and Cecil pulled it on the ground to shortstop. Now in the sixth inning, Leyritz calls for the fastball and sets up inside. If we didn't know it anyway, this sequence of pitches in three at-bats proves that the pitchers don't consider Cecil a one-dimensional slugger with a glaring weakness that can be exploited in every at-bat.

Yes! Go after the guy with the inside fastball. NO! The pitch is over the inside half of the plate, not the black, and Cecil turns on the fan. But he gets just a fraction under the ball and lifts it to straightaway, medium center. You can read the relief on Kamieniecki's face—anytime Cecil Fielder makes an out with men on base, the pitcher is happy—and the frustration on Cecil's. Count that pitch as a mistake that the pitcher gets away with it. Happens all the time. Round bat, round ball, as we say, with a tiny margin of error for the hitter. By the way, in these last two at-bats Jim Leyritz behind the plate doesn't seem to be sliding in and out while setting his location against Fielder, leading us to believe that the maneuver in the first inning was some kind of aberration. Cecil wouldn't dream of peeking, right?

Two outs now, Lou Whitaker still on first. Kamieniecki sees the clearing ahead, but he's still not out of the woods. Kirk Gibson stands between him and side retired. Kirk has seen what happened with Fryman and Fielder, but he also knows that he may be pitched completely differently, not just for the sake of change, but because Kirk bats left-handed. Totally different story here. I'm going to guess a change-up on the first pitch to Gibson. (I'm guessing; Kirk isn't.) No! Leyritz flashes "1" again and slides inside. Oh, I'd be careful coming down and in to Kirk Gibson in Yankee Stadium. Then again, Kamieniecki got Gibson swinging on a pitch low and away in the first inning and pitched him mainly away in the fourth inning before Kirk got the squib hit. And Kirk is generally pitched away because he's so dangerous inside, especially down and in. So coming inside on the first pitch isn't a bad idea in theory, but it's dangerous. Be sure it's belt-high or higher. Kirk is blind up there. I exaggerate, of course, but it is his toughest hitting zone; the same goes for most left-handed batters, including myself.

Kamieniecki turns and throws to first, and this does make sense. With two outs, it's more likely that Lou might try to steal. Now Leyritz flashes the sign for the fastball again, and again he slides inside. Well, here goes…Ball one, low and inside. I'd be shocked if Kamieniecki throws inside this time. Leyritz calls for the fastball but slides outside, the safer pitch…ball two, high and outside. Oh, what a difference that second pitch in the at-bat makes. After the second ball, Kirk is in the driver's seat. He can pick his pitch or location. Kamieniecki doesn't want to walk him and move the tying run into scoring position, with the go-ahead run on first, Mickey Tettleton coming up. Tettleton has had some good swings against Kamieniecki tonight.

Nasty! Change-up, swing and a miss, strike one. That ball really darted down and away. Another change-up, swing and a miss, strike two. That ball also really darted down and away. Kamieniecki has an outstanding change-up going for him right now. With the count 2-2, Leyritz flashes the sign—"1"—and taps his left thigh, indicating location outside. Kamieniecki waits, and a split-second later Leyritz flashes the "1" again and taps his right thigh. This is the location Kamieniecki wants—inside—and only on television can you know how it came about. The tube is good for something. Leyritz slides inside and the fastball is right there, jamming Gibson at the belt, but he fights it off for a foul. Good pitch, good hitting. Now Leyritz calls for the inside fastball again, but this one runs just about over the middle of the plate and Kirk gets a good rip. Foul, straight back off Leyritz's chest protector. Mistake! I guarantee Kamieniecki took a deep breath and said, "Thank you, Lord." That was Gibson's pitch to hit, and that's twice this inning Kamieniecki got away with one, once with Fielder, now with Gibson. Keep these pitches in mind when you go back over a pitching chart to count up the balls and strikes. There are strikes and there are strikes. The change-up is working great this inning but a couple of these fastballs have flirted with disaster.

With the count still 2-2, Kamieniecki can do whatever he wants to, chooses the change-up, but the pitch is way low and outside and Gibson isn't even tempted to swing. Ball three, full count. With old-style pitching, this would be the heater. With new-style pitching, it could just as likely be the change-up. Kamieniecki chooses…new-style pitching! So does Gibson because he's right on this change-up, but the location is good enough—toward the outside edge—and Kirk can only pull the ball sharply on the ground, right at Don Mattingly for the third out.

And has Kamieniecki developed a pattern now against the left-handed batters, or what? Fastballs inside for starters, then if he falls behind he goes to his change-up, and if he gets even he comes back with fastballs inside. Mix in the occasional breaking ball. This is solid strategy, a lot of good pitchers have this approach, but it can be overdone, too. Are the Tigers watching from the dugout? Are they going to sit on a couple of these pitches in the next inning?

3-2, Yanks, and all those runs crossed the plate in the first inning.

Bottom of the sixth, Boggs, Mattingly, and Leyritz up for the Yankees. Critical for Mark Leiter. Go to enough games and you'll often see one of the infielders trot over to the pitcher before the start of the sixth or seventh inning—whichever one features the meat of the order—and say a few words. Those words are, more or less, "Big inning. Bear down." Watching on TV, I don't see anyone do this for the Tigers, but I'd bet somebody said something to Leiter as he left the dugout. It's a small thing but it can't hurt, and it might help. But you have to know your pitcher and his mood this day. Tom Seaver, for one, wouldn't be interested in your pep talk on certain days.

Wade Boggs. What a way to start an inning. Hard work for the pitcher practically guaranteed. As I said earlier, I like the theory that you might as well throw the best strikes against these pesky guys and let the chips fall. Wade takes a first strike, as usual, then swings and misses at another fastball for strike two. Now, go get him, I say. Don't fool around. But Leiter wastes a pitch outside, then doesn't get the call on a slider at the knees. Strike three in my opinion! But it's true that hitters with a reputation for having a good eye get the calls, just as some pitchers with a reputation for excellent control get the calls. I had an excellent eye, if I do say so, thanks to all the pitches I saw from my dad, who called out the location—"Inside, Keith" or "Outside corner, too close to take with two strikes"—and I did often get the benefit of the doubt on close pitches. Boggs does, too. And Ted Williams? They joked that if Ted didn't swing, especially with two strikes on him, it wasn't a strike.

So Wade Boggs stays alive, fouls back a slider, and then takes two pitches that aren't even close and walks to first base. There you go. A lot of Detroit fans and neutral fans know enough to mutter, "Walking the guy—the leadoff guy—after having him down two strikes!" But they might not realize what's really bad here is that Leiter walked Boggs with two breaking balls that completely misfired. Boggs is leading off the inning. He's not a home run hitter. Throw your fastball for a strike! In my humble opinion. Then again, Leiter threw a higher percentage of his breaking balls than fastballs for strikes in the previous two innings. He must feel confident with it. And he's the pitcher, not me. You have to wonder whether Leiter lost his concentration after he didn't get the call on the slider. It's definitely a possibility, something to think about. What could Leiter do about the call? Not much. He has to let his catcher do the bitching from behind the mask.

The give-and-take between players and umpires is often behind the scenes or behind the masks, but watching carefully in certain situations can pay off for the fan. One way the pitcher can express his displeasure without irritating the umpire is to do what John Smoltz of the Braves did in the Wednesday matinee in Philadelphia, the third game of that series. Smoltz didn't like a couple of Jeff Kellogg's calls in the first inning. He got out of that inning unscathed, but heading for the dugout on the third base side Smoltz followed a semicircular route that brought him within fifteen or twenty feet of home plate. Walking past Kellogg but looking at the fans, not at the umpire, Jim said to Jeff, "Darn, those pitches were close. You're squeezing me."

Something like that, and umpires don't mind this. If you think the pitcher is generally unhappy with what he considers a small strike zone, you'll often see this kind of maneuver or something similar. Of all the pitchers active today, Nolan Ryan may get away with more on the mound than anyone else. But what the hell, he's a living legend and he's retiring, too. Nolan seems to be glaring a lot lately, hands on hips, the whole bit, but I'll bet he chooses the younger umps for his more "outspoken" demonstrations. I'll bet he's not doing it with a crew chief like Dave Phillips. When Nolan was in the National League, I'll bet he didn't glare much at Joe West. West doesn't put up with that stuff or anything else. Ryan knows his umpires, that's for sure. The players have to. Young umps coming into the league tend to fall into one of two categories, polar opposites. Either they're overly assertive from the get-go or they're unsure and intimidated. In the National League, Bruce Froemming had about as short a fuse as you can have, especially for a new guy, but then Bruce settled down and now he's great and deservedly gets a lot of postseason games. Jim Quick lived up to his name early on. He was quick on the draw—we had a few run-ins—but then he settled in. Gary Darling had a great attitude from his first day in the league.

What a player has to be careful about, I think, is trying to take advantage of the insecure guy. Don't try to badger him. Umpires have long memories. Make your point, but do it politely. The best way for the fan to get a reading on the umpires is find out who the new man is on the crew, watch him handle any argument, and watch closely when he's behind the plate. How often are the players griping? How does the umpire react? You'll get an idea of how much lee-way the players are taking with him.

In my first All-Star Game, 1979 in Seattle, Tommy Lasorda sent me in to pinch-hit against Jim Kern in the seventh inning. That's when Kern was having those awesome years with Cleveland, mainly, then Texas. Marty Springstead of the American League was calling the balls and strikes. I was nervous, but Kern's first pitch, a fastball, was at least six inches outside, so I heaved a sigh of relief. At least I was now up in the count. But Springstead called the pitch a strike. I turned to him and said, "Strike??" And he said, actually said aloud, "Swing the bat, *sonny*."

If that had been the regular season, I'm ejected. But he was just baiting me. He knew this was my first All-Star Game. What am I going to do, get thrown out after seeing one pitch?! Asshole. This was also a couple of months after the umpires' big strike finally ended, and they weren't happy with the players, that's for sure. But there was no excuse for that remark, and it made me as mad as I ever got at an umpire. But I held it in. I usually held it in, because arguing with the umps is a no-win proposition. One time that I didn't control myself cost me. This was '85 or '86, I guess, one of those years when the Mets were in contention, and this was a tight game at Wrigley Field. I was on second base, bases loaded, two outs, we needed to score, and our ace reliever, Jesse Orosco, was hitting. The count was 3-1, I wanted Jesse to walk, and Doug "The Lord" Harvey behind the plate called strike two on a pitch outside and, worse, at the ankles. In a competitive moment, I raised my arms and yelped "Holy Cow!" Then I reached down to swipe a hand across my ankles. Doug got mad, walked out in front of the plate, pointed his mask at me, and yelled, "Here's the mask. You come umpire." For the rest of that series in Chicago, everything close was a strike when I was batting. And in the next couple of series the Mets played, the veteran umpire on the crew working our games made it a point to say to me, "We hear you're getting out of line." Do they have some kind of hot line? Yes. This convinced me I had to go to Doug Harvey my next opportunity, and I did. You just need to pull out the peace pipe sometimes. I apologized and blamed those day games at Wrigley Field! I preferred playing at night. In the interests of full disclosure I should also note that Harvey's call turned out to be a break for us. Orosco singled home two runners on the full-count pitch.

Moments after Wade Boggs walks in the Yankees' sixth following the tough call against Mark Leiter on the slider, the phone rings in the Tigers' bullpen in left-center field. They've probably been waiting for it because Leiter has averaged less than six innings per start. Mark has used his breaking stuff effectively, but if these last two breakers to Boggs are going to be indicative, the batters will forget about that pitch and sit on his fastball. So left-hander Bill Krueger leaps into action. Why a left-hander? Left-handed batters Paul O'Neill and Dion James are due up third after Mattingly and Leyritz, and that's when Sparky Anderson might want Krueger if the inning falls apart with the next two hitters.

Does Buck Showalter have a play on with Don Mattingly batting? We'll find out, but working against the hit-and-run is the short right field at the Stadium. If Don pulls the ball with a sharp liner, Boggs would not be guaranteed third base. And that's one thing about baseball in the American League that I do prefer over the National—the older, asymmetrical parks that affect the strategies of the game. The best example I can provide of how this works, and one of the best stories about baseball strategy that I know of, period, happened in the fourth game of the '86 World Series at Fenway Park in Boston. The Red Sox had won two of the first three games. The Mets had to win this one. Everyone knows that the short wall in left field at Fenway, the Green Monster, usually keeps runners on first from scoring on any hit off that wall. Darrell Johnson, our advance scout at the time and a former manager in Boston (including in 1975, when they lost to Cincinnati in the Series), made certain that our left fielders understood a more subtle effect of the wall: With a runner on first, Boston batters sometimes assumed that the left fielder would automatically play the hard hit off the wall in the standard fashion, throwing to the cutoff man stationed between him and the plate in order to hold the lead runner at third base, but allowing the batter to reach second. The papers made a big deal of the fact that the Met outfielders didn't spend hours practicing with balls caroming off the Monster, but they didn't know that Darrell Johnson told our outfielders to forget the lead runner, who would stop at third base out of habit at Fenway, and to throw directly to second base instead!

When Rich Gedman hit a bullet down the left-field line with Dwight Evans on first in the sixth inning, Mookie Wilson played the ball perfectly off the Monster and threw out Rich going for second. That was the third out. The normal play would have left us facing runners on second and third, but this peculiar play in a peculiar field was crucial for the Mets in that Series, I've always believed. The Green Monster affects a lot of plays in Boston at second and third bases and at home plate. At Yankee Stadium the short wall is in right field, but it has a similar effect on plays on the bases. One of those plays is the hit-and-run, which it works against because the right fielder plays relatively closer to the infield.

With Boggs on first, Mark Leiter starts Don Mattingly off with a slider outside, just in case Don is overanxious with the idea of pulling the ball into right field. Don doesn't bite. Ball one. Now Leiter throws a terrible fastball that Mattingly jumps all over. Deer goes back, back, back...and catches the ball at the wall in right-center. There's only one reason that ball didn't leave the field: Leiter's tailing fastball that runs away from left-handed batters did so in this case at the last moment, moving away just enough from the meat of the barrel toward the end. One away.

Jim Leyritz at the plate. Leiter's first slider is outside for a ball, but his second one is right over the plate and Leyritz lifts a fly to Deer in right field. Leyritz was definitely trying to drive the ball in that direction. Another mediocre pitch that the pitcher gets away with, this time because the batter was overswinging. Jim was trying to hit that ball onto the train tracks. The wrong approach. The ball goes just as far with a smooth, relaxed swing.

Paul O'Neill walks to the plate, and this is the first critical decision of the game for either manager. With a runner on first, there's no pitching around O'Neill, even though he has rocked Leiter for a long homer and a hard single. Does Sparky Anderson bring in Bill Krueger? No. Sparky stays with his right-hander, who has to try to set aside memories of the previous confrontations with O'Neill and go after the guy. He immediately gets a nice break on a fastball six inches outside. That was not a strike! O'Neill just stares diplomatically at the outfield fence. When Leiter follows with a second fastball that is a strike over the outside edge, O'Neill finds himself in the proverbial big hole. And since the waste pitch on two strikes is outside, Leiter predictably but shrewdly follows with a fastball inside, but he overthrows it. Wild pitch. Not a pitch you want to make. Boggs hurries to second base so we have the open base, and this changes everything in this at-bat, for better or for worse for

Mark Leiter. The "better" is that Cecil Fielder at first base can now assume his regular fielding position against O'Neill and Leiter can follow the rules in this situation—be careful, work the corners, don't give O'Neill anything to hit, blah blah blah—and, if necessary, pitch to Dion James with runners on first and second. But the "worse" is that Boggs is in scoring position regardless. There's no question here; the wild pitch was for the worse.

With the runner on second, Mickey Tettleton changes his procedure behind the plate, giving a long series of signs that will probably be impossible for Wade Boggs to decipher and will definitely be impossible for the television viewer at home to understand. As with the signs from the third-base coach, you have to know the code, and it's not worth trying to figure out; there are too many ways to set up the catcher's signs. However, teams have pulled it off. The '84 Cubs team that won the NL East before losing to the Padres in the playoffs was one of the best at this. We got suspicious when Cub batters started getting hits on Doc Gooden's curve on the first pitch of their at-bats. One time, okay, but twice, not likely. They were sitting on the pitch. The situation got so bad with them that year that we had to change the code with *each batter* if there was a runner on second. Larry Bowa was one of their ringleaders that year, as he confirmed when he joined the Mets late the following year. When one of their veterans watching the game on television in the clubhouse thought he had the code, he passed it up the line to the players. When the next runner reached second base he watched for a few pitches to make certain the signs hadn't been changed. If the code was right, this runner would signal to the batter with an inconspicuous gesture, tugging at his left shoulder with his right hand, as I recall, or maybe vice versa. When the pitcher took his stretch, the runner got into his crouch. If he then looked at the hitter, the pitch was a fastball, if he looked back at second base it was a breaking ball.

But isn't that "cheating"? Absolutely not.

When I talked about batters sometimes peeking at the

catcher's location, I suggested watching to see whether the catcher slides back and forth or sets up at the very last moment in an attempt to deceive them. These maneuvers can also be used by the catcher if he thinks the runner at second base is indicating location to the batter. That's a rare trick for the offense to play, but it could happen, obviously. I'll tell you another trick that's been pulled. If the guy in the on-deck circle yells, "Let's go!" the catcher has set up outside; no shout of encouragement, inside. This ploy has to be set up between the two players beforehand and used rarely, and I mean rarely, key situations only. You could easily get caught.

Wade Boggs on second, the 2-2 count to Paul O'Neill, and Mark Leiter throws the splitter outside. On the full count, he does it again. You can't second-guess that. The questionable choice of the two breaking balls to Boggs leading off the inning was a different situation entirely. In this at-bat, Leiter prefers to pitch to the next batter, Dion James, and who can blame him? If O'Neill was going to get a hit, it would be on a tough pitch.

Two men on, two out, the pitcher clearly struggling. All eyes turn toward the Tiger dugout, then toward the Tiger bullpen in left-center field, where the left-hander Krueger is getting ready to go against the left-handed-hitting Dion James, if that's Sparky's decision. But why is Krueger out there all alone? What about having a right-hander ready, too? One idea for Sparky Anderson in this and all future situations in this game is to keep right-hitting Danny Tartabull on the bench, or if Danny comes in, at least have him facing a right-hander. Tartabull is the Yankees' big power guy, getting the evening off but ready for pinch-hitting duties. If Sparky comes in with a left-hander to face Dion James, Showalter might send up Tartabull or another right-handed hitter instead, because James is a platoon player, and Sparky would be stuck because a pitcher has to face at least one batter, while one pinch hitter can be lifted for another pinch hitter before he faces a pitch. Happens all the time. So I wouldn't think a lefty would be the move in this situation. In fact, Sparky might want to come in with a right-hander right now; maybe that would keep Tartabull on the bench. And there's another reason to have a right-hander in the pen. Following Dion James in the batting order is Mike Gallego, who bats right-handed. He's having a great year and Showalter isn't going to pinch-hit for him in the sixth inning, so what about the option of having a right-hander ready to face Mike? In short, why is Sparky satisfied either to stay with his struggling starter or to come in with a left-hander against right-handed batters?

In the first game of the series in Philadelphia, Jim Fregosi did a lot of maneuvering with his bullpen when he was down six or seven runs. In the second game featuring Pete Smith and Danny Jackson as starters, the bullpen moves by both Fregosi and Bobby Cox were pretty straightforward. Tonight at Yankee Stadium we may see some really interesting maneuvering. If I've said this before I'll say it again because it's important for the advanced fan to understand: The managers' handling of the bullpen is a great opportunity for second-guessing that we often overlook. All you have to do is watch the bullpen, study the list of prospective pinch hitters, and study your own lineup in the National League because you have to factor in when the pitcher's spot is due at the plate. Finally—and this is the tricky part—you have to know who's available for relief, which side they throw from (you might need a book for this), who's overworked, who needs work.

I could reiterate my point that these decisions are easier in the AL because of the DH. I won't bother. That's a dead horse, I'm afraid, but just one final point: The only good reason for the designated hitter is more offense in the game. The others sometimes put forth, such as the one about the DH allowing guys like Dave Winfield the opportunity to stay in baseball and get that three-thousandth hit, are too silly to consider seriously. Dave's a great player, and he'd be starting for somebody in right field, and getting a lot of games off, if the AL didn't have the DH. No, the only good argument for the DH is offense. But if you believe there's more to baseball than offense, if you believe that a lot of interesting ramifications flow from the fact that your most important player—your pitcher—is, by way of contradiction, probably a weak hitter and that having him bat for himself, or not bat for himself, makes the game more complicated in a dozen ways, then you're with me.

I should make clear that I am not a diehard sports purist. I like the twenty-four-second clock in pro basketball, which adds offense without subtracting anything basic from strategy or defense. More power to it. I also like the three-pointer (although the line is too close in college ball), which adds offense while actually complicating matters for both coaches and defenses late in the game. This is good. But the designated hitter in baseball adds offense at the price of simplifying the game. This is too high a price to pay.

As complex as the situation in this ball game is, it would be more so without the DH because the pitcher's spot comes up fourth in the Tigers' next at-bat in the seventh. That's a fact. Another fact is that Sparky Anderson only has two right-handers in his bullpen, along with four left-handers. I don't know the reasons for this imbalance. Managers like lefties out of the bullpen for purposes of holding runners on, but most batters are right-handed, so right-handed pitchers come in handy, too. The best bullpen is two righties, two left-ies, plus your closer. Sparky has one more reliever and one less right-hander than normal. One of the right-handers is his ace closer, Mike Henneman, and he isn't coming into the game in the sixth inning. That leaves Kurt Knudsen, who pitched an inning on Sunday, two days back. What if your starter is a left-hander and he's knocked out early in the game and you have only the one right-handed middle reliever? Your options are severely limited.

Tonight in Yankee Stadium, you would figure that Knud-sen would be warming up right now for the reasons I've explained and for a whole range of scenarios created by the fact that all the potential pinch hitters for the Yankees tonight bat right-handed (catcher Matt Nokes went on the DL yesterday). Every left-handed batter is in the starting lineup. In fact, this lineup is a shrewd move by Buck Showalter. With the day game tomorrow, Buck wants to give some guys a rest. Tomorrow's starter for Detroit is David Wells, a left-hander. By starting all his left-handed batters against the right-hander Leiter, he has a nice selection of right-handers for pinch hitting duty, knowing that Sparky only has the one right-handed middle reliever to counter with if Leiter fades. Smart.

In this critical situation in the sixth inning, Knudsen keeps his seat in the bullpen. Why? We almost have to conclude that Sparky has no confidence in Kurt Knudsen. What do the stats show on Kurt? He's had a stint in the minors, his overall ERA is good at 3.25, but ten of sixteen inherited runners have scored, and seven of the last eight, over four appearances. There you go. As often happens, the reliever's ERA doesn't indicate squat. Knudsen is giving up hits and/or walks to the first batters he's facing, and therefore giving up other people's runs. With a big losing streak in the works, Sparky just doesn't want to give him the ball. And sitting out in the pen, Knudsen must know this.

Sparky makes no move at all at this juncture. He sticks with Leiter against Dion James, two on, two out. Ball one, high. Ball two, high. Strike one, barely. Ball three, outside. Leiter is losing it. The crowd is roaring with delight. Leiter may have already lost it. If he doesn't get James, he'll be invited to take a shower. What happens when a pitcher "loses it"? The legs get tired, the velocity drops, he starts throwing horrible breaking balls (we've seen that with Mark in this inning). Mostly, however, the pitcher loses it "up here." Mental lapses. When the legs go, the head goes with it. The pitcher has to be sharp. He cannot lose focus and lay the ball over the middle of the plate. But on the road, especially, it's tough to keep that focus. Almost 40,000 Yankee fans are screaming bloody murder right now, and this racket is much tougher on the opposing pitcher than on the opposing batters. Leiter is standing all alone on the mound, his neck is on the line right here, the fans want to see the guillotine drop, and he knows it.

197

KEITH HERNANDEZ

On 3-1, Dion James should get something to hit or he'll walk. And so it is, but Dion proceeds to take a nothing slider dead over the heart of the plate for strike two. Oh, Dion. You've got to hack at that pitch! Make him pay for that pitch! You work hard for 3-1, get your reward—and then don't even swing! Talk about nonaggressive! Ball four on a high slider saves the at-bat for Dion, on paper, at least, but he still lost a great opportunity to break the game open on that 3-1 pitch. It's easy to sit and contemplate these mystifying events, and it's perfectly fair, I think, because we've paid our money, but while we're exclaiming, "Oh, why did he take that pitch!" we can also use the situation to think about the possible reasons. Maybe Dion was geared for the fastball and wasn't able to pull the trigger on the slider. Unfortunate, but it happens. But when you've got the pitcher in trouble, bury him.

Bases loaded on three walks. Two outs. Bye-bye, Mark Leiter. That's it for you, of course—or is it?! Pitching coach Billy Muffett, not Sparky Anderson, walks to the mound. Sparky always does his own dirty work. This is just a confab with Muffett. They're going to leave Leiter in! Amazing. I thought he was gone. Good-bye. Thank you for your services. I mean, Leiter has thrown twenty-three pitches in this inning alone by my count, fourteen of them for a ball, and a handful of the strikes caught too much of the plate for comfort. Sometimes it seems to me that there are a lot of nonmoves in the American League. Or else Sparky just has no confidence in his bullpen, particularly Kurt Knudsen, or maybe they're dogtired from overwork during all the consecutive losses, but if that's the case, why even warm them up? If you're going to warm them, use them, I would think, and if you're going to use them, isn't now the time? Sparky apparently doesn't think so. And he's the manager who's won 2,039 ball games, not me. (That's one victory behind Walter Alston—and holding.) Maybe Sparky is giving top consideration here to the fact that Leiter has handled Gallego in the two previous at-bats. Still, I say Knudsen should be up and ready and probably in the game, but he's not.

Mike Gallego steps in. Leiter works from the stretch and throws a breaking ball inside. Ball one. Boy, I don't understand that, after two walks in a row, three altogether in the inning. Then again, you know that he thinks Gallego might be sitting first-ball fastball. But now you've got to throw a fastball, don't you, son? I'm looking dead-red as the hitter because this is like a 3–1 count. If you throw something else, I take it. You want to throw a breaking ball, I spit on it unless you hang it. But throw me cheddar and I'm all over it...like that! Right down the middle, and Mike hits the ball hard but foul just off the line. Now on 1-1, the batter should have the same strategy and the same advantage. Sit on the fastball. This pitcher's control is going, going, gone. He's in labor. You don't lose your control after all these pitches—over one hundred—and suddenly regain it. Pitching doesn't work that way. So Gallego will be thinking, "If you want to throw some dippity-do pitch on 1-1 with the bases loaded, be my guest. If you locate a great breaking ball, I tip my cap and bear down with two strikes. But you'd better throw it for a good strike. Me, I'm looking dead-red again."

This is the key pitch in the at-bat, the inning, and the game. Fastball away, please, Mark. That's your pitch, in my opinion. Tettleton flashes an array of signs, slides a bit to the outside, Leiter takes his stretch, delivers...Ohhhh! A breaking ball with not much on it, catching a lot of the plate, too. Maybe Mike could have adjusted, but he didn't. He glances back at Rick Reed as though he thinks the pitch was a ball, but it wasn't. What it happened to be was a nice pitch to hit. If the pitcher locates a breaking ball on the black, take it, but if it's a hanger, take a rip! Oh, well, bear down. On 1-2, the complexion of this at-bat has changed entirely. Advantage lost. It's hard now for Gallego not to press. He's had a bad night so far, he's not only protecting the plate, he's protecting those three runners with two outs. There's pressure and a tendency to press. Everyone knows that the idea for the pitcher here is some kind of bait pitch. It's a free pitch for Leiter, you might say, except that he's been wild in this inning—those three walks and the wild pitch in the dirt to O'Neill—and another wild pitch here scores a run. So does Leiter want to risk a blatant bait pitch in the dirt? Not only is the wild pitch a possibility, but if Gallego has the discipline to refuse the lure, then it's 2-2 and you have to throw a strike. How much liberty the pitcher will take with a bait pitch depends on his assessment of the batter. Gallego can be struck out, Leiter knows that. Mike swung at strike three on a pitch almost in the dirt in the second inning. It also depends on his faith in his catcher. Major consideration. Does Leiter feel Tettleton can block the ball? Pitchers want a goalie back there, a guy like Gary Carter who stopped everything.

Tettleton flashes a bunch of signs and Leiter delivers...a big slurve in the dirt. Gallego swings nevertheless and misses. Strike three. Side retired and Leiter gets out of the inning. He risked the bait pitch and trusted Tettleton to stop it, which he did. But I still don't believe Mark should have been in there at the end. He got away with two "meat hangers" when behind in the count—one to James, one to Gallego. Buck Showalter wanted more aggressive hitting from his men and Sparky Anderson rolled the bones and came up seven.

CHAPTER 9

After six innings we're still 3-2, Yanks, and Scott Kamieniecki comes out to the mound after a long rest. Twenty minutes, just about. While failing to score, the Yankees sent six men to the plate, three of them walked on full counts, and Mark Leiter threw twenty-seven pitches. You often hear that the pitcher sitting on the bench while his hitters take an extended turn at the plate runs the risk of stiffening up. I don't believe it. I never saw it. The pitcher stays warm. I think a nice, long rest is good for him, especially in the late innings and because that rest usually means his team scored some runs. Anyway, Kamieniecki starts the inning and immediately gets two quick outs on six pitches: Mickey Tettleton hits a fastball right down the middle for an out to center field and Alan Trammell lines a slider to third base.

Outs, but these are the type that raise the eyebrows of managers and coaches, especially in the later innings. I've seen hundreds of pitchers jerked when they were recording outs on bad pitches and hundreds of others jerked when they were giving up singles on good pitches. In the first case, the series of hard shots in a late inning could mean your man is losing his stuff, regardless of whether the balls are caught. With a nice lead, you might hang with the pitcher, but in a close game, you're probably going to go with a fresh arm once the first, maybe the second, man gets on base. In the second case, the same logic might seem to dictate staying with the pitcher who has been victimized by a blooper, a bleeder, a squib, and an error. "He's still got his stuff, the batters are getting the breaks, our luck will turn." But it doesn't work this way in baseball most of the time, for some reason. More apt is the adage "When it rains, it pours," or maybe Murphy's Law, take your pick. The pitcher can appear to be throwing fine, technically, but *bad things are happening.* He has to be tiring a little, physically and mentally, he has to be rattled, and when the pitcher is rattled, the odds for overthrowing go way up, leading to a hanging curve or fastball over the heart of the plate. The manager does not intend to see that blooper, bleeder, squib, and error followed immediately by a 450-foot orbiter. He'll jerk the pitcher.

Therefore, just getting outs or just throwing good pitches is not good enough in the late innings. You have to do both—get the outs with good pitches—in order to stay in the game. With two fortunate outs within seconds of each other, it seems, Rob Deer steps in and the television coverage happens to show both Mattingly at first base and Boggs at third base guarding their lines. This strategy is within the common-sense rules—Deer presents the tying run—but I still don't believe it's automatic that the first baseman guards against the dead-pull-hitting Deer, who bats right-handed.

While you're checking the position of the infielders, you might as well also look at the outfield. Against Deer, they're deep, but they're always deep against him. The difference in the late innings will be against a guy like Lou Whitaker. With a one-run lead, the Yankees will play him a little deeper than normal the next time he's up, trying to protect against the extra-base hit.

Kamieniecki's fastball still has good velocity and movement and he's throwing it for strikes, and this does reflect the idea that the sinker sinks better as the pitcher tires a little. So what if the Tigers are a fastball-hitting club? That cliché doesn't mean anything anyway. Every club is a fastball-hitting club. Against Rob Deer, Kamieniecki throws five consecutive fastballs, and the location is instructive. The first one is right down the middle, strike one. So we can conclude Rob wasn't looking first-ball fastball or he would have swung at that pitch. Next comes a pitch outside, then one way inside that Deer pulls deep into the stands down the left-field line. The knee-jerk reaction might be that that swing was another warning sign for Buck Showalter regarding his pitcher, but in fact that was one of those long foul fly balls that shouldn't fool you. Jim Leyritz was set up inside; if Kamieniecki's intention was to come way in for a ball, that was a good pitch because the only place to hit that ball is foul. It's the hitter Deer who has to be questioned for swinging at what should have been ball two. Instead, it's 1-2. The next fastball is high, evening the count, and the next one is a mistake that Deer jumps all over. Jim Leyritz sets up on the inside corner and that's exactly where the pitch is. Fair enough, but that makes three straight fastballs inside. At least one too many, I would say, and not just in retrospect. I respect the reasoning behind the Gene Tenace rule about pitching inside to a power hitter late in a close game.

After three consecutive fastballs inside to Deer back in the fifth inning—the last one rapped sharply for a single—I suggested that Kamieniecki might use that at-bat to set up this one, showing Deer the fastball inside here in the seventh, then working him mainly outside. I was wrong. Clearly, he thought he could get this guy out inside. He was unsuccessful.

Credit left fielder Dion James for getting over toward the line quickly to cut the ball off before it gets all the way to the wall, holding Deer to the single. Speed in the outfield has changed the game of baseball probably more than any factor in the last twenty years other than the rise of the relief pitching corps. On artificial turf, especially, you can't survive with slow outfielders because the speed allows you not only to catch more balls, but also, and just as important, to cut off more line drives and prevent them from racing through the gaps or down the line for doubles and triples.

Range in the outfield is easy to observe. Range in the

infield is tougher to judge. The only way I could recommend would be to watch closely over the course of a series and try to get a "feel." I know if you compared any other shortstop to the Dodgers' José Offerman, you could see how much greater Offerman's range is. He's one of those sharp Dominican infielders from San Pedro de Macoris, and he gets to everything. But he also makes a lot of errors. Match up José against Cal Ripken, say, and the difference in range would be noticeable, but so would the difference in dependability and errors. I'd take Cal on defense alone.

Scott Livingstone arrives at the plate for the Tigers. He bats left-handed, and this might seem to be one of those cases in which the first baseman should play behind the runner and fill the hole on the right side because Rob Deer isn't going anywhere. But in this instance Mattingly doesn't want to fill the hole. In fact, Boggs and Mattingly both want to guard the line a little more closely because the double might score the tying run and put the go-ahead run in scoring position. Watch closely in these late-inning situations as the first and third basemen shift their positions according to the batter and the number of outs.

Also check the bullpen, where Steve Howe has just started throwing for the Yankees. He's a left-hander and a short-stint man, and the reason for this choice by Buck Showalter is obvious. After Livingstone, the next two Tiger hitters bat left-handed. If Livingstone gets on versus Kamieniecki, Buck would almost certainly bring in Howe to face Tony Phillips and/or Lou Whitaker. And since right-handed-batting Travis Fryman would be third up after Livingstone, Buck will probably also get a right-hander up to prepare for him if Livingstone gets on. We'll see. In any event, if Fryman hits this inning, the Yanks have blown the lead.

Kamieniecki tosses to first. Something to do, I guess. Now he throws to the plate, fastball outside, ball one. Another, ball two. He throws to first again, with authority. Does he know something I don't? Hard sinker, strike one. Leyritz slides inside to set the target for the next pitch. Be careful in there. Ooops, Kamieniecki misses the target with his fastball. Doesn't even come close. Leyritz is reaching out to catch the ball over the middle of the plate just as Livingstone's bat beats him to it and rips a shot to right field. Single. Deer bolts to third base. Wait a minute. Did Sparky slip in a surprise hit-and-run on the advantageous 2-1 count? No. The ball hit the infield dirt and then died in the grass in front of Paul O'Neill. The replay verifies this.

Anderson immediately dispatches Milt Cuyler to run for Livingstone at first base, and Cuyler is quick: forty-one stolen bases in 1991. Before Tony Phillips steps in to bat, Leyritz looks into the Yankee dugout for instructions, then steps in front of the plate and gives the signal to the infielders about how to play in the event Milt takes off from first base, either as a straight steal or as the initial move in a double steal. I've already noted how the catcher changes the signs on pitch selection, gesturing from behind the plate on his mask and chest protector and shin guards. When he steps in front of the plate to give signs, it's almost always in this runners-first-and-third situation, and you'll see him do so before every pitch.

Showalter has to make a decision here and Leyritz has to give the sign, but either play strikes me as inconceivable in this situation for the Tigers. The straight steal of second base, even though it would put the go-ahead run in scoring position if successful, jeopardizes the inning with the tying run on third base and a good hitter at the plate, and it would also relieve Mattingly of his duties at first base, allowing him to play deeper down the line. The double steal with runners on first and third, two outs, is equally dicey. That's a last-ditch strategy with a weak hitter at the plate and two good base runners. For the record, though, I'll outline Sparky's three main options on the double steal:

1. The runner on first base gets intentionally picked off, forces the throw to first, the runner on third base comes down the line and reads the ensuing rundown play between first and second, and makes his break accordingly.

2. The runner on first takes off on a steal, draws the catcher's throw to second, forces a rundown, the runner on third reads the rundown and makes his break. Or the runner can break immediately when the catcher throws. That's extremely dangerous because one of the manager's options on defense is to throw short to second base, with either the shortstop or second baseman cutting in front of second base for a quick return throw home.

3. Just as the pitcher takes his stretch, the runner on first breaks, so the pitcher has to step off the rubber. The key here is that the pitcher has been taught his whole life to run directly at the runner. If he does so now with the runner at first, his back will be to the runner on third. I think this is the best of the three options for the offense because the pitcher is involved, and he's not used to this. If you're the offense, always try to get the pitcher involved in the play. He has a better chance than the infielders of bungling it.

As a fielder, I feared the double steal for years—botched it royally a couple of times with the Cardinals—until one day early in my tenure with the Mets I realized how I should play it. Once I had the ball in the rundown, I could look at the *shortstop's* regular position and see both runners in my peripheral vision, one to the left, one to the right. Holding the ball, I'm on the infield grass and closing the gap between myself and the shortstop, running the base runner toward second base. (The shortstop is the other fielder in this play unless he's playing so deep in the hole against a right-handed pull hitter that he can't get there in time; then it's the second baseman.) I'm "inside" the runner so that he doesn't impede my throw to the shortstop, who is inside, too; if I'm working with the second baseman, I'm outside the line because he's coming to the play from that direction. Never throw across the base path because that risks hitting the runner.

Okay, I'm running the runner toward second base with the runner on third in my peripheral vision. If the runner on third strays as much as twenty feet from the bag, I turn immediately and charge directly at him. If he tries to return to third, I throw to that base on the run. If he bolts for home, I do *not* throw home immediately. Remember, he's closer to third base in this scenario. If he breaks for home and I throw to the plate immediately, he'll retreat to third safely. Therefore, when he breaks I run straight at him. If he continues toward home, I throw to the plate. If he stops, I throw to the catcher, who is now running up the third-base line to narrow the distance between himself and the runner. Now the catcher and the third baseman are responsible for executing their rundown play with two throws, preventing the runner who started all this, the guy on first, from rounding second and reaching third himself. And I race behind the catcher to back up the rundown.

But say the runner on third base stays near third base initially. With the ball, I drive the runner on first almost to the shortstop, toss the ball to my teammate, back up quickly to avoid interference with the runner, stay in the rundown backed up by the pitcher, and key the shortstop to what's happening with the guy on third. If this runner now breaks for the plate—and he's not bluffing, I have to make sure of that—I shout "Home" and point home, and the shortstop throws to the plate. If the runner strays that critical twenty or so feet off the bag at third but doesn't break, I shout "Run him!" and point at the runner, and the shortstop breaks immediately in that direction. He participates in the rundown on the third-base line the way I would have if the runner had strayed off third when I had the ball.

At some point in this play the runner on third base should make a move because that's the whole point for the offense. The best time for him to do so is exactly when I throw to the shortstop the first time or after the shortstop has the ball and has to rely on the first baseman's instructions. If for some reason the runner on third doesn't break, the shortstop and I execute the rundown between first and second with the maximum of two throws.

With the Mets, Rafael Santana, Tim Teufel, Wally Backman, and I had that play down pat. It was one thing we never screwed up, and teams stopped trying the double steal against us. I don't think highly of the play in general. It's fun to foil on defense, and fun to describe here, but it's strictly desperation. After seven straight losses on this road trip, Sparky may be desperate tonight in Yankee Stadium, but running here is not his style, certainly not with a good hitter at the plate in Tony Phillips. But should Milt Cuyler stun the crowd and take off on a steal, I don't think the Yankees want to concede second base to the go-ahead run. Jim Leyritz has signaled the Yankee infield that he'll either throw to second to try to get the third out on Cuyler or he'll throw short to one of the infielders. I don't think he would hold the ball at home and concede that base. And remember, a slow runner is on third. If Deer were Otis Nixon, that would be more precarious situation for the defense.

But I can't imagine Sparky trying any version of that play in the first place. More interesting than the question of a double steal is why Sparky has Cuyler running for Livingstone at first base, representing the go-ahead run, and not for tying-run Rob Deer when *he* was at first base. Presumably Livingstone is about as fast, or as slow, as Deer. Is this a really subtle example of the rule about the visiting team playing to win, the home team to tie? At first glance this rule might seem exactly backward, but it does make sense. The idea is that the visitors, who don't have the advantage of the last at-bat, might as well go for the winning run in a given situation, whatever it is, since this may be their only chance; they could lose a tie game without coming to the plate. The home team, on the other hand, has the luxury of playing relatively conservatively if they're behind—going for the tying run rather than the go-ahead run—because they'll get another at-bat, regardless.

The difference plays out most commonly on the decision whether to send the runner home on what may be a close play. If that runner is the go-ahead run, the third-base coach for the visiting team might be slightly more likely to do so than the coach for the home team. Or say the tying run reaches first base with nobody out. The visiting team might be less likely than the home team to go for the sacrifice bunt. There are a million scenarios with which you can test the logic of the rule that the home team plays for the tie while the visitors play for the win. I can think of one instance when I would not follow the rule: Last week of the season, close pennant race, down one run late in the game, nobody out, seventh batter gets a single, .220 hitter coming up. You're not going to have this man bunt just because you're the visiting team? I am.

Tonight maybe Sparky Anderson is letting the slower Deer fend for himself as the tying run while going with the fast guy as the winning run! Novel, and it might be a factor, but I think Sparky has something else in mind, too. There are two outs, remember. Deer would have been running on contact with any hit, so he would score from first base on most doubles at Yankee Stadium. Not all, but most. And if Cuyler runs for Deer he is *not* going to score on a single, so what's the advantage of the faster guy? Two outs—running on contact—is the key. Also, with speed on first in the first-and-third situation, the pitcher has a great deal more to think about. The steal is a possibility. The more I think about it, this substitution that looks odd at first glance is pretty shrewd on Sparky's part.

We're all set here. Slow Tiger on third, fast Tiger on first, two outs, Detroit needs a run in the top of the seventh. Buck Showalter does not make the move to Steve Howe in the Yankee bullpen. He stays with his starter Kamieniecki in this situation facing Tony Phillips. But checking the bullpen, we do see that Buck has indeed got a right-hander warming up next to Steve Howe. This is Bobby Muñoz, and by the size of him, he must throw hard, and he might need to against Travis Fryman and Cecil Fielder.

Kamieniecki takes his stretch, Cuyler holds at first, Kamieniecki delivers, and Phillips looks at a fastball way high, a sinker way low, and a curve nowhere near the plate. You take here, absolutely on 3-0. It's true that if Phillips walks, loading the bases, Mattingly can then play back, but in return the Yankees would have to face the red-hot Lou Whitaker. Phillips is good, but Whitaker is better. Sparky would love to see him at the plate. The 3-0 pitch is a fastball outside—a broom wouldn't have reached that pitch—but it's called a strike nevertheless, the semiautomatic strike on the 3-0 count.

On 3-1, Kamieniecki fires a fastball low in the zone and Phillips fouls it back. Good pitch! This guy has some hair on him. He hasn't given in, even though he knows one more ball and he's out of the game. Now on 3-2 and with two outs, Mattingly drops behind the runner. He'd much rather be able to cover more ground from a deeper distance than keep Cuyler one step closer to the bag. Many times the announcer will declare that with the count 3-2 and two outs, the offense gets a break because the base runners get a free jump, in effect. True, and I said earlier that a few games a season turn on just this situation. However, the defense also gets its own advantage, especially against left-handed batters. But the net advantage is still with the offense. Cuyler scores easily on a double.

The Yankee fans are on their feet, yelling for the strikeout. This is a game situation, and everyone knows it. What will Kamieniecki throw here? The fastball! Just inside, ball four. Barely inside. *Was* it inside? That was a tough pitch to take. Kamieniecki bounces off the mound and leaps high in the air in frustration. He wanted that call. He could have gotten that call. He shakes his head. Great pitch, great location, surprised me. Maybe it surprised Tony Phillips, too.

Buck Showalter sprints to the mound—that's his style— and signals for the left-hander, Steve Howe. Kamieniecki gets a big hand as he walks off the mound because he pitched a fine game. The first two Tiger batters of the game got hits and scored, then Kamieniecki shut them down. And they haven't scored here yet. Actually, Kamieniecki's lucky he stayed in the game this far. He might have been relieved of his duties after Scott Livingstone's hit. Showalter could have brought in Howe to face Phillips, who's a switch-hitter anyway. If Howe had walked Phillips, at least he'd have a few pitches under his belt before facing Lou Whitaker. It's tough for a reliever to come into a bases-loaded situation, especially for a guy who has had his problems this year. But Howe has been better since coming off the disabled list earlier in the month (3.65 ERA), and he hasn't walked many guys all year—four. That's good news when the bases are loaded. But the main reason Showalter let Kamieniecki pitch to Phillips is revealed by a check of Phillips's stats batting from each side. "Turning Phillips around" is not a fifty-fifty proposition. He feasts on left-handed pitching.

One theory holds that the American League in general has shaky middle-relief pitching because of the designated hitter. It could be. Obviously, the middle relievers are not used as often in the AL because the starters don't have to come out for pinch hitters. But without a choice now, Showalter brings in Howe to face—and get—Lou Whitaker, lefty versus lefty. This is a tough spot for Howe, bases loaded, two outs, one-run lead, tough, disciplined hitter at the plate. Whitaker strikes out about once every ten at-bats.

Howe has a good fastball and a good breaking ball, and you have to figure that Whitaker will see more of the fastball until Howe gets ahead in the count. A walk is a run. As it turns out, Howe does not get ahead in the count and throws five fastballs, only one of which, the second, is a strike. The final three miss badly, Whitaker trots to first, the three base runners advance, Rob Deer steps on home plate for the tying run, Buck Showalter sprints to the mound to give this pitcher the rest of the day off, and Howe only makes matters worse with a flippant doff of his cap to the fans, who are booing him for all they're worth. An ugly scene, really, but it is bad when your left-handed reliever walks their left-handed batter in this situation. He's paid to get this out. The camera picks up Kamieniecki in the dugout, not booing, but not happy, either. He has been up and down this year; he needed the victory, his team needed the victory. Now he has no shot at the win, a no-decision at best, and he might pick up the loss if Milt Cuyler on third base scores what proves to be the winning run. That sounds self-centered, but how could a pitcher not think like this?

Now pitching for the Yankees, Bobby Muñoz, a big kid who has pitched a total of fourteen innings in the big leagues, most of them scoreless outings. Travis Fryman is the batter. He's having a tough day—a line-out, strikeout, and pop-up—but this is still a tough situation, the crowd is anxious and restless, and Leyritz calls for the slider on the first pitch! This youth on the mound is not likely to brush off the catcher's selection. I would have called for the cheese and taken my chances. As big as Muñoz is, he has to have a good one. But Travis Fryman does Muñoz a favor by swinging at the pitch probably outside, so it's strike one instead of ball one. And that's why the selection might have been shrewd by Leyritz, figuring Fryman would be sitting on the fastball. And in this situation—bases loaded, young kid on the mound—Fryman should look fastball. But if he gets the slider, and certainly the slider outside, he should take it. A good eye is so important.

Now Leyritz calls for the curve, and Muñoz misses the plate and the count evens up, 1-1. Here comes the fastball, finally, and this pitch also misses the strike zone, but again Fryman does the Yankees a favor and swings and misses. He hasn't swung at a strike yet. The count should be 3-0, not 1-2. The hard slider might work here. No, cheese upstairs! And of course Fryman swings at this, too. Bad at-bat, but he doesn't need me to tell him this. He's disgusted that he's the one who looked like the rookie. Critical at-bat, critical out, critical gift to the Yankees. Detroit just got a gift of their own with the bases-loaded walk to Whitaker. Fryman hates to return the favor so quickly.

Score now tied, 3-3, thanks to the two-out rally.

We saw how Kamieniecki handled his long rest before the start of the seventh—okay, with two quick, fortunate outs, and he could have gotten the third one on that close pitch to Tony Phillips—and now we'll see how Mark Leiter responds after his own vacation. The Tigers were at the plate for a long time, but Leiter needed the rest. He was shaky in the bottom of the sixth. Sparky has the full compliment throwing in the bullpen at the start of this inning: left-hander Bill Krueger, who was up in the sixth while I was wondering where Kurt Knudsen was, and now the right-hander Knudsen himself. And note the defensive changes for the Tigers necessitated by the removal of third baseman Scott Livingstone for pinch runner Milt Cuyler: Alan Trammell moves from center field to third base and Cuyler takes over in center, batting in the ninth position. This defensive alignment can only help the Tigers because Trammell doesn't belong in the outfield and Cuyler does.

Leiter starts off against Kevin Maas, and all he has to do here is stay away from this guy, who won't hurt you too badly away, but can take a fastball middle-in all the way to the bridge. After a fastball high and some kind of odd pitch also high, Maas hits a fly ball to center field on a good sinker. One away. With Spike Owen up, if Leiter doesn't handle him with good pitches, he's gone (I think) because a set of three good left-handed batters follow.

But Mark just can't do it. He was all sold out in the last inning but managed to hang on. Now he proves he's finished by throwing four balls in a row to Owen, all fastballs way wide of the plate. Spike heads for first and Sparky Anderson drags himself to the mound in his accustomed fashion (pretty much the opposite of Buck Showalter's) and brings in Krueger to face Bernie Williams. Why the lefty Krueger? Sparky wants Williams to bat right-handed. That has always been his somewhat weaker side (in contrast to Tony Phillips, the Tigers' switch-hitter whom Buck Showalter wanted to bat left-handed). And Sparky knows Buck isn't going to pinch-hit for Boggs or Mattingly, so the left-hander makes sense against three batters in a row, and the decision on facing right-hand-hitting Jim Leyritz can come later, with Knudsen ready. Also, the left-hander helps hold the runner close, but if the choice is between holding the runner close and having the matchup you want at the plate, you take the matchup at the plate. That's where the game will be decided, not on the base paths.

The moment Krueger leaves the bullpen, another left-hander, Bob MacDonald, gets up to warm. This is no time for the manager to get caught flat-footed. Krueger might not have his stuff tonight. Against this Yankee line-up, a left-hander has to be ready for the rest of the game, and a right-hander has to be ready for Danny Tartabull and all the other Yankee right-handed pinch hitters.

Showalter could hit-and-run in this situation. Owen isn't a base stealer, and if Williams could at least get him to second, the Tigers would have their choice of facing Boggs or walking him to face Mattingly. They'd take Boggs, of course, wanting no part of Don Mattingly with runners on base.

Decisions made, signs flashed, Bernie Williams steps in for the first time hitting from the right side. Krueger greets him with a fastball outside. No play was on with the runner at first. Owen holds again and Williams swings at a low fastball and fouls it off. Krueger tosses to first. Then the pitch to the plate is a curve way low, ball two. Now the count is perfect if Buck wants to run Owen...but he doesn't. Spike holds and Williams lines a fastball into right field. The ball might carry all the way to Rob Deer, so Owen has to be cautious. By the time he decides the ball will fall, he can't go past second. Even if he had been running on the play, he might have had to hold up. There's also the factor of the short porch in right.

So Krueger will have to face Mattingly anyway unless he can get Boggs on a double play, and he'll try hard to get that ground ball. This at-bat will be choice. Runners at first and second, one out, one of the best, if not the best, contact hitters in the game at the plate. Put on a play here? Never. Don't run yourself out of an inning. Boggs can hit. Let him hit. And I seem to recall something out of Boston about Wade's not liking the hit-and-run. Even if he does, not here, not now.

With Krueger's first pitch to Boggs, we get another indication that Wade gets the calls from the umps. A real close pitch on the outside corner at the knees is called ball one. Boggs now takes a strike and a ball—the first curve of the at-bat—and with the count 2-1, Wade is in great shape. He's seen Krueger's hard stuff and soft stuff. He's ready for anything, and he's swinging. Indeed, the fastball is down the middle and Wade gets a good rip, but doesn't get all of it. Foul ball straight back, strike two. With the count 2-2, you're hoping for a ball if you're a Yankee fan in order to make the count 3-2 so the runners can be put in motion, staying out of the double play. Boggs seldom strikes out, remember. Also note that in this situation the first baseman would not get an advantage by playing back because he's already playing behind the runner with second base occupied.

Ball three. The fastball barely misses outside at the knees. Same pitch as the first. Rick Reed is consistent in this at-bat, at least. But a good pitch. Now Showalter will let the runners take off. They study the signs. But they don't run! The fastball is fouled off, almost predictably, with Boggs batting. Unbelievable, really, that the runners were holding. How can you tell from your seat on the couch if the television director doesn't happen to show them and the announcers don't say? Watch the catcher. If he maintains his crouch, the runners are holding. If he springs up prepared to throw, they're running. Tettleton remained in his crouch on that foul ball.

Krueger delivers again, Boggs fouls another fastball back, and this time Owen and Williams are running. Why this time and not the first time? I have no idea. Ask Buck the next chance you get. Or maybe Spike Owen on second base missed the sign (the runner on first keys off the runner on second, obviously, in case that lead runner does miss the sign).

Yet another outside fastball, yet another foul, the runners running again. This is the thing that makes Boggs so effective in these situations. He has the eye and the bat control to torture the pitcher with fouls until he gets something he can drive. Having Mattingly batting behind Boggs doesn't hurt him, either. Krueger has to throw strikes.

On the fourth full-count pitch, Boggs finally gets something a little more acceptable—a fastball low in the zone and right about in the middle of the plate—and Wade drives it hard but right at Milt Cuyler. Out! Spike Owen, running on the play, makes a bad read on the ball. He retreats, but too late. He's dead at second base for the third out. Terrible base-running blunder! No percentage whatever, with Don Mattingly batting next. If you're running with the pitch in that situation, the correct procedure is to stop and read the play. Make sure the ball drops. If it does, you can't be faulted for not scoring and with one out the sacrifice fly scores you from third base anyway. If the ball is caught in the outfield, you can get back to second. Safety first all the way.

Horrible play! The worst we've seen in Philadelphia or New York by far.

How will the big sinker baller Bobby Muñoz pitch to Cecil Fielder with the game just about on the line in the top of the eighth inning? This should be good. Scott Kamieniecki used curves the first at-bat, mostly fastballs the second and third times around. You have to imagine that Jim Leyritz isn't going to ask Muñoz to play around with his curve against this guy. Make him hit your best pitch, something hard, and remember Gene Tenace's advice: Stay outside. But the dilemma here is that Fielder likes the pitch outside. Well, nobody said it would be easy.

Did Gene Tenace also say something about staying low, because Muñoz's first four pitches to Fielder are down: two fastballs, two sliders; three balls, one strike. This is a problem because you can't walk the big guy. You have to throw a strike…oh, bad hitting. Cecil tried to pull the low, outside fastball with predictable results: a slow roller to short. He's disgusted with that swing, no doubt. But like I say, it's easy to do the right thing while sitting up in the stands or watching on the tube. And Muñoz made an excellent pitch on 3-1. Nevertheless, you want a solid chance on 3-1, and Cecil didn't get one. He's tired of this losing streak, too, and maybe tried to hit a ten-run homer.

Muñoz now makes a bad pitch to Kirk Gibson—down and in, of course—and Gibson hammers it hard, but right at Paul O'Neill in right field. Two outs, Tettleton up. I just noticed, sixty-three RBIs on sixty-two hits for the big catcher, production numbers like Pete Incaviglia's in Philadelphia. Muñoz's program this at-bat? Pitch away. Oh, some kind of breaking ball, check swing, strike one. Surprised everyone in the park with that selection. Four pitches later, a big, looping curve finishes the at-bat. Boy, Muñoz looks good. However, I was wrong in my estimation that his size means he throws real hard. He doesn't. His fastball has good sinking action.

We move to the bottom of the eighth, score tied 3-3, and we have a new man on the mound for the Tigers, Bob MacDonald, and he pitches from the stretch in all situations. (I believe Bruce Sutter was the first reliever to do this, although I could be wrong.) The left-hander MacDonald is in the game because Mattingly and O'Neill are coming up for the Yankees. Fair enough, but why is the left-hander Krueger out of the game? He only faced two batters and he hadn't pitched since Saturday. He shouldn't be worn out. What if this tie game goes thirteen innings? Sparky will need all the pitchers he can get. The manager's hook (Sparky was nicknamed Captain Hook during his tenure in Cincinnati) seemed slow with Leiter and now fast with Krueger.

MacDonald starts off Mattingly with one of those accidental backup curves that misses the inside corner, and with the count 1-0 in the late innings, Don could now look for the fastball inside and wail away if he gets it. He does get exactly that pitch but doesn't offer. Ahead in the count, he had the luxury of taking. Maybe he wanted to get a reading on the fastball. After another breaking ball misses outside, Mattingly is in great shape on the 2-1 count and takes advantage of it, smashing a fastball down the middle, but directly at Tony Phillips in left field. One away.

Curve for strike one against Jim Leyritz batting cleanup. Obviously, MacDonald has confidence in his curve. Uh-oh! You're the cleanup batter, right-hander against left-hander, and you're bunting in the eighth inning!? Leyritz even misses the low pitch. Questionable, in my opinion, very questionable, even if Jim is not the regular cleanup guy. (Tartabull is the main man for the Yanks in that position.) Leyritz finds himself in a hole 0-2, MacDonald wastes outside, then gets his man on what I believe is the change-up in the dirt.

Paul O'Neill has had a good day at the plate, with a homer and a single, but he's making a mistake if he's dreaming about topping it off by pulling the ball over the wall for a heroic homer. He will not see an inside pitch in this situation if MacDonald knows what he's doing and has decent control. If anything, O'Neill should be looking away. For the third batter in a row, MacDonald starts off with the curve, outside corner, check swing by O'Neill, strike one. That check swing might indicate that he was looking inside, after all, or he was just fooled. A fastball is low, and two curves sweep across the plate for strike two and a foul ball. That's the correct program. Throw those pitches outside. He can't kill you there. Oh no! MacDonald catches too much of the plate with this one—not a hanger, but close to it. And give O'Neill credit. He's all over the pitch and drives it on one bounce against the wall in the right-field corner. Deer gets a good carom, makes an accurate, quick throw to cutoff man Lou Whitaker, who makes a crisp play on the short hop and fires a strike to Fryman at second base. Really nice work out there, but all for naught. O'Neill slides in safe on a close play. If O'Neill had been thrown out, is that a bad base-running play? No. In a tie game or down a run, two outs, don't get thrown out at third base or home plate because you're already in scoring position, but go for scoring position—second base—if you get the chance.

Buck Showalter will probably pinch-hit here for Dion James, bringing in a right-handed batter, and that move will probably be matched by Sparky Anderson, bringing in a right-hander from the bullpen. If Danny Tartabull is Showalter's choice, Sparky will intentionally walk him, with first base open and two out, and then wait to see if Buck pinch-hits for Mike Gallego. Showalter wouldn't have done that in the sixth, but he might in the eighth. Mike hasn't fared well this evening. Showalter must know that Tartabull will be walked, so if he puts him in for James anyway, we can conclude that he's satisfied with Gallego or another hitter at the plate, and with two men on, not just one. Another strategy for the Yankees' manager would be to use another pinch hitter for James, the dangerous right-handed Mike Stanley, for example, and at the same time send Tartabull into the on-deck circle, or just instruct him to put on a helmet in the dugout, giving Sparky second thoughts about walking Stanley. But a drawback to using Stanley is that he's the only catcher on the bench, I believe. Matt Nokes is out of action. Managers always want a spare catcher available. Still, I'd forget that wisdom and go for the victory.

However this situation plays out, the first move is for Showalter to replace Dion James, and he does so with...Danny Tartabull. This makes no sense to me. Isn't the least good option for Buck Showalter the one in which your power hitter is used as fodder for an intentional walk? As it is, the big guy is wasted. I think the better move was to send up Mike Stanley, put Gallego in the on deck cicle, and have Tartabull pace up and down the dugout with his batting helmet on and waving his bat. Sparky would have seen Tartabull; he would have pitched to Stanley. If Stanley gets a hit, giving the Yankees the lead, Gallego stays in. If Stanley is unintentionally walked, Tartabull bats for Gallego. Plus, as we will soon see, Sparky's right-hander in the pen—now Mike Henneman—isn't ready, so Stanley would have been assured of batting against the lefty MacDonald. Perfect.

Instead, MacDonald issues the free pass to Danny Tartabull, who trots to first base. Now Sparky has to come in with a right-hander to face Gallego or somebody else. But Sparky doesn't do it. What's going on?! Oh, the old stall maneuver. Kurt Knudsen had been throwing but he's taken a seat, and now Mike Henneman is warming up. A little indecision from Sparky? Mike's not ready, but he should be.

I noted earlier that a left-hander has to be ready to face all the Yankee left-handed batters in tonight's lineup and a right-hander has to be ready because the Yankees are left with only right-handed batters on the bench. Nevertheless, Henneman needs more time, so first the catcher Tettleton goes out to talk to MacDonald, then Billy Muffett walks out to the mound as slowly as he can (pretty slowly), talks as long as he can, then returns to the dugout as slowly as he can (pretty slowly).With prodding from the umpire, Sparky Anderson finally emerges and makes the move to Henneman. By hook or crook, the manager will usually get the pitcher he wants in the game, but he can't stall forever. The umps know what's going on. If the manager or his pitching coach has been to the mound once in the inning, the second time is an automatic pitching change, and the umpires won't wait for the managers to trudge all the way to the mound. They'll signal for the pitcher the moment the manager steps on the field. I've even seen the third-base umpire sprint to the bullpen to try to force the reliever to quit his warm-ups and get in the game. But the guy will get in two or three final throws and then look up and go, "Oh! Who? Me?" It can be amusing to watch the manager stall, but it also might be a sign that he was caught short in the strategy wars. And it's not funny when a pitcher hasn't had enough time to warm up and hurts his arm as a result. That's happened more than once.

Mike Henneman is Sparky's ace, his closer. At other times, in other games, Anderson would think twice—no, three times—about bringing him into the eighth inning of a tie game, but the Tigers have lost seven games in a row. They need a victory, and it could slip away right here. Henneman sort of makes sense. This guy is good. We know Knudsen's stats with inherited runners. Both pitchers are right-handers, and in the seventh inning Sparky might have gone to Knudsen in the crunch, but with two outs in the eighth, he's hoping Henneman can get Gallego, hoping the Tigers can score in the top of the ninth, hoping Henneman can get three outs and the victory in the bottom of the ninth. That's a lot of hoping. If Sparky had a balanced bullpen, with three right-handers, he'd have a lot more leverage.

After Henneman is announced, does Showalter pinch-hit for Gallego? Mike Stanley is sitting there, ready to go. But Buck stands pat. Gallego walks to the plate, so we must conclude that Buck is as satisfied with him at the plate as with any of the other potential pinch hitters. There isn't any reason to save them, not even Stanley the catcher. This is it. The game is on the line now. But if Buck had a left-handed hitter available, you know he'd be in the game.

At long last, we're set to go with O'Neill and Tartabull on base, two outs, Henneman on the mound for Detroit. On the first pitch to Gallego, we see what I think is another difference between the two leagues, as luck would have it. The first-base ump, Durwood Merrill, calls a strike after Gallego checks his swing on a tough slider on the outside edge. In the American League, that call on the check swing is almost automatic. In the National League, not so.

A slider on the outside edge makes strike two on Gallego and another in the dirt is the perfect bait pitch, swing and a miss, strike three. Gallego's bat ends up in the seats beyond the Yankee dugout. Mike is enjoying a great year with the Yankees, but this has not been his night. We have no way of knowing how Gallego felt stepping up to bat in this situation, he may have been full of confidence, but any honest ballplayer will confess to coming to the plate in similarly tight situations when things haven't been going well, certainly in the middle of a prolonged slump (not the case with Gallego), and thinking that he had just as soon be watching someone else hit in this situation. In a basic, competitive way, you want to be up there, but you're also thinking, "Wow, I'm in trouble against this guy." You've got to get rid of that thought. When you see batters in these situations walk off for a moment after one or two strikes, they're probably trying to get rid of any negative thoughts. You've got to bear down and try to deliver. Gallego's best opportunity for the clutch single in that at-bat was on that second pitch.

Once he went to two strikes against Henneman, he was in trouble big time, and he knew it. Score still tied, 3-3.

Take a moment to reconsider the previous two and a half innings, from the bottom of the sixth through the bottom of the eighth. Only one run scored, but 25 batters came to the plate, eight were left on base, five pitching changes were made, the managers were managing for all they were worth and made several moves that were ripe for analysis. That was fascinating baseball. By comparison, the ninth is lackluster, frankly, and why spend a lot of time on it? We have a couple of defensive changes for New York, with Danny Tartabull staying in the game in place of Dion James, but playing in right field, with Paul O'Neill shifting to left field. Both are right fielders by trade, and of the two, O'Neill must be more comfortable in left. Plus Tartabull has a bad shoulder, and the left fielder has the greater odds of making some throws against the Tiger hitters coming up, two of whom bat right-handed, and the short fence in right gives Tartabull a shorter throw.

But Trammell, Deer, and switch-hitting Milt Cuyler make three outs on eight pitches from Bobby Muñoz. For the Yankees, Maas, Owen, and Williams make three outs on eight pitches from Mike Henneman. Spike Owen did get a hit, but Williams grounded into a 4-6-3 double play. Buck Showalter decided against putting on any kind of play with Owen on first and Williams batting. That's twice late in the game Buck chose not to force the action with a hit-and-run with Owen running and Williams batting. That's not a criticism, just an observation.

Extra innings. Bobby Muñoz returns to the mound for the Yankees, and he's throwing to Mike Stanley, defensive replacement for Jim Leyritz. There goes the possibility that Showalter didn't use Stanley to pinch-hit because he wanted to save him. Mike's in the game anyway! I still say that Stanley pinch-hitting for Gallego (or for Dion James) sounded like a pretty good deal. But here we are, and Muñoz uses four fastballs while getting Tony Phillips on a grounder to shortstop. Lou Whitaker gets his chance and falls behind, 1-2, all fastballs. Advantage, pitcher, but Muñoz proceeds to lose it with a couple of breaking balls that miss by six feet. With the count full Muñoz returns to the fastball...outside, ball four. Ouch.

Now Muñoz will have to face Cecil Fielder unless Travis Fryman grounds into a double play, and he doesn't. In fact, he hits a long fly to deep right-center on a high, outside fastball that Bernie Williams runs a long way to catch. So we get the anticipated rematch with Fielder. Back in the eighth, Muñoz induced Cecil into pulling the fastball on the outer half and got the ground ball to shortstop, but many relievers aren't as effective after the batters have seen them once. We'll see here. Muñoz begins with a sinker that bites hard on Cecil's hands, and he fouls it off. After a slider just misses and a fastball is high, Bobby makes the mistake of his brief career on 2-1 and grooves one. What a cut by Fielder, but he's just a hair under the ball and hits an incredibly high drive to deep left-center for the long third out. I said earlier that Jack Clark was as dangerous and as exciting to watch as any player back in the mid-eighties. That's Cecil Fielder in the nineties thus far. He pounds his bat into the ground when he realizes he just missed home run number twenty, and for the second time in the game. Good work on the instant replay.

Wade Boggs starts the Yankees' tenth exactly three hours and thirty-seven minutes after Tony Phillips led off the first inning for the Tigers. Thirty seconds later, it's all over. Boggs turns on Tom Bolton's second pitch, an inner-half fastball, and hits his first home run in a New York Yankee uniform. This blast hits the façade of the upper deck in right field. The crowd erupts with joy. Yanks win. Toronto trembles. They're dancing in the aisles in the Bronx.

Did I say right-field line? Wade pulled that ball? Shocker! He said after the game that this at-bat was all a mistake, that he got out in front of the pitch. This comment just goes to show how he thinks about batting because he had a great swing on that pitch. He wasn't out in front by anyone's standards but his own! I think Wade is skilled enough to adapt to the new surroundings. He should turn on more of those pitches in Yankee Stadium.

But let's back up a minute. Tom Bolton is pitching? That's right, Bolton, a former teammate of Boggs's in Boston. Tom was in the game for a couple of reasons, I guess. Maybe Sparky didn't want to extend his closer Henneman for more than one and a third innings. Also, Bolton is a left-hander to face Boggs and Mattingly starting off the inning. Whatever. The bottom line is that Sparky's gamble that the Tigers could score in the ninth (or even in the tenth) didn't pan out. He might wish he had used right-hander Kurt Knudsen against Mike Gallego as the last out in the eighth, then brought in Bolton to face Maas, Owen, and Williams in the ninth inning. He must not have any faith in Knudsen at all. As it turned out, Sparky used his best reliever against the bottom of the Yankees' order and second-best against the heart of that order, and he paid the price with the Tigers' eighth consecutive loss on this miserable road trip. But the Tiger fans in the stadium tonight don't have to walk away empty-handed. They saw a good, although long, ball game, and they have plenty of opportunity for second-guessing.

EPILOGUE

Y ou know what happened in the end. Detroit and New York hung on as long as they could in the AL East but eventually faded and left the field to the favored Blue Jays. Cecil Fielder failed in his effort to become the only player to lead the majors in RBIs for four consecutive years, but 117 is hardly peanuts. Mickey Tettleton continued his terrific productivity per hit: 128 hits, 110 RBIs. The Tigers traded Rob Deer to Boston, where he once again led the league in strikeouts, and Detroit acquired the often-injured Eric Davis from Los Angeles, proving again that the organization's focus these days is power, power, power, despite the fact that their winning teams were built around—what else?—pitching. Go figure. Mark Leiter wound up with a 6-6 record and a 4.73 ERA in '93.

The Yankees sent Kevin Maas to the minors for a while, then recalled him in September. Wade Boggs did start pulling the ball more at Yankee Stadium, although not for homers. He ended up with two for the year, along with a .302 average. Scott Kamieniecki pitched brilliantly in Yankee Stadium all year, less so elsewhere, and ended up 10-7, with a 4.08 ERA. Mike Gallego hit .283 for the year; Kevin Maas .205. The Yankees fired big Frank Howard after the season.

In the National League, Philadelphia appeared to have it wrapped up on August 15, then got a scare from Montreal in September, whom they had led by 14 1/2 games about a month earlier, before finally winning the East in the last week of the season. Then came that roller-coaster postseason. Danny Jackson for the Phillies continued to pitch pretty well, although following the series with Atlanta in June he lost more games than he won. His final record was 12-11, with a 3.77 ERA. Lenny Dykstra led the league in runs scored with 143, an enormous number. He also led in hits and walks, a rare, rare combination, yielding a .420 on-base average. And he was unbelievable in the playoffs and Series. Pete Incaviglia matched Tettleton with his productive hitting, with 89 RBIs on 101 hits. Mitch Williams finished the regular season with forty-three saves, a Phillies record. Then came the World Series he would like to forget.

Atlanta started playing great ball not long after the series in Philadelphia, helped enormously by the fire-sale acquisition of Fred McGriff from San Diego. A couple of immediate home runs from Fred seemed to free up the whole Braves offense. Three players—McGriff, Gant, and Justice—ended up with at least thirty home runs, but without McGriff I don't think it would have happened for Atlanta. That was as extreme a turnaround as you'll ever see following one mid-season trade. The only comparable deal I recall was in 1984, when the Cubs acquired Rick Sutcliffe from Cleveland. With the Indians, Rick had gone 4-5 with a 5.15 ERA; with the Cubs, 16-1 with a 2.89 ERA. He led them to the division title. The Braves got that quality of pitching from just about everyone in '93 as they caught, then passed San Francisco when the Giants went into a tailspin in late August and early September. But they didn't win their third consecutive division title until the last day of the season. When they fell to the Phillies in the playoffs, some called the entire season a failure. Thanks to all the days off, Bobby Cox only needed four starters for the last month or so and Pete Smith therefore became a reliever. His record for the regular season was 4-8, with a 4.37 ERA. The Braves were so strong in pitching, Pete wasn't even on the twenty-five-man roster for postseason play. But he was in the dugout.

❋   ❋   ❋

For our purposes, none of that really matters. I didn't pick the Philadelphia-Atlanta series because I thought they'd win their divisions. All I really wanted for this book were two good, representative games and four good teams that would give me the opportunity to cover all the bases. I think I got them.

There's no doubt that baseball is a game of small differences and details that come into clearer focus with careful scrutiny and are missed otherwise. I've tried to prove that the more you know, the more you enjoy. But that doesn't mean you have to watch every game with the attention I've just lavished on these two. You won't. Impossible! What I hope is that you'll find some carryover the next time you're out at the park with family and friends and a bucket of soda pop. Why did the shortstop cover on that hit-and-run with a right-handed batter at the plate? That question might nag you until you figure it out. Then again, it might not. Either way, here's to the game!

ACKNOWLEDGMENTS

Within major league baseball, a special thanks to Larry Shenk with the Philadelphia Phillies. Also contributing in various ways were Arthur Richman and Willie Randolph with the New York Yankees, Jay Horwitz with the New York Mets, Jim Schultz and Bruce Benedict with the Atlanta Braves, and Kirby Puckett.

Jeannie Dubinsky and Joe Fox were helpful with travel and accommodations; Mary and Ted Jones, Andy and Louis Grigar, and Ruth and Bill Jacobs were more than generous with room and board in Tincup, Colorado, where much of this book was put together.

Agents David Katz and Joe Spieler and attorney Richard Basch did a good job on that end, aided and abetted, in Spieler's case, by Susan Hobson. At HarperCollins, Eileen Campion handled a hundred phone calls and requests with aplomb.

Among the readers whose comments and criticisms were valuable were Lisa Arning, Ed Dinger, Steve Hanks, Gary Hernandez, Mark LaBarbiera, Doug and Tim Magee, Tim Ungs, Ed Walters, Paul and Chantal Weinhold, and Rob Wilson. Gay Talese was an early and enthusiastic supporter of the idea.

For assorted services rendered—marketing, mainly— thanks to Elaine Kaufman and Bobby Zarem.

It's tough to write about baseball these days without getting into the numbers, and this book has quite a few throughout. Three books helped us cope: *The Scouting Report: 1993*, Bill James's *STATS 1993 Major League Handbook*, and *Total Baseball: The Ultimate Encyclopedia of Baseball*, edited by John Thorn and Pete Palmer.

Thanks to Patty Bryan for all her help.

Finally, we wouldn't be here without our editor, Wendy Wolf. The book was her idea. This particular writing team, united again, was her idea. The oddball cover, which we like, may not have been her idea, but she fought for it. In short, Wendy is responsible for this whole mess, and we thank her no end.

POSTSCRIPT:

THE GAMES BY THE NUMBERS

Phillies 5
Braves 3

ATLANTA	AB	R	H	BI	BB	SO	AVG.
Nixon cf	3	1	0	0	1	2	.234
Blauser ss	3	1	2	1	1	0	.325
Pendleton 3b	4	0	0	0	0	0	.253
Gant lf	3	0	0	0	1	0	.272
Hunter rf	4	0	1	1	0	0	.136
Cabrera 1b	4	1	2	1	0	0	.283
Berryhill c	4	0	0	0	0	0	.256
Lemke 2b	4	0	1	0	0	0	.265
PSmith p	1	0	0	0	0	0	.238
a-Pecota ph	1	0	0	0	0	0	.276
Mercker p	0	0	0	0	0	0	.000
Wohlers p	0	0	0	0	0	0	.000
b-Olson ph	1	0	0	0	0	0	.206
TOTALS	**32**	**3**	**6**	**3**	**3**	**2**	

PHILLIES	AB	R	H	BI	BB	SO	AVG.
Dykstra cf	2	0	0	0	2	0	.282
Morandini 2b	4	1	1	0	0	1	.230
Kruk 1b	4	1	0	0	0	1	.358
Daulton c	3	1	1	0	1	1	.262
Incaviglia lf	4	1	1	3	0	2	.292
Eisenreich rf	4	1	3	0	0	0	.347
Batiste ss-3b	4	0	1	1	0	2	.315
Manto 3b	4	0	0	0	0	1	.000
Millette ss	0	0	0	0	0	0	.200
DnJackson p	3	0	0	0	0	2	.088
MtWilliams p	0	0	0	0	0	0	.000
TOTALS	**32**	**5**	**7**	**4**	**3**	**10**	

Atlanta	002 001 000 — 3	6	1
PHILLIES	100 130 00X — 5	7	1

a–grounded out for Smith in the 6th. b–grounded into double play for Wohlers in the 9th.

E—Blauser (7), Batiste (4). LOB—Atlanta 6, PHILLIES 6. 2B—Blauser (15), Cabrera (2), Daulton (16), Eisenreich (11). 3B—Blauser (1). HR—Incaviglia (12) off PSmith, Cabrera (3) off DnJackson. RBIs—Blauser (28), Hunter (6), Cabrera (6), Incaviglia 3 (47), Batiste (17). SB—Dykstra 2 (21). S—PSmith. GIDP—Olson.

Runners left in scoring position—Atlanta 3 (Nixon, Hunter, PSmith); PHILLIES 3 (Morandini, Incaviglia, DnJackson).

Runners moved up—Lemke, Kruk.

DP—PHILLIES 1 (Millette, Morandini and Kruk).

ATLANTA	IP	H	R	ER	BB	SO	NP	ERA
PSmith L, 2-7	5	7	5	5	2	5	91	4.56
Mercker	2	0	0	0	1	3	29	3.43
Wohlers	1	0	0	0	0	2	11	2.57
PHILLIES	IP	H	R	ER	BB	SO	NP	ERA
DnJcksn W, 7-3	8	5	3	3	3	2	101	3.35
MtWilliams S, 22	1	1	0	0	0	0	9	2.81

IBB—off PSmith (Daulton) 1. WP—PSmith.
Umpires—Home, DeMuth; First, Kellogg; Second, Runge; Third, Reliford.
T—2:28. A—41,557.

How they scored

PHILLIES FIRST: Dykstra led off with a walk. Dykstra stole second with one out. Kruk grounded into fielder's choice, pitcher Smith to third baseman Pendleton to second baseman Lemke, Dykstra out at third. Daulton doubled down the right-field line, Kruk to third. On Smith's wild pitch, Kruk scored. 1 run, 1 hit, 1 error, 1 left on.

Phillies 1, Braves 0

BRAVES THIRD: Nixon led off with a walk. Blauser tripled to right-center, Nixon scored. Hunter singled to center with two out, Blauser scored. 2 runs, 2 hits, 0 errors, 1 left on.

Braves 2, Phillies 1

PHILLIES FOURTH: Eisenreich doubled past third with two out. Batiste singled to left-center, Eisenreich scored. 1 run, 2 hits, 0 errors, 2 left on.

Phillies 2, Braves 2

PHILLIES FIFTH: Morandini beat out an infield single to shortstop with one out. Kruk grounded out to third baseman Pendleton, Morandini to second. Daulton was intentionally walked. Incaviglia hit a home run down the left-field line on 2-1 count, Morandini and Daulton and Incaviglia scored. 3 runs, 2 hits, 0 errors, 1 left on.

Phillies 5, Braves 2

BRAVES SIXTH: Cabrera led off with a home run down the left-field line on 0-2 count. 1 run, 1 hit, 0 errors, 0 left on.

Phillies 5, Braves 3

Yankees 4
Tigers 3

DETROIT	AB	R	H	BI	BB	SO	AVG.
Phillips lf	4	1	1	0	1	1	.302
Whitaker 2b	3	1	2	2	2	0	.324
Fryman ss	5	0	0	0	0	2	.271
Fielder 1b	5	0	1	1	0	0	.273
Gibson dh	4	0	1	0	0	1	.251
Tettleton c	4	0	0	0	0	1	.248
Trammell cf-3b	4	0	0	0	0	0	.308
Deer rf	4	1	2	0	0	1	.220
Livingstone 3b	3	0	1	0	0	0	.281
1-Cuyler pr-cf	1	0	0	0	0	1	.217
TOTALS	**37**	**3**	**8**	**3**	**3**	**7**	

YANKEES	AB	R	H	BI	BB	SO	AVG.
BWilliams cf	5	0	1	0	0	0	.256
Boggs 3b	4	2	2	1	1	0	.311
Mattingly 1b	4	1	1	1	0	1	.279
Leyritz c	4	0	0	0	0	2	.340
Stanley c	0	0	0	0	0	0	.311
O'Neill rf-lf	3	1	3	2	1	0	.337
James lf	2	0	0	0	1	0	.299
a-Tartabull ph-rf	0	0	0	0	1	0	.223
Gallego 2b	4	0	0	0	0	3	.325
Maas dh	4	0	0	0	0	1	.206
Owen ss	3	0	1	0	1	0	.254
TOTALS	**33**	**4**	**8**	**4**	**5**	**7**	

Detroit		200	000	100	0 — 3	8	0
YANKEES		300	000	000	1 — 4	8	0

No outs when winning run scored. a–was intentionally walked for James in the 8th. 1–ran for Livingstone in the 7th. LOB—Detroit 7, Yankees 7. 2B—Whitaker (19), Boggs (14), O'Neill (18). HR—Boggs (1) off TBolton, O'Neill (11) off MLeiter. RBI—Whitaker 2 (40), Fielder (65), Boggs (33), Mattingly (23), O'Neill 2 (39). SB—O'Neill (2). GIDP—Livingstone, BWilliams. Runners left in scoring position—Detroit 2 (Fryman 2); Yankees 4 (Gallego 4). DP—Detroit 2 (Cuyler and Whitaker), (Whitaker, Fryman and Fielder); Yankees 1 (Gallego, Owen and Mattingly).

DETROIT	IP	H	R	ER	BB	SO	NP	ERA
MLeiter	6⅓	4	3	3	4	5	119	4.20
Krueger	⅔	1	0	0	0	0	13	3.71
MacDonald	⅔	1	0	0	1	1	13	3.62
Henneman	1⅓	1	0	0	0	1	11	1.78
TBolton L, 1-3	0	1	1	1	0	0	2	5.54
YANKEES	IP	H	R	ER	BB	SO	NP	ERA
Kamieniecki	6⅔	8	3	3	1	4	113	4.55
Howe	0	0	0	0	1	0	5	8.50
BMunoz W, 2-0	3⅓	0	0	0	1	3	40	2.50

Howe pitched to 1 batter in the 7th, TBolton pitched to 1 batter in the 10th. Inherited runners-scored—Krueger 1-0, Henneman 2-0, Howe 3-1, BMunoz 3-0. IBB—off MacDonald (Tartabull) 1. WP—MLeiter.
Umpires—Home, Reed; First, Merrill; Second, Hirschbeck; Third, Welke. T—3:37. A—37,692.

How they scored

TIGERS FIRST: Phillips singled to left. Whitaker doubled to center, Phillips scored. Fryman lined out to shortstop Owen. Fielder singled to left, Whitaker scored. Gibson struck out. Tettelton grounded out to first baseman Mattingly. 2 runs, 3 hits, 0 errors, 1 left on.

Tigers 2, Yankees 0

YANKEES FIRST: B.Williams flied out to right fielder Deer. Boggs doubled to left. Mattingly singled to center, Boggs scored. Leyritz struck out. O'Neill homered to right on 2-1 count, Mattingly and O'Neill scored. James grounded out to second baseman Whitaker. 3 runs, 3 hits, 0 errors, 0 left on.

Yankees 3, Tigers 2

TIGERS SEVENTH: Tettleton flied out to center fielder B.Williams. Trammell lined out to third baseman Boggs. Deer singled to left. Livingstone singled to right, Deer to third. Cuyler ran for Livingstone. Phillips walked, Cuyler to second. Howe relieved Kamieniecki. Whitaker walked, Deer scored, Cuyler to third, Phillips to second. Munoz relieved Howe. Fryman struck out. 1 run, 2 hits, 0 errors, 3 left on.

Tigers 3, Yankees 3

YANKEES TENTH: Bolton pitching. Boggs homered down the right-field line on 1-0 count.1 run, 1 hit, 0 errors, 0 left on.

Yankees 4, Tigers 3

PLAYERS	Pos.	1	2	3	4	5
NIXON	8	F-9			K	
Sub.						
BLAUSER	6					
Sub.						
PENDLETON	5	F-8		5-3		F-6
Sub.						
GANT	7			F-9		F-2
Sub.						
HUNTER	9	4-3				F-8
Sub.						
CABRERA	3			F-C		
Sub.						
BERRYHILL	2		1-3		E-6	
Sub.						
LEMKE	4		6-3		K-2	
Sub.						
SMITH	1		5-3		1-4	
Sub. PECOTTA T-6th PH						
MERCKER B-6th	1					
Sub. WOHLERS B-8th	1					
OLSON T-9th	PH					
Sub.						

SUM.	RUNS / HITS	ERRS / LOB	1	2	3	4	5
	RUNS	0	0	1	2	0	0
	HITS	0	0	1	0	0	0
	ERRS		2	0	0	1	1	0
	LOB						1	0

K ①

F-7 ②

F-8 ③

F-4 ①

F-4 ②

6-3 ③

WILLIAMS

1-7 ①

6-4 ②

OLSON

6-4-3 ③
DP

| 1 | 0 | 0 | 0 | 0 | | | 3 | 6 |
| 0 | 0 | 0 | 0 | 0 | | | 1 | 6 |

PLAYERS	Pos.	1	2	3	4	5
DYKSTRA	8	1-5-4 ②		F-8 ①		F-7 ①
Sub.						
MORANDINI	4	①		F-8 ②		
Sub.						
KRUK	3	PC		Kc ③		5-3 ③
Sub.						
DAULTON	2			F-7		INT. BB
Sub.						
INCAVIGLIA	7	F-9 ③			K ②	
Sub.						
EISENREICH	9					
Sub.						
BAST			K ①			34
Sub.						
MANTO / Sub. MILLETTE T-9th			F-7 ②		E-6	
JACKSON / Sub. WILLIAMS			K ③		1-3 ③	
Sub.						
Sub.						

SUM.	RUNS / ERRS	HITS / LOB	1 / 0	0 / 0	0 / 0	1 / 1	3 / 0
			1 / 0	0 / 1	0 / 0	1 / 1	2 / 2

6	7	8	9	10	11	12

WOHLERS

KERKE

0 0 0 0 0 5 7
1 0 0 0 0 1 6

Team **TIGERS** vs. **YA.**

PLAYERS	Pos.	1	2	3	4	5
PHILLIPS	7			Kc		1u
Sub.						
WHITAKER	4					
Sub.						
FRYMAN	6	F-6		K		
Sub.						
FIELDER	3				5-3	
Sub.						
GIBSON DH		K				
Sub.						
TETTLETON	2	3u			F-7	
Sub.						
TRAMMELL 8-7th	8		6-3		F-9	
Sub.						
DEER	9		Kc			4-6
Sub.						
LIVINGSTONE	5		F-3			4-6-? DP
Sub. CUYLER PR T-7th	8					
KRUEGER B-7th	1					
Sub. MacDONALD B-8th	1					
HENNEMAN B-8th	1					
Sub. BOLTON B-10th	1					

SUM.	RUNS / HITS	2 / 3	0 / 0	0 / 0	0 / 0	0 / 0
	ERRS / LOB	0 / 1	1 / 0	0 / 0	0 / 0	0 / 0

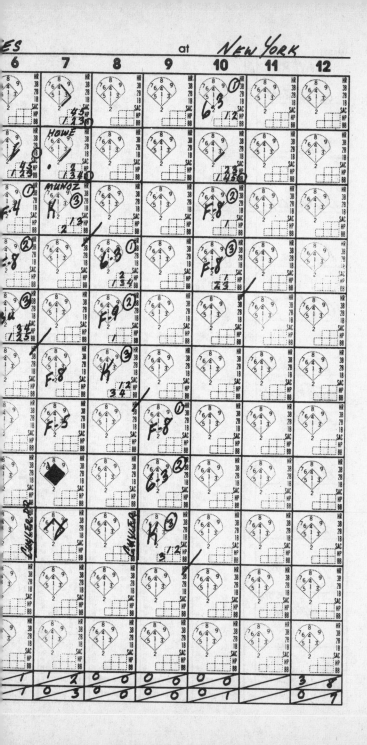

at NEW YORK

Baseball Scorecard

Team _____ vs. _____

PLAYERS	Pos.	1	2	3	4	5
WILLIAMS	8	1-2 ①		F-6		F-7
Sub.						
BOGGS	5			4-3 ②		
Sub.						
MATTINGLY	3			K ③		
Sub.						
LEYRITZ / Sub. STANLEY T-10th	2 / 2	K ②			1-3 ①	
O'NEIL T-9th-7	9				① 6 8	
Sub.						
D. JAMES 8-8th / Sub. TARTABULL	7 / 9	4-3 ③			F-6 ②	
GALLEGO	4		K ①		5-3 ③	
Sub.						
MAAS	D4		F-5 ②			K
Sub.						
OWEN	6		6-3 ③			F-8
Sub.						
HOWE T-7th / Sub. MUNOZ T-7th	1 / 1					
Sub.						

SUM.		1	2	3	4	5
RUNS / HITS		3 / 3	0 / 0	0 / 0	0 / 1	0 / 0
ERRS / LOB		0 / 0	0 / 0	0 / 0	0 / 1	0

6	7	8	9	10	11	12

KRUGER

BOLTON

MACDONALD

INT. BB

HENNEMAN

INDEX

ABOUT THE AUTHORS

Keith Hernandez played baseball for seventeen years in the major leagues with the St. Louis Cardinals, the New York Mets, and the Cleveland Indians. During his career, he won the National League batting title in 1979 and was co-MVP that year; he appeared on six National League All-Star teams; he won the Gold Glove Award for first base eleven times; and he played on World Championship teams in 1982 with the Cardinals and in 1986 with the Mets. This is his second book with Mike Bryan. He lives in New York City.

Mike Bryan collaborated with Keith Hernandez on *If At First: A Season with the Mets* in 1985. His other books include *Baseball Lives, Dogleg Madness,* and *Chapter and Verse: A Skeptic Revisits Christianity.* He divides his time between his native Texas and New York.